The BDMA Direct Marke
Desk Reference

The BDMA Direct Marketing Desk Reference

Edited by Sandra Carter and Tessa Kelly

McGRAW-HILL BOOK COMPANY

London · New York · St Louis · San Francisco · Auckland · Bogotá
Caracas · Hamburg · Lisbon · Madrid · Mexico · Milan · Montreal
New Delhi · Panama · Paris · San Juan · São Paulo · Singapore · Sydney
Tokyo · Toronto

Published by
McGRAW-HILL Book Company (UK) Limited
Shoppenhangers Road, Maidenhead, Berkshire, SL6 2QL, England
Telephone 0628 23432
Fax 0628 770224

British Library Cataloguing in Publication Data
The BDMA direct marketing desk reference.
1. Great Britain. Direct marketing
I. Carter, Sandra   II. Kelly, Tessa
658.81

ISBN 0-07-707486-6

Library of Congress Cataloging-in-Publication Data
The BDMA direct marketing desk reference: the essential guide to all aspects
of direct marketing, by the experts / edited by Sandra Carter and
Tessa Kelly
    p.   cm.
Includes bibliographical references and index.
ISBN 0-07-707486-6
1. Direct marketing—Handbooks, manuals, etc.   2. Direct
marketing—Great Britain—Handbooks, manuals, etc.   I. Carter,
Sandra.   II. Kelly, Tessa.   III. British Direct Marketing
Association.
HF5415.126.B38   1991
658.8'4—dc20   91–11750

1234PB9321

Typeset by Cambridge Composing (UK) Ltd, Cambridge
and printed and bound in Great Britain by Page Bros, Norwich

Contents

About the BDMA

The British Direct Marketing Association is the largest direct marketing trade body in the UK. It represents all types of direct marketing, not just direct mail. Members include companies who use direct marketing techniques to sell their goods and services and companies who supply services to the industry.

It is a trade association run by its members for its members, and aims to promote the industry for the mutual benefit of advertisers and consumers.

About the editors

Sandra Carter has a background in publishing and is the author of three books. She is currently a journalist specialising in consumer and property markets.

Tessa Kelly is assistant director of the BDMA. She has over 10 years' marketing experience in industrial and service companies operating in the business-to-business market.

Preface

The British Direct Marketing Association is very proud of the publication of its first major work, reflecting one of the most significant initiatives of the organisation—that of education and training in direct marketing techniques and practices. The book combines the expertise of many of the leading authorities in direct marketing today—expertise which for many of them has been learnt through great personal commitment and many years of hard work.

By sharing their knowledge and experience, they are making a great contribution to the continued rapid growth of direct marketing. The measurability of this powerful medium will ensure that all developing companies will include 'direct' techniques in the marketing mix of the future.

So whether you are a marketing director of a large multinational wishing to re-examine current trends or to train new staff, a small business owner trying to make a very tight marketing budget yield the highest return, or a student learning the marketing methods of today and tomorrow, this work contains invaluable information for you.

The BDMA is confident that this book will become indispensable to anyone involved—or thinking of becoming involved—in direct marketing in the 1990s.

Ruth Naylor-Smith
Chairman, BDMA
1991

Acknowledgements

Thanks are due to Dr Peter Tomkins for helpful comments on the entire text of this book; and to Derek McKeown and Tony Book for input on individual chapters.

Introduction

TESSA KELLY

The BDMA Direct Marketing Desk Reference is a unique and comprehensive compendium of the essentials of direct marketing: a neat collection of ideas, information and advice. All the contributors are experts in their own field, making this a truly authoritative publication.

The book is full of practical do's and don'ts, useful tips and guidance—all gained from the hard won experience of these experts—and fills a niche between the weighty textbooks on direct marketing (most of which are American) and the technical how-to-do-it manuals covering, in the main, just one area of this vast subject. We recommend that this desk reference be kept within easy reach of all marketing practitioners, whatever their disciplines or specialisations.

The book is easy to follow through its design and layout, with four main sections: channels of distribution, markets, services and controls and regulations. We would suggest that newcomers to direct marketing identify the most likely channels for promoting their product or service and follow these by the most appropriate market sector chapter. The service section provides essential information on the wide variety of specialist services available. Further detailed information on suppliers can be found in the BDMA Members Handbook which is available from the BDMA's offices.

All BDMA member companies agree to abide by the Association's Direct Marketing Code of Practice and the other self-regulatory codes of practice, details of which you will find in Part IV and the appendices.

The industry has to be aware not only of the self-regulatory codes but also of a variety of legislation including the Data Protection Act, the Financial Services Act, and the Consumer Protection Act to name just three. Many of the queries coming into the BDMA office concern legal aspects of direct marketing. The chapter on legislation affecting the industry should therefore be an invaluable aid in helping the direct marketing practitioner through this potential minefield. Even household name companies have made mistakes in prize draw promotions. As infringements against some laws can involve companies and individuals in criminal proceedings, check your ideas with the advice given in the chapter on Direct marketing and the law.

Direct marketing can be defined as a process of interactive marketing by which an organisation seeks to generate a direct and measurable response to advertising which offers goods, services or information.

All direct marketing channels are experiencing dramatic growth throughout the Western world. (At the time of writing the BDMA has already been approached by an Eastern bloc country looking for advice, so perhaps direct marketing will play its part in *perestroika*.) One reason for this growth is that direct marketing—more than any other form of advertising or marketing—mirrors the changes happening in today's society: the shifting emphasis from mass markets to the small targeted niche markets; the home as a focus for leisure activity; and the increasing emphasis on service and customer care.

Direct marketing enables companies to profile their customers and prospects and target offers based on a knowledge of purchasing patterns, lifestyle and propensity to buy. Today's powerful and sophisticated computer hardware and software are the tools the direct marketer uses to store, manipulate and analyse this proliferation of data. The days when the term 'individual communications' conjured up an image of an overkill of personalisation are over.

Home shopping, either by mail order catalogue or by interactive telecommunications, with instant ordering over the 'phone, 48-hour delivery services, etc., offers a time-saving comfortable home-based alternative to shopping in the High Street on a busy Saturday afternoon. In today's competitive marketplace, and with pressure on budgets, direct marketing scores through its measurability and, hence, accountability. By using direct marketing you should know which 50 per cent of your promotional budget works!

Many of the chapters mention testing: this, too, is one of the advantages of direct marketing methods over other forms of marketing or advertising. Statistically valid testing, properly analysed and backed by research, identifies what will work best in your particular marketplace.

There is a growing realisation that the marketplace does not contain an infinite number of new customers. Spending a lot more money trying to win a few more customers is not a sensible use of costly resources. It is more sensible to use direct marketing methods to keep your present customers and maximise their value. How many companies quantify the lifetime value of a customer? Meaningful communication, customer care, the catchwords of the nineties, can be implemented through the power of the direct marketing database.

A direct marketing database is the tool enabling this interactive approach to marketing. It has been described as the engine that drives direct marketing. Keeping accurate records on customers and analysing those data means that customers can be contacted with messages relevant to them. A knowledge of current customers helps to target future prospects accurately.

Direct marketing today is not a one-off mail shot or a press advertisement that happens to contain a coupon. Long gone are the self-liquidating off-the-page offers in the Sunday supplement. Direct marketing involves conducting your business in a totally different way. It is not merely a case of trying to manipulate your accounts database for marketing purposes. Direct marketing requires commitment, resources and vision: commitment to long-term strategy and perhaps longer term pay-offs; resources such as investment in computers or in staff training; and vision in seeing customers as having lifetime values. For instance, car manufacturers no longer wave goodbye to customers as they drive off in their new cars. Those customers will be written to, telephoned, nurtured with news, advice, offers—all carefully timed to ensure that next time they buy a car they will return to the company they know, trust and feel at home with. Direct marketing is a sophisticated business. It is neither an answer to short-term problems nor a route for the faint-hearted.

There is also one other factor to be taken into account when considering direct marketing and its future potential. Direct marketing has come of age, and with that status comes responsibility. There is no denying, the industry suffers from an image problem and certain elements in direct marketing deservedly receive some consumer criticism. The industry has to be committed to implementing and maintaining high standards. Much has already been done in this area, particularly in the establishment of the Mailing Preference Service, the proposed Telephone Preference Service and, as mentioned above, the self-regulatory codes of practice, but more needs to be done. The industry's trade bodies and educational establishments need the industry's support. Your support.

In conclusion, we hope this publication will give you ideas, answer your queries and point you in the right direction to find out more about these exciting routes to a successful business.

PART I

CHANNELS OF DISTRIBUTION

1

Direct mail

JOHN FRASER-ROBINSON

Get to know the medium
Direct mail as an advertising or communication medium is exceptionally powerful; so much so that, occasionally, it is abused, misused and over-used. Therefore we shall start by highlighting some of its qualities and peculiarities to ensure that you select direct mail for the best reasons, fully understand its capabilities and reap its full potential.

Many of the basic benefits are shared with other 'direct' media. Like them, direct mail is selective, creative, flexible, riddled with test opportunities, easy to respond to, cost-effective, etc.

Notably, however, most other direct media will offer you one or two of these qualities while direct mail offers you all—whether you use them or not—every time you mail.

Yet it is not so much these qualities which will lend power to your proposition and praise to your media selection. For direct mail sells differently. It has a different character. Readers have a different perception of it. And it pushes different buttons within them.

A lot of the 'direct mail differences' has to do with the potential charm, trust and amicability of one of its essential components: *the letter.*

Letters have a pleasant, almost disarming lack of formality without being pretentious, precocious or presumptive. They are also polite. They wait until you're ready for them. They don't shout over you like the radio and television. They're not inherently silly like posters and more and more press advertising. They 'talk' in an easy, conversational way. Most are lively and fun to read. Some are stimulating. Some are newsworthy. Some are quite valuable. Some are very moving.

Letters are intimate. For example, you read them to yourself. And if you decide to let someone else see your letter, then you do. Some of this intimacy has to do with the way they, as letters, are perceived. Some of it has to do with the fact that they are undoubtedly the only advertising message that starts 'Dear' and ends 'Yours'—a final pledge of faith, sincerity or truth. Moreover, mailings are safe to handle, to read and to use. Unlike a human salesperson, they can be ignored, put down or curled up into a ball and thrown on the fire. And, unlike a human salesperson, if a letter confronts you, you can't lose. You don't feel as though you've offended anyone. You never feel guilty or threatened or intimidated. With a letter the advantage stays with you.

And what of the phone? What do most people feel when the average (not the best, the typical) telephone salesperson gets to work? Defensive. On guard, and therefore threatened.

Articles have been written about how to hang up on telephone salespeople. They bandy techniques of how to dispense with people quickly and painlessly. They resent the often awkward and intrusive timing.

So direct mail has an often overlooked comfort factor. With mail, the prospect is always in control. It's passive. It's certainly persuasive in most cases, but not threatening, intrusive or intimidating. And you are always, silently, alone with the reader. Other components of the package have similar advantages. Which is easier and preferable to deal with: a well-designed response piece or a pushy salesperson hurrying you along, completing an application for you? And so on through the pack.

Direct mail is expensive advertising. But it's *selective*. It gets you in front of the right people: the kind of people who will be more interested in what you have to say, and what you have to sell. It can give you their undivided attention. What you make of it is, ultimately, up to you. If you press all the right buttons, they'll give you a proper hearing.

Direct mail is also *creative*. It gives you more opportunity to hold their attention than any other advertising medium. You can include colour, smell, sound, texture, shape. You can fashion your communication more artfully, more convincingly, than any other apart from actually sitting down with them and talking it through. Because, apart from all these things, you have the space to do it. Be confident. Your enthusiasm will show. Your conviction will prove infectious. The crunch is not whether it will, but for how many.

The importance and scope of the creative process
The role of creativity in direct mail is changing. There is a resurgence of factors other than the response effect. Far greater attention is now being placed on the advertising effect—brand-building, image, the customer care aspects, and so on.

For perhaps 20 years or so direct marketers have greedily followed short-term objectives. The Holy Grail of the Cost per Sale. This kind of direct marketing has more to do with the rapidly fading era of exploitation selling than the far more fashionable new process of satisfaction marketing.

It is the creatives particularly who will need to understand this. And it is vital that they do, for something like 80 per cent of their work is aimed at advertisers' existing customers. A nucleus too precious to be mishandled!

Weak, ineffective or low-quality direct mail creative is most usually the result, not so much of bad creative people, but of those people not understanding the medium—or being badly briefed. Here, therefore, is a suggested briefing document. Note that the creative brief need not be different from the agency brief, but can be part of it.

Briefing document
A THE OBJECTIVES
    1 *Sales objectives*
      The precise targets (quantity percentage, quality percentage, cost per . . .)
    2 *Business objectives*
      The relevance of the sales objectives to the business as a whole
    3 *Timing required*

B THE PRODUCT/SERVICE
    1 *What is it?*
      What does it do, how does it work, how much does it cost, etc?
      Is it complete, or has it on-going or after-sales elements?
    2 *Is it any good?*
      What's wrong with it (weaknesses)?
      What's right with it (strengths)?
    3 *Who says so?*
      And how do they know?
      Can we quote them?
    4 *Is it unique?*
      Or merely different?
      Specifically, how?
    5 *Any guarantees?*
      Or other added customer/service benefits?
    6 *Is it mail order—or how is it to be sold?*

C THE MARKET
   1 *How big is it?*
      Market shares?
      Where do you 'sit' in the market?
   2 *What does a buyer 'look' like?*
      Research and sources
      Geographies/demographies/psychographies/RFM   (Recency,   fre-
      quency or monetary value data)
   3 *Who makes decisions?*
      How many involved?
      Any third parties or other considerations?
   4 *Previous and latest experiences*
      Samples
      Any customer correspondence
      Case histories
   5 *Selections/segmentations/lists*
      Exploitable affinity or intermediary involvement
      Relevant endorsements
      Other activities: PR, advertising, sales promotion
   6 *The competition*
      Run through same list as above where possible

D THE MEDIA
   1 *Why direct mail?*
   2 *. . . and why not other media?*
   3 *How is audience data held?*
      Customer or file record layout
      Processing requirements
      Processing times
      Processing constraints, restrictions
   4 *Any other media factors*
      Codes of practice
      Restrictions

E THE BUDGET
   1 *Total*
      Any specific allocations
   2 *How budget is calculated*
      Mathematics of sale
      Dynamics of financial success/failure
      Breakeven point

3 *Highest cost/risk factors*
Of mailing
Of project

F CREATIVE
  1 *Corporate*
  Positioning/image requirements
  Brand/product positioning and image requirement
  2 *Product/service*
  Benefit/feature analysis
  Offer/proposition rationale
  In-house or other products, services or resources available as enhancements (old stock/supplies, etc.; ancillary or consumable items)
  3 *Review of previous creative work*
  And results
  4 *Systems/response handling/legal*
  Procedures
  Timing
  5 *Specific test requirements*
  Statistical data/viability
  Variants identified
  Outline matrix
  6 *Information gathering*
  Any data for future activity
  Repeat sales
  7 *Buyer attitude statement*
  Before
  After

G FOLLOW-UP PROCEDURES
  1 *Methods/systems*
  2 *Despatch or follow-up times*
  3 *Capacity/constraints*
  Manpower
  Resources

H RESULTS ANALYSIS
  1 *Who and how?*
  2 *Reporting and review disciplines*
  Short term—when?
  Long term—when?

I EFFECTS ON FUTURE
 1 *In event of . . .*
 Success
 Failure
 2 *Development/growth potential*
 3 *Any 'if it works . . .' factors*

Given a comprehensive document like this and—most important—a full, if long, meeting to discuss it, there is obviously no reason why your message shouldn't get through in a clear, articulate, informed and effective manner.

A word of advice: make sure you have the briefing meeting with the documents already written. Don't be tempted to use it as a confirming document. Worse still, don't even think about trying to prepare it as the meeting proceeds. This will be a meeting of quite a few people and quite a few disciplines, and quite a few strong points of view. It should be for discussions, not strategic decisions.

IT'S TIME TO PRESS THE BUTTON . . .
Having chosen direct mail for the best reasons, understood its unique qualities and considered methods of achieving optimum creativity, we arrive at the process of production.

In fact the production team's responsibilities, as the checklist shows, begin as early as those of the rest of the team.

Direct mail production checklist
A Mailing production
   1 Preliminary discussion
   2 Method of approach developed—strategy prepared
   3 Strategy discussed, amended, approved
   4 Brief prepared, circulated, discussed, amended, approved
   5 Briefing meeting—creatives and as many others involved as possible; discussion to cover all aspects but *must* include budgets and lists/database capabilities and timing
   6 Mailing concepts developed, formats agreed, outline production specification prepared
   7 Product specification passed to suppliers for estimating with outline timing requirements
   8 Estimates received
   9 Creative concepts reviewed against prices and any discrepancies and specification or cost problems considered and resolved
  10 First timing schedule issued

11 Creative given go ahead
12 Copy and visuals presented
13 Photocopies and full specification passed to suppliers for submission of first written estimates
14 Copy and visuals processed to full approval, materials gathered, studio briefed to proceed to finished artwork
15 Schedule reviewed and re-issued if appropriate
16 List or database specification finalised
   (Go to B list routine)
17 Finished artwork received; photocopies to all appropriate parties
18 Amendments gathered, merged, and consolidated
19 Final changes and amends re-circulated
20 Studio briefed for amends; schedule reviewed and re-issued if appropriate
21 As 17 to 20 until approval received from all parties
22 *Signed* proofs obtained as appropriate
23 Meeting to pass finished artwork for printing; prices and timing checked and problems resolved
24 Revised photocopies, coding instructions and any other 'special treatments' or requirements re-instructed to suppliers
25 Process work carried out and completed
26 Machine and/or proofs prepared, circulated and signed off
27 If any amends—review and re-issue schedule if appropriate; postage payment checked
28 Final samples prepared for lettershop from machine proofs and/or photocopies
29 Print complete, finished samples checked and circulated; lettershop instructions re-checked; deliveries confirmed; quantities and coding details re-verified; made-up samples signed off
30 Lettershop commenced, mailing dates and response handling details re-checked
31 Lettershop complete; counts completed and checked; spot check on finished items; release sanctioned
32 Release confirmed; postal dockets received; response handling alerted
33 Invoices received, verified and passed
34 Cost discrepancies analysed and noted
35 Guard book entries, with job history and log entered
36 Responses processed; surplus material arrangements checked and confirmed
37 Response pattern logged and reports prepared

38 One month from mailing: interim figures reviewed and reports passed
39 First de-briefing: all suppliers attend—report on response to date and feedback; financials circulated
40 Two months after: final figures reviewed, responses and financials circulated
41 Final de-briefing with computer analysis and review and reports circulated and discussed
42 Nixies dealt with
43 Guard book entry finalised

B Lists/database (*from A16*)
1 List and data specification agreed
2 All segmentation, availability, coding and costs drawn up
3 List owners circulated with copy and visuals for approval
4 List details, segmentation, codings, prices and dates finalised; addressing or tapes ordered
5 If appropriate, magnetic tape dump and record formats checked, details passed to computer print bureau
6 Go ahead to bureau with instructions issued *per tape* including coding details

C Personalisation/addressing (*from A5*)
1 Requirement feasibility checked and costs estimated
2 Bureau confirmed all details of selections, formats, codes, mail preference, samples (copies of copy and visuals at the least) agreed
3 Bureau estimate, timing and provisos received and verified
4 List security requirements reviewed and instigated
5 Bureau received copies of finished artwork for addressed/personalised items, production details checked thoroughly
6 Format proofs received, reviewed and approved
7 Live proofs on actual printed stocks prepared, reviewed and approved; timing checked if amends required
8 OK to run
9 Run computer, counts and samples provided, checked and verified
10 Finished production delivered to lettershop
11 Deliveries checked for quality and against quantity counts

Sixty steps to follow. A lot to get right. Don't let the apparent complexity of the task worry you. It's a system you need. Once you develop one and discipline yourself not to skip the safety steps you'll find it's all straightforward.

Personalisation, individualisation . . . and then what?
The nature of direct mail is changing. It gets increasingly difficult to get your voice heard above the noise level.

At one time, 'matching in' the name and address on to a printed letter would have done it. Then, to add that special touch to an 'executive' level mailing, at extra expense, a personal salutation and date were added. The first generation of personalisation.

With the advent of computers came the second generation of personalisation. As it became easier, the price dropped. And large mailers started making strategic corporate decisions that 'all our mailings will be personalised to demonstrate the way we feel about our customers and the level of service we give'.

The database is the catalyst for the third generation of personalisation, smoothing the way for the new era of individualisation. It makes possible the level and style of approach needed to put direct mail at the forefront of those media that will deliver the integrated blend of marketing and direct marketing currently referred to, accurately but rather unsatisfactorily, as relationship marketing.

Strapped to the marketing database, direct mail currently represents the only medium that enables you to talk to your existing customers, all in one go (or not) and all at one time (or not). Face-to-face and the 'phone are the other two major methods; so direct mail is suddenly price competitive and more convenient—whether delivered electronically, by fax, or by a postperson. (See Appendix 4 for industry statistics.)

With the increasing awareness of the power of direct mail as a customer care delivery medium and the reblending of techniques into a mix that recognises long-term strategic marketing objectives, direct mail will stay at the top of many media selectors' lists for many years to come.

2

Telephone marketing

ROBERT LEIDERMAN

Gone are the days when telephone marketing meant the telephone call one received in the middle of dinner. That call inevitably concerned some product you couldn't care less about, and was delivered by an individual who would try to keep you on the phone until you said 'yes'.

While marketing people recognise that high-pressure telephone selling is actually counterproductive, they often miss opportunities that the use of the telephone can provide. Telephone marketing is more than making or receiving calls, just as direct mail is more than printing and posting letters.

By defining telemarketing in a direct marketing context, however, we can begin to take advantage of its many benefits.

Telemarketing is any measurable activity using the telephone to help find, get, keep and develop customers.

Working to this definition, telephone is seen as one of the elements of the direct marketing mix, rather than an end in itself. You choose telephone as the route to the customer, when you need to use its strengths—for example, its speed as a method of responding to radio or television commercials, or its convenience when you want people to answer questions.

Devising the plan
The only way to determine that the use of telephone will help you find, get, keep and develop customers is to have a plan which clearly lays out your business objectives, the resultant marketing objectives, the strategies that will be used to achieve the marketing objectives and the tactics that will turn the strategy into workable applications. Think about the potential applications, such as 'Let's call all our new customers and welcome them

to the club', only after you have clarified and quantified your objectives and your strategies. Look at the major issues:

- What opportunities are there in the life cycle of the customer?
- How will telephone help in exploiting those opportunities? How will the other media help?
- Which opportunities will be best served by the strengths of telephone? Mail? Broadcast? The salesforce?, etc.
- What volumes might there be for each of those applications?
- What are the cost implications?
- What applications will give the best return to the company?
- What is the impact on resources?
- What tests do we design and how do we measure them?
- What are the timescales?

Agency or in-house?
If you need to be up and running quickly and have no in-house resources, the agency route is really your only choice. Some advantages of the agency option are:

- An agency can usually make or receive calls out of business hours.
- An agency should be able to shorten the learning curve, having conducted many different types of projects for their clients.
- An agency should be able to offer advice on creative and approach.
- An agency should have premises, trained communicators, supervisors and managers.
- Using an agency could help overcome headcount or resource problems.

On the other hand, a number of companies simply won't entertain the idea of using an agency, for a number of reasons:

- It would be totally against their culture
- Confidentiality
- The need to have on-line systems or database
- The product or service is incredibly complex.

Even in these situations, though, it could be a good idea to develop a relationship with an agency—not only for advice, but also as a way to set a benchmark for in-house operations.

Is cost an issue?
According to the BDMA survey of the telemarketing industry, 99 per cent of companies gave cost as one of the reasons they would not consider

using an outside telephone operation. Nonetheless, cost really is not an issue. When you look at the real costs involved to set up and run an in-house operation—space, management and overheads, not to mention labour, supervision and telephone costs—the differential becomes small. Also, a good agency is often more efficient in their calling procedures than most in-house units and that will also reduce the differential on outbound calls. It's also difficult to use the cost argument for setting up an inbound operation in-house because the capital cost of setting up a unit that could handle high volumes of inbound calls could be quite significant.

Working with an agency
When using a telemarketing agency it is crucial to allow for the fact that some time will elapse before the agency learns about your business and 'beds-down' your project. No one can work efficiently in an environment where the goalposts are constantly moving, or where someone is constantly threatening to take the ball home. The agency want to do a good job but they will make mistakes, and so will an in-house operation. Be honest with the agency; document the problems, deal with the agency early, and work with them to solve those problems. Get to know the people making or receiving the calls as well as the people handling your account. Also, whether you are working with an agency or an in-house unit, make sure that you have agreed objectives, budgets and reporting requirements because that will avoid the confusions that tend to lead to mistrust.

SELECTING AN AGENCY
If you have decided to use a third party, ask yourself a few questions before entering into a contract. You should also make sure that you are satisfied with the answers your in-house unit provides.

1 Do they understand what you want to do?
2 Do their proposals meet your needs and reflect what *you* want to do?
3 Do they have the capacity to do your work in the timeframes you require?
4 Who will be looking after your business and how will they do it?
5 Are there sufficient measurement procedures and agreed reporting times and standards?
6 What do the people on the telephone sound like?
7 Do they have any testimonials?
8 Are they members of their direct marketing association and do they subscribe to the telephone marketing guidelines?
9 What kinds of production systems do they have?

10 Do they understand costing?

11 Do they want your business?

12 Would you bring your board to the agency and say 'These people are working for us'?

Choosing an automated telemarketing system

When considering an automated telemarketing system, it is important to recognise what it can do and what it can't. The installation of a computer system will not help you to determine the objectives and strategies of a campaign. Nor will it help you to manage your people; but it will, however, force you to organise your thinking, and then, if you have installed the right system, it could help you to execute efficiently the applications you have decided upon.

SPECIFY WHAT YOU REALLY WANT THE COMPUTER TO DO

The primary objective of installing an automated telemarketing system is to improve the service you provide to your customer.

In writing the specification, therefore, think of your marketing applications—that is, what you want your system to help you with. If your software supplier asks you to compromise on what you need, or tells you that what you want to do is not really important, find another supplier. If you are considering computerising, answer the questions in the following checklist before going any further:

- What is the computer strategy of your company?
- Do you need an inbound system, an outbound system, or do you need a system that handles both?
- Will the system be able to interface with other systems in the business?
- Is software support available?
- How easy is it to implement new applications?
- How easy is it for the communicators to use?
- Will the system be able to grow as you grow?
- What value is the addition of the computer system adding to my customer service?
- What is the cost?

WHAT WILL IT ALL COST?

Costs are basically divided into direct and indirect costs, which are sometimes referred to as variable and fixed costs. Direct costs can be attributed to doing the job; they are 'variable' because costs are not incurred unless a job is actually done. For example, unless you actually make calls to customers, you do not incur telephone call charges. On the other hand, since you must have premises whether you have additional work or not, the cost of premises is an indirect or fixed cost.

Costs will be a totally different order of magnitude for large operations than for small ones. So it makes more sense to look at the elements involved in the process, which are the same whether you are setting up an in-house unit or using an agency.

Look at the figures in hourly equivalents, i.e. analyse what happens for each hour that a person is employed making or receiving calls. Aside from being easier to work with and simpler to understand, the use of hourly pay figures, telephone and list costs, and hourly determination of indirect cost, will quickly show you if your costs for making the calls are too high, (i.e. if your direct costs exceed your income) or if your support costs—your overheads—are too high, and need to be adjusted.

Toll-free numbers for inbound calls

The use of calls that are free to the caller has risen in popularity in recent years, largely because of the introduction of the 0800 LinkLine system, which allows for automatic free calls. (The Freefone system required the caller to dial the operator first.) A number of tests show that response increases with toll-free calls or reduced rate calls (0345 calls are charged at local rate regardless of the origin and termination point of the call). What you must calculate, however, is whether the increased revenue offsets the increased costs involved in using these calls.

When using a telephone number in your advertising:

- Feature the number prominently. Use a graphic device or put a box around it. DON'T reverse it out.
- Use it in the body copy as well as on its own.
- Provide a benefit for calling.
- Make it clear when to call; if you are open 24 hours, say so.
- If you advertise on Sunday, be available to answer calls on Sunday.
- If the call is free, say so.
- If you are advertising on television, leave the number on the screen and announce the number at least twice in a voiceover.

Scripts

There are certain creative approaches that you know work in other media, such as the AIDA formula: Attention, Interest, Desire, Action. You should be able to apply approaches like this to telephone as well. You also have to be sure that the things that are being said are true. However, word-for-word scripts are sometimes not practical, and in such cases you should present a guide. You should consider guiding if:

- you have a stable workforce
- you have sufficient time and money for extensive product training
- the types of calls handled will require a lot of technical knowledge
- you pay a commission.

In any case, remember that the telephone is an aural and oral medium. Not only is someone actually listening to the words, but someone is also saying them. The phone call is a conversation, so don't worry about accurate grammar; and before you do anything else, buy a thesaurus to make sure you use words that are easy to say and easy to listen to.

3

Direct response advertising: print

GRAEME McCORKELL

People like direct response ads. We know that, because they consistently attract higher noting and reading scores in advertising recall research than conventional ads. The problem is that more people like them than respond to them.

Direct response advertising, like all advertising, is simply a means to an end. Obvious, perhaps, but many would-be entrepreneurs have tried and failed to generate the business needed to meet the whole of their sales targets from sell-off-the-page advertising. An enterprise which seeks to generate all of its sales from new business and none from past customers deserves to fail. And that is what it does, sooner or later.

One-step or two-step?

While there are many *uses* for direct response advertising—ranging from advertising designed solely to generate cash receipts to advertising which, purely as a by-product, generates brochure requests—there are fundamentally only two *types* of direct response advertising. In direct response jargon these are *one-step* advertising and *two-step* advertising. The former seeks to complete a sale, the latter merely to pave the way to a sale.

Successful advertisers evaluate both forms by *the total worth of the business that results*. They look at their direct response media advertising dispassionately, perhaps comparing its cost-effectiveness alongside their direct mail and house-to-house distribution activities. A one-step ad may produce £10 000 worth of immediate business. But that is not the *total worth* of the business generated; for, with a well-planned customer mailing programme, repeat business may be worth a great deal more than the initial £10 000 of new business.

It is not realistic in most markets to expect a profit from new business advertising. The profit arises from dealings with identified prospects and customers created by new business advertising. Even the advertisers fortunate enough to do more than break even on their advertising investment will miss the main opportunity if they fail to recognise that it is cheaper and, therefore, more profitable to sell to identified customers and prospects than to the entire readership of any publication.

At the risk of labouring this point, we have now established that there is no difference *in principle* between one-step and two-step advertising. Each is designed to start a profitable relationship. The difference is purely one of directness. It follows that those advertisers who are using direct marketing as a method of distribution have a choice. (Naturally, the advertisers who seek only to generate prospects for distributors have no choice. They must employ two-step advertising if they are to use direct response advertising at all.)

How to choose

Any such consideration aside, the choice between one-step and two-step advertising may be arrived at either rationally or empirically, from the results of testing. We may make the rational judgement that it will not be practicable to sell a round-the-world luxury cruise off-the-page; it would be unrealistic to expect our would-be passengers to shell out £30 000 on the basis of whatever persuasion we can cram into a colour page. But be careful. Rational judgements have their limitations. It is very *likely* that we shall need to send our glossy 48-page brochure to sweet-talk our prospects into stepping on board, but it is not a *certainty* that we shall need to do this.

It could just be possible that those with £30 000 and time to spare will accept our invitation almost on impulse. And that, if we use our ad to sell our brochure instead of our cruise, we shall spend a fortune mailing it to 40 000 dreamers who could not afford the fare to Southampton.

Test, don't guess

The beauty and fascination of direct response advertising is that, budget permitting, we can test each reasonable alternative. It is wise to do so rather than attempt to second-guess the consumer or business prospect. The major variables that will determine our success are *the product, the media, the offer, the creative treatment* and *the timing*. They are all important enough to merit testing.

Once we have executed a test programme we have results that will enable us to make business forecasts that will become progressively more accurate as our store of back-data builds up.

How do one-step ads work?

There is more than one type of one-step advertising. Most commonly, the respondent is expected to mail a cheque or send his credit card number (or give this information over the telephone). In this case he or she is *paying in advance* and we shall need to submit to the media bodies (the NPA and the PPA) evidence that the consumer's money will be safe and that we have sufficient stocks to meet demand promptly before our advertising can be accepted. The National Newspapers' Mail Order Protection Scheme (MOPS) may also require us to open an independently administered account in which consumers' money is held until the merchandise is despatched.

Less commonly, we may take the risk of mailing out our product to the consumer (or business buyer) on *free approval*, asking the recipient to return the merchandise if it is unwanted. We are more likely to do this in a market where product cost is relatively low and selling costs are relatively high, because the effect of free approval offers is to reduce advertising expense at the cost of some bad debt, increased administration expense and a less advantageous cash flow.

The reason advertising expense will be reduced is that our advertising will now pull, perhaps, almost twice as many orders. An example showing the comparison can be seen in Table 3.1.

In this simplified example we have improved our profit on net sales from 22.4 per cent to 24.7 per cent by switching to free approval. This may or may not be enough to justify the loss of cashflow, depending on the cost of funds. However, since diminishing returns set in fairly quickly in direct response advertising, the return on our advertising investment is a very important component of the equation, because the next £25 000 spent on advertising may pull a lower return than the first £25 000.

The reason for diminishing returns

In any campaign, we construct our plan around the most efficient activities and build outwards from that core. As one medium will be more effective than another, the use of a second medium will increase our cost per sale. To avoid that problem we may repeat our ad in the best medium, but later ads in a series nearly always pull less response than the first. A typical response curve is shown in Figure 3.1.

To avoid using less efficient media and taking too many ads in the most

Table 3.1   A comparison of 'cash' and 'free-approval' offers

	Cash-with-order	Free approval
	£	£
Gross order value	100 000	180 000
Less Bad debt	(—)	(12 000)
Less Returns/refunds	(5 000)	(18 000)
Net sales	95 000	150 000
Less Cost of product	(47 500)	(81 000)
Less Non-resaleable returns	(1 250)	(4 500)
Less Advertising	(25 000)	(25 000)
Less Account collections	(—)	(2 500)
Total costs	(73 750)	(113 000)
Profit before operating	21 250 (22.4%)	37 000 (24.7%)

efficient media we may increase the size of our spaces. But ads larger than the optimum size (and the optimum size can be arrived at only from testing) will pull proportionately less response. This is because readership generally increases by no more than the square root of the increase in the size of an ad.

ARE INSERTS THE ANSWER?
We may try to break out of this trap by using loose inserts, bound-in inserts, or tip-ons (pieces spot-gummed onto space ads). As a generalisa-

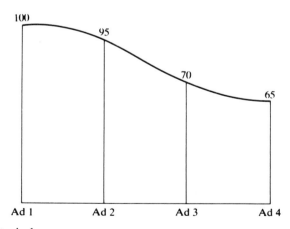

Figure 3.1   A typical response curve

tion these formats are more likely to work for us in two-step advertising than in one-step advertising because, apart from the greatly increased attention value, they also offer convenience in response. Convenience in response is more important in two-step advertising because an enquiry is more likely to be made on impulse than is a purchase. Since these formats are relatively expensive, they must be given every advantage if they are to pull new business at a lower cost than space advertising.

The pros and cons of two-step ads

Two-step advertising is a trade-off between quantity and quality of response. The optimum mix of quantity and quality depends on the relative costs of securing an enquiry and following it up. Typically, a colour page ad with a simple tip-on enquiry card will pull between two and three times as much response as a colour page ad without a tip-on card. A loose insert may pull five times as much response as the colour page with no tip-on. Such massive increases in response are at the cost of some loss in conversion rate. If the cost of following up enquiries is, say, five times the cost of securing them, there would be little point in experimenting with expensive gimmick formats, or freebie offers, to increase response.

Most often, however, the relatively high cost of advertising can be reduced by the use of inserts. These must be used sparingly in any one publication because they exhaust the supply of potential responders very quickly. Diminishing returns may be offset by the use of incentives.

When to add an incentive

Incentives are most often conditional on purchase, so that they impact both response and conversion rate favourably. However, where the enquiry cost is high, and conversion rate is also high, it may be beneficial to offer a separate reply incentive.

Any incentive will work better if we can close date our offer. However, the close date must be genuine. The Code of Advertising Practice and Code of Sales Promotion Practice from the Advertising Standards Authority give guidelines on this, and copies should be kept on hand for reference.

What will soon emerge from test experience is that the response and conversion characteristics of individual media vary widely. This may necessitate different approaches in alternative media in order to hit on the right format, space size, or offer for each publication.

The results of the use and non-use of a reply incentive are compared in Table 3.2. On the face of it, it would appear that we would be better not to use an incentive in this example. However, in direct response advertis-

Table 3.2   The use and non-use of a reply incentive

	No incentive	Incentive
	£	£
Cost of advertising	10 000	10 000
Response	1 000	2 000
Cost of incentive	—	4 000
Cost per response	10	7
Cost of follow-up per response	5	5
Total costs	15 000	24 000
Total cost per response	15	12
Sales	150 (15%)	200 (10%)
Cost per sale	100	120

ing the next question is, 'How shall we spend the £9 000 we have saved?' If the answer to this question cannot recover the 50 sales we have lost, then we should opt for the incentive.

Use back data to plan forward

Media planning for direct response is simplified by the ability to forecast from back data. This may be done by building a model that can be used on a computer, or manually, according to the number of variables the planner has to contend with and the volume of back data he or she can access. Either way, there will usually be:

1 a requirement to achieve a specified volume of business;
2 a requirement to keep within a given budget; or
3 a requirement to keep within a specified advertising cost-per-sale.

Whichever of these three briefs the media planner is given, the forecasting model will enable expenditure to be cut off when the target is achieved.

HOW TO ALLOCATE RESOURCES

However, with experience, media planners will quickly discover that it is unwise to commit all the resources available to them too quickly. Since they are in a position to 'know' what any given space is worth, they are in an excellent position to negotiate on a rational basis. They may therefore opt to spend, say, 60 per cent of the budget on the best media and positions, negotiating as well as they can in advance. A further 10–15 per cent may go on tests of new media, with the balance being reserved for late dealing. This will give flexibility to adjust the plan when results do not come in exactly as forecast. These proportions will depend on the state of the media market and the degree to which particular positions or timings are crucial to the success of the advertising.

Bargains in late dealing

Success in late dealing depends on having a decision maker at the end of the telephone and being able to supply copy instantly. Since the media buyer should have been given parameters within which to make decisions, the best results can be achieved by trusting the buyer to get it right. The buyer who advertisement sales staff know can make an immediate decision is the one who is called first when late space becomes available. Success is therefore determined by careful pre-planning in which forecast response for any given space is on tap, copy is always available, and advertisement code numbers (to track response) are issued in advance or follow a logical sequence.

Make it easy on the reader

Once the product is right, the offer is working and our media planning and buying are functioning well, we may believe that we have done all that is necessary to ensure success. Nevertheless, how we decide to fill the space we have bought can make the difference between a comfortable profit and a catastrophic loss. Direct response advertising is essentially functional. It should start with a consideration of what we want the readers to do.

If we want them to order, do we care how they order? Are we able to cope with telephone orders and to accept all major credit cards?

If they are enquirers, what do we want to know about them? Their telephone numbers? Their postcodes? The reason for their interest? Their job titles?

The easier we make it to respond, the more response we shall get. The more personal detail we want from readers, the less likely they are to respond. Again we are in a trade-off situation. The more information we have, the more precise can be our follow-up. However, this information will usually be obtained at the cost of losing some part of our response.

Don't be too clever

It is impossible to write and design direct response ads well unless we have started by thinking about the people we want to respond, how we want them to respond and why they should bother. Once we have these points settled we can create soundly based advertising. We already know how much space will be taken up with the response mechanism because we have worked out what we want the respondents to tell us. We are halfway to our headline and main illustration because we understand what the main benefit in responding will be and who will benefit most from responding. By now it will be quite impossible for us to execute clever advertising. Clever advertising is the kiss of death to direct response because it attracts readership for the wrong reasons and, therefore, largely from the wrong people.

If our ad is merely to seek an enquiry then it need only say enough to qualify our respondents. It is a mistake to think that long copy works better. All it does is to weed out potentially casual enquiries. Our success will depend on the headline, main illustration and reply device. These are the elements worth testing. On the other hand, if our ad is selling off-the-page, we must set out all the supporting benefits and imagine all the major sales objections so that we can counter them.

Testing
Once ads are created it is not always easy to test them. Split-run facilities, permitting alternative ads to appear in alternate copies of a newspaper or magazine, may not always be available and seldom are in such abundance that we can test different combinations of offers and copy simultaneously. It is useful in these circumstances to turn ads into simple loose inserts of identical format so that six or eight variants can be interleaved and tested in a couple of media. While the absolute results may not be meaningful the relative results will be—providing our test is large enough to produce statistically significant findings.

Conclusion
It is always worth keeping some money in reserve for experimentation. It has been found that some of the variables that determine success remain fairly constant, while others can change quite suddenly and inexplicably. Some of what works today will work tomorrow. And some of it won't. That is the only certainty in direct response media advertising.

Checklist
1 Is it practicable to sell directly out of ads, or do my distribution channels require me to generate enquiries only?
2 If I can sell direct, have I planned to test the cost-effectiveness of both one-step and two-step ads?
3 Do I have a realistic plan for securing repeat business from my advertising respondents?

4 Do I have the option to test alternative products?

5 What media tests are incorporated in my plan?

6 Have I planned to split-run alternative offers and creative treatments?

7 Have I ensured that my tests are large enough to produce valid results and that they are pure—that is, they test only one variable at a time?

8 Do I know the ideal timing for my ads or should I test to find out?

9 Would it make economic sense to sell on free approval? If so, do I have the administration to cope with collections?

10 Have I set up a system to give me a detailed, day-by-day analysis of results?

11 Does my ad meet the guidelines of the Code of Advertising Practice and the Code of Sales Promotion Practice? If accepting cash in advance, have I secured MOPS approval?

12 Am I sufficiently organised to take advantage of late deals in the media?

13 Does my coupon ask for all the data I need—but not enough to deter response?

14 Am I organised to handle telephone response and to accept credit card orders?

4

Direct response advertising: television

ANTHONY DARELL-BROWN

Television is, almost without dispute, the most powerful advertising medium available. The United Kingdom is extremely well served both in channels and in commercial audience delivery. In terms of national display advertising, television is certainly the most successful medium.

Advertising revenue for independent television companies in 1989/90 totalled £1680 million. ITV and Channel 4 together transmitted 16 062 programme hours, reaching 99.4 per cent of the UK population. Satellite cable channels, although having small audiences at the moment, are likely to see growth in the 1990s.

Why, then, is television so often overlooked by direct marketers? Probably because, until very recently, direct marketing advertisers have not understood how to use television. They have thought that television advertising was too expensive or too ephemeral, or both. This is inaccurate except at the most simplistic measure in that it probably is not sensible to use peak airtime for a mail order product.

One can pay just a few pounds or many thousands of pounds and buy spots reaching a few hundred people or a few million people. What matters is that the direct marketing industry does not waste the opportunities provided by television because of lack of interest or lack of information.

Lately, however, direct marketers have begun to seize the opportunities offered by this most powerful medium.

When to use television
The best use of television has not in the past been for mail order, but for two-stage direct marketing.

If you look at the client lists of the largest direct marketing agencies, you will find the bulk of their work is two-stage and often they are working for organisations that have a high profile, either generally or within their own industry—i.e. they are, to some degree, branded.

These same criteria apply to many users of television direct marketing. When you start using television it helps to be fairly well known by the audience. If you are not well known then you must allow for the fact that some of your early television expenditure is going to be spent in making you well known and not pulling in response. The less well known you are, the longer it will take for television to become a fully effective response generator.

How to use television
There are several uses for television direct marketing:

- response address and phone number
- response phone number
- referral to another medium
- advertising another medium
- business-to-business.

RESPONSE ADDRESS AND PHONE NUMBER
This is used, very often, for trade support commercials and, especially, local commercials. As often as not the reason seems to be that no one has had the courage to leave anything out, rather than a conscious decision to include both elements. Generally, you need to give the audience the simplest instructions on how to obtain the advertised product or information.

RESPONSE PHONE NUMBER
This is the most popular form of response mechanism for television direct response. It has two major functions. The first and most important is that it signals to the viewer that you, the advertiser, want a direct response. In fact it does it more strongly than an advertisement that also includes an address. The larger the numbers appear on screen, or the more often you say them, the more obvious it is that you want a response.

Secondly, you are communicating a piece of information to which you want the viewer to respond. Since very few people watch television with a pencil and paper beside them, your choice of telephone number is extremely important. Response mechanisms are discussed below.

REFERRAL TO ANOTHER MEDIUM

This has become a well-established technique, much used by sales promotion and holiday advertisers. We have all seen the words 'Look out for our advertisements in the *TV Times*'. The financial community, particularly unit trust companies, who use the *Daily Telegraph* on Saturday and *The Sunday Telegraph* as a 'retail outlet', have for some time used television as a referral medium to their couponed ads in the quality papers.

The rationale is not hard to find. Their retail outlets are limited, there is intense competition within them and the money spent on television to support their couponed advertising can significantly lift response as well as help with branding.

Advertisers such as Bonus Print and Truprint, who use television to support the house-to-house distribution of their film envelopes, also fall into this category. So do double-glazing and central-heating advertisers who may well include a telephone number in their television advertisements while knowing that most response will come through referral to other media, in particular, *Yellow Pages* or the telephone directory.

ADVERTISING ANOTHER MEDIUM

This is one of the most widely used and effective applications. Indeed, at one time London Weekend Television operated a system designed specifically to work on this basis, using selective house-to-house distribution as the main medium. Perhaps the best example is Reader's Digest with their annual, multi-million mailing supported by a major television campaign.

They directly advertise the imminent arrival of their mailing shot promoting the accompanying competition, but without describing the contents of the mailing shot or the product that is being advertised. This more than pays for itself in that it prompts a greater number of people to open the envelope.

When you consider the enormously high cost of putting together a package and paying for the postage, it doesn't take a very large increase in response to a major mailing to justify the cost of a television support campaign.

BUSINESS-TO-BUSINESS

'Business-to-business' direct marketing is a very different discipline from consumer direct marketing. Assuming the product appeals to the target market sufficiently, the response mechanism is much less important. If you see a commercial for a car phone or a computer and decide to find out more, or arrange for a sales call, it is a fairly straightforward affair for you, at work, to find out how to contact the company. You do not have to remember the response mechanism, you merely have to remember the name of the company.

It is, however, very important that a response mechanism is included in the advertisement and, indeed, given some weight. Your emphasis on the response mechanism is a signal to the consumer that you want a response and that you want it now!

Response mechanisms

The options in response mechanisms are:

- Standard number
- 0800—advertiser-paid
- 0345—caller pays local rate, or 0898/0839—premium charge
- 081 200 0200—bureau number
- Freefone number
- Freefone name.

Standard number   This can be far and away the best choice, especially if it is an easy number. Properly promoted, your number becomes a very valuable property. One good example is: Plumbing Mate—8, double 8, double 8, double 8. Another is the classified number for *The Evening Standard* (in London), which was heavily branded on television a few years ago: 35 35 000 (you have to sing it, and sing 'oh, oh, oh' at the end). The disadvantages are that you really have to spend some time and money branding the number. This is not a one-off option. Also, you ought to have someone available 24 hours a day to answer the telephone. An answerphone is better than nothing, but not much.

0800   In the last year or so these advertiser-paid numbers have become fairly well understood by the public. This has coincided with a dramatic increase in their use on television by companies as diverse as Western Union, Peugeot cars, and Prudential Assurance. With the introduction of much more easily remembered six-figure accompanying telephone numbers they are, I think, the wave of the future.

In general, it is not too difficult to remember a simple telephone number. If you are in the direct response business for the long term it might be worth branding an 0800 number back to your product or corporate base.

0345   These are advertiser-funded numbers for which the caller pays only a local charge. I suspect that viewers will become familiar with this number, in time, and appreciate the courtesy. In the meantime I think it is sensible to stick with one of the other options.

081 200 0200   This, I think, is a terrific number. Almost everyone in London knows the number, as do most people in the south of England and quite a lot of people in the rest of the country. It is a kind of walking coupon which people carry around in their heads. Its one serious disadvantage is that the number belongs to whoever pays to use it, and its use makes no contribution to your long-term business.

Freefone name/number   Despite its cost and the difficulties of having to go through the operator, Freefone name can be the best response mechanism for television. If you choose a sensible name (preferably the product or company name, if it is not too long) it is by far the easiest to remember for most of us.

I have noticed, lately, that use of Freefone name is declining on television. Looked at purely from a response viewpoint, I think this is a pity because it brands the product with the response mechanism. The two messages become one and the effort needed to recall is minimised.

Freefone number is a very poor substitute. If you are prepared to spend the money, use a name not a number.

0898/0839   These premium-price lines have become very familiar lately for all kinds of services from chat lines to health and investment tips. A number of advertisers have attempted to use them as a response-gathering mechanism. The attempt is doomed to failure. One needs to decide what business one is in (premium phone line or direct response) and act accordingly.

However, as a side comment, the voice-activated services spawned by the 0898 companies will, I believe, usher in a new era in broadcast response gathering.

Tips
Before entering television direct marketing, consider the following points:

TESTING
TV is a truly regional medium—more regional than almost any other national advertising medium. It is easy to test and it does not have to cost the earth. But remember that you are not testing for a one-off. Test over time.

BUYING AIRTIME

When you first start out, the local stations will be very helpful, especially with a test. But, before you roll-out, if you do not have enough experience in buying, find someone who has and pay for his or her experience. Television is not the easiest medium to understand and the day-to-day mechanics of the airtime market are not for the uninitiated.

PRODUCTION

Television is a very powerful medium. It is just as powerful when you communicate badly as it is when you communicate well. You can spend a lot of media money and, with a poorly prepared commercial, you may even damage your product or service rather than increase your sales. If in doubt, be as uncomplicated as possible in your approach. Avoid over-clever devices. Above all, tell the truth. By that I mean don't try to glamorise your message unrealistically.

BUDGET LEVELS

Television can be much less expensive than you might imagine. What would you expect to spend on a direct mail test? Why not telephone a television station and ask what they will sell you for the same money?

PERSEVERANCE

Television is not like print. You can't target so tightly, but your message is more powerful. If you are in business only for today, television is probably not for you.

THE MEDIA MIX

In most cases television is just one component, to be used as well as, not instead of, other media opportunities. Usually it should not be your first choice, but it may be your best choice in the long term.

5

Direct response advertising: radio

CHRIS HARVEY

Direct response is probably subject to more 'rules' and formulae than any other kind of advertising, and a cursory glance at direct response ads or mailing pieces would suggest that the rules apply more or less equally across all print media.

Radio, however, is a very different medium, and before good direct response advertising can be created, it is important to understand how radio is used by the listening audience. But first, a word on the merits of radio as a direct response medium.

What does radio offer the advertiser?
Radio's greatest virtue is its flexibility. It offers short production lead times allowing the advertiser to respond quickly to a market opportunity. It offers geographic flexibility through the independent local radio (ILR) network, and flexibility to copy test because production costs can be reasonable and copy rotation easy to organise. It also offers flexibility in terms of withdrawing advertising if targets are achieved or circumstances change. (Be aware that you may still be committed to the airtime, but postponement is not usually difficult.)

There is, however, one drawback. Precise targeting, a big factor in successful direct marketing, is more difficult to achieve. Close scrutiny of programme schedules is important and the advice of a good media planning/buying operation is essential. ILR stations offer many special airtime packages to assist planning. Weather-related and drive-time packages, for example, with the careful addition of certain fixed spots, can minimise wastage.

Using radio

The most important thing to remember is that radio, unlike print or television, is frequently consumed by an audience who are actively involved in some other pursuit. They may be working, driving, ironing or socialising, but almost certainly most will not be concentrating on the advertising. This fact has a significant bearing on the role of the advertising, and especially on the creative approach. (Information on listening patterns and coincidental activities is available from radio stations and from media planning companies.)

The role of radio

Radio can be used as the prime medium, or can play a supporting role. In its capacity as a support medium, it can be a highly effective method of creating awareness and initial interest in a proposition that is the subject of a more conventional direct approach. As a pre-sell, it can increase response significantly. It is particularly useful as a method of influencing a tertiary audience, i.e. those people who may be in a position to influence a decision but who are not the key, and therefore targeted, decision maker. In a business-to-business context, secretaries would be a good example, and in a consumer context, wives of target males.

If radio is to be used as the prime sales-generating medium, the serious consideration of targeting must be addressed. That done, the big issue is the commercial itself.

Creative considerations

Given the nature of radio advertising, attention must be earned; it cannot be demanded. This requires a significant level of consumer involvement. Since only the aural senses are used, it is critical that the creative treatment succeeds in involving the audience by creating a mental picture. Any script idea should be interrogated against this criterion.

An execution that interests or entertains is more likely to be listened to and thus provoke a response. So, while the execution must never bury the message, the need to provide stimulating creative 'packaging' cannot be stressed too highly.

Achieving audience involvement sometimes takes time, so although a typical time length is 30 seconds, serious consideration should be given to extending this to 40 or even 60 seconds. Although longer commercials cost more, they are often more effective. It is also worth considering a mix of time lengths—for example, 40 seconds with a 10-second reminder. Most radio stations will accommodate a top-and-tail approach.

While in certain circumstances a fast-moving, jam-packed commercial can be effective, in general a slower, more involving style is preferable. Don't be afraid to use silence as a way of achieving impact and adding power and conviction to the message. When in doubt, less is more.

The proposition

The golden rule of clarity and single-mindedness is as true in radio as in any other medium. There is no substitute for a clear, motivating and simple proposition, which should be repeated several times. It is after all the proposition that the audience will be responding to.

Response mechanisms

The single biggest misconception in radio advertising is that the audience can remember a multi-digit telephone number fired at them in the last two seconds of the commercial. There are three options:

1 If you are using your own telephone number, say it slowly and repeat it several times during the commercial.
2 Use a freephone number with a descriptive and memorable name. (In my view this is the best option, although call charges can be expensive.)
3 Use an 0800 number with a set of simple and memorable digits.

Details of these and many other facilities are available from British Telecom. Bear in mind that setting up telephone response mechanisms can take six weeks, so plan ahead.

Radio production

Let me explode a popular myth—that writing effective radio commercials is easy. It is not, and the general low standard of most radio commercials bears witness to this fact. An experienced radio writer should be employed, either through your agency or on a freelance basis.

Local radio stations do have facilities for writing and producing commercials. But bear in mind that they are more experienced in radio programming and broadcasting than in the skills of direct response advertising.

The best option is to talk directly to your advertising agency or a specialist radio production company. Although this can increase production costs a little, the quality of the end result is worth it. They will also book artists on your behalf, negotiate fees and buy-outs etc.

As a general rule all broadcast advertising must be approved by the independent television authority (ITVA). They will often insist on the inclusion of certain disclaimers and caveats, so get the script approved well before production.

Checklist

1 Have I considered the differences between the radio medium and print?
2 What is the real purpose of my radio advertising—awareness, an enquiry or a direct sale?
3 Have I considered talking to a professional media planning/buying operation to help achieve cost-effective targeting?
4 Apart from my prime targets, who else may I be able to influence?
5 What distractions are my commercials competing with during broadcast?
6 Is my script idea capable of involving the audience to the degree that they will *actively* listen?
7 Have I considered variable time lengths?
8 Is the proposition clear and have I repeated it?
9 Have I made the response mechanisms as easy as possible?
10 Have the ITVA approved my script?

6

Direct response advertising: new electronic media

STEWART PEARSON

The new media for the 1990s have one factor in common: the communication of information by electronic methods. What formats does this definition embrace?

'Newness' suggests important, perhaps revolutionary, change. Here we shall bypass well-established technologies such as facsimile and electronic mail, and deal with the most significant development facilitated by 'electronic' communication of information: interaction among users or between users and information.

Electronic media can be classified as either broadcast (point to multipoint) or interactive (point to point). Media which offer only broadcast capability, such as Ceefax and Oracle, are limited in application.

Here we consider the revolutionary interactive new media technologies which are poised to play a major role in business and in society: videotex, audiotext, optical storage, cable and satellite.

Videotex

Videotex is the generic term for all systems which communicate textual and graphic information electronically to low-cost terminals. Information is stored on a large host computer, and transmitted to the user by one of a number of alternative methods—broadcast, cable, satellite—but most frequently by telephone. The user controls receipt of the information, using simple procedures.

The key advantages of videotex are its low-cost and readily available communication (telephone networks) and display (television receivers) technology.

In the UK the oversophistication of system design and the high cost of terminals (adapted TV receivers) have restricted usage principally to business. The public system Prestel was the first in the world, yet only 90 000 terminals have been connected (40 000 to residential users). Over 2000 companies provide information. High-profile services include home banking (e.g. Bank of Scotland) and teleshopping (e.g. Littlewoods). The travel industry is a major user: over 90 per cent of travel agents are on Prestel, and over 85 per cent of bookings are made through the network.

The development of videotex in France could not have been more different. The French PTT launched Minitel in 1984, and there are currently more than three million users. Minitel terminals are low-cost and easy to use. The majority have been distributed free. Users can access any information provider's service via a three-digit 'kiosque' identifier, and billing is automatic.

Elsewhere videotex has not flourished. Various US ventures, heavy investments, have folded. The latest—Prodigy, a joint venture between IBM and Sears—is PC-based.

Usage of information services has, with the exception of Minitel, been disappointing. Some observers believe that the future lies in systems which transmit selectively to the user—it calls you rather you go to it. This preserves the information provider's added value role as selector and editor of information.

For the European Community a videotex network offers huge potential benefits (which only the transport industry has as yet seized). The challenge of standardising the protocols that control access to different networks remains to be overcome.

The electronic shopping opportunities created by videotex are clear, and (in France) early ventures have been successful. Direct marketers can also seize new opportunities to use videotex for the communication of messages and the display of marketing information.

Audiotex

Audiotex is the audio equivalent of videotex, using the telephone instead of the TV or PC. At the heart of an audiotex system is the voice-mail processor. This consists of a central processing unit which addresses, stores, and forwards messages. Line cards, which connect the processor to incoming telephone lines, detect tones and signals from the caller's telephone, and have the ability to digitise incoming speech. Typically, users are presented with an electronic message, and interact with this message via simple voice choices or touch-tone telephones.

Usage is significant in the US. TWA operate a number of audiotex systems, including a flight crew scheduling system handling thousands of enquiries each day. In the UK early usage has included sales promotions. And, while other banks set up home-banking networks on videotex, the TSB chose audiotex for its Speedlink service (users pay £10 for a keypad tone generator which fits onto the phone).

As business increasingly uses the telephone to give the public access, audiotex will grow in importance. It eliminates personal intervention and is thus highly cost-effective; it can deliver highly selective and detailed information (especially if linked to optical storage); and interacts with users.

Other applications are likely to use systems to dial-out selective messages (investment information) to voice mail boxes or, more controversially, to collect data from recipients of automatic calling (e.g. market research).

As a medium which permits selective communication and selective information capture, audiotex has a major role to play in direct marketing. The major opportunity is to capture data from and deliver data to inbound telephone calls.

Optical storage

Optical storage systems hold recorded information as small spots or pits in a spiral track, read by a tightly focused laser beam. The benefits are high capacity (600 Mb on a 12-cm disc), high security (data are permanent and secure), cost-effectiveness (low manufacturing costs), and flexibility.

The major optical storage media began with CD-A, the now ubiquitous audio compact disc.

The CD-ROM is a read-only memory compact disc on which computer data is recorded. The high storage potential and low distribution and manufacturing costs of CD-ROM have encouraged a growing number of applications. These include encyclopaedias (notably Grolier), specialist publishing (e.g. medical and software) and reference material of many kinds.

Newer developments in optical storage technology include CD-WORM (write-once-read-many-times) and fully erasable storage memory CD-E.

The development of CD-ROM may be threatened by more sophisticated technologies. CD-I supplements text and data with visual material—still pictures, animation, graphics. CD-V incorporates live video on a CD. Applications include sophisticated training, self-instruction, and enhanced sales presentation—in particular in retail outlets.

The volume capabilities of optical storage make it an ideal 'safebox' for major marketing information systems. Users will be able to access and interact with new volumes of data without recourse to large mainframes or complex communication links.

Cable

Cable has a specific application in the provision of television channels. Yet arguably (in Europe at least) TV can be provided more cheaply by radio and by satellite. Cable must compete by exploiting to the full its potential for broadband communications, and thus its ability to deliver a wider range of services.

Potential applications begin with HDTV (high definition TV), CATV (community antenna TV, an example of closed user group broadcasting being pioneered in Croydon), pay-per-view networks. But the most interesting possibilities are interactive services. Cable permits video telephony and video-conferencing. It can be used for surveillance, security and traffic monitoring. A broadband network can also permit high-volume data transmission.

Another new development is the video library. British Telecom have tested this concept in Westminster using their Switched Star network.

In the UK there remain only about a quarter of a million cable subscribers, with a total of just over one and a quarter homes passed by cable networks.

On a grander scale, Cable & Wireless set up an international broadband communications network, the Global Dynamic Highway.

Satellites

The development of VSATs (very small aperture terminals) as microterminals for reception of satellite messages has created the potential for the mass communication of information via satellites.

The major application in Europe has to date been data communication. The French Polycom system, for example, uses the Eutelsat F-1 satellite, and major users include Agence France-Press (for simultaneous transmission of pictures and text) and the Paris Bourse (for financial data).

DBS (direct broadcast satellites) permit transmission of signals to a defined geographical area of the earth, the 'footprint'. Eutelsat F-1 carried TV programming such as Music Box/Superchannel, but was low power, and required expensive reception equipment and large reception dishes. Newer, higher powered satellites will transmit to smaller and cheaper terminals, and have opened the way to the battle for the mass satellite TV market.

In the US more developed applications include transmission of market and financial data (Reuters), and data and video communication to retail outlets (K-Mart).

Satellites offer a potential means of communication to information providers who have to supply a large number of users over a wide geographical area. The key benefits of satellite are its range of coverage and the low cost of adding more receivers to the network.

Cable and satellite in direct marketing

Cable and satellite television will fragment television audiences, increasing the importance of finer targeting and of response advertising. Marketing will thus exploit the secular media trend towards 'narrowcasting'.

7

House-to-house distribution

BARRY ATTWOOD

Booking a door-to-door distribution has been likened to walking through a minefield, with each step taking you or, at least, your reputation closer to oblivion. In many instances, this can be true. Too many promoters actually create this minefield themselves. They put together costly promotions, steer them skilfully through numerous budget meetings and detailed planning sessions and, finally, look for a distribution company to deliver their items. The temptation, at this point, to accept the cheapest rate on offer, can easily backfire.

Choice of distributor

Buying on price alone, almost inevitably, results in a poor quality distribution. Unless the distributors are properly remunerated and payments made commensurate with contract requirements, the dream promotion can become a total failure.

So, how do you avoid the pitfalls, when faced with the wide selection of distribution companies listed in the back pages of *British Rate & Data*?

The best recommendation is a personal one. Unfortunately, many of your colleagues might have heard of companies, but never used them. Therefore, you should look at trade bodies, such as BDMA or ISP. They should be able to supply you with a list of member companies within the door-to-door industry. This process can eliminate the 'cowboy' operators and produce a limited selection of reliable companies.

When you contact your short list of companies, don't be afraid to probe:

- Ask about the number of full-time employees currently on their PAYE payroll.

- Ask about the companies for whom they have recently completed distributions. Can they name contacts within those companies?
- Find out how many area or regional managers are in their full-time employment. This is essential, as the area and regional managers actually control the distributions while they are in operation.
- Press for details about the organisational departments within the company, or even ask if you can pay a field visit, prior to booking a distribution.
- Finally, a visit to the company's head office can often provide a revealing insight into the quality of the management and the overall standard of administration.

A reputable company will welcome direct questions about their field operations. It is the hub of their business. Flashy sales brochures count for nothing unless the company can demonstrate its ability to mobilise an army of casual workers and turn them into an efficient unit under the supervision of a professional management system.

Types of distribution
There are really only three types of delivery.

SHAREPLAN
This is the most popular method of door-to-door distribution. It is normally a monthly facility, which entails the distribution company distributing a package of between three and five non-competitive items, against a common schedule to the same households. Items as large as 120-gramme brochures can be delivered within the shareplan, although smaller, lighter coupons or product samples are the norm.

There are only two companies who are large enough to offer this facility. These are Circular Distributors and MRM, both of which can supply you with guaranteed dates and timing for your product. They can also offer distribution schedules based on any marketing information which you may have at your disposal.

SOLUS OR SINGLE-ITEM DISTRIBUTION
The distribution is limited to one client who, therefore, has complete control over timing, coverage and market selection. This service, obviously, is more expensive than either of the other two options, but it is often the only way of meeting the marketing objectives. It is, for example, the only method by which you can make a personal call and place a

product sample in the hands of a prospective user. A questionnaire can also be incorporated.

FREE NEWSPAPER-LINKED DELIVERY
Weekly free newspapers are growing in popularity as a vehicle for leaflet delivery. Its main benefits include the ability to deliver your items within a 36-hour period, together with a very high penetration figure, as their distributors are normally the same people doing that round week in and week out. This system does have a few drawbacks, i.e. the workforce is mainly made up of 13–16 year olds, coupled with a 1–2 week delivery deadline prior to your distribution date.

Costs

This, obviously, depends on size, weight and, at times, bulk of the item, together with the quantity, area of coverage and targeting requirements. Very broadly, an average A4 single sheet item would cost:

Shareplan £10.95 per thousand
Free newspapers £11.00–£13.00 per thousand
Solus £25.00–£27.00 per thousand

Targeting

With the advent, in recent years, of geodemographic systems, such as ACORN, PINPOINT, LIFESTYLES and MOSAIC, the ability to target specific consumer groups has both increased the effectiveness of promotional companies and attracted new users into the marketplace. Many of these companies offer complete targeting and selection systems, which make it possible to reach your selected audience, whether it be by TV region, county, town, store catchment or administration area.

Creativity

Once you have chosen your friendly, well-established, highly motivated and conscientious distribution company and your leaflet or brochure has, finally, fallen on the doormat, then your creatively designed and well-thought-out item is on its own. Unlike conventional press ads, with their inherent production restraints, the scope for creating high impact mail shots with doormat appeal is virtually limitless. New print technology has spawned a range of intriguing involvement devices such as rub and reveal, fragrant bursts, scratch and sniff, pop-ups, window peel-offs, etc. Therefore, with some lively imagination, a mildly interesting communication can be transformed into a dynamic sales promotion device. Provided that your item is legal, non-toxic and is not larger than a letterbox, there is no limit to creative possibilities.

As long as you choose a reputable distribution company, coupled with proper targeting and creative design, then door-to-door is certainly a medium that makes walking through a minefield well worth while.

PART II

MARKETS

8

Business-to-business markets

STUART HEATHER, DAVID READ AND
WANDA GOLDWAG

Every year companies in this country spend over £1 billion on advertising and sales promotion to sell their products and services to other companies, to local authorities, government departments, nationalised industries and to people in the professions. And that expenditure excludes the cost of the salesforce.

What we now define as 'direct marketing' is what companies engaged in business-to-business marketing have been doing for years. They pioneered direct response press advertising for products and services, and were among the earliest users of direct mail. They have, in most cases, built their companies by dealing direct with their customers. And being able to identify their customers enabled them to build databases, measure the value of each customer in terms of sales value and identify prospects for sales leads.

Targeting

Targeting in industrial and commercial market sectors is relatively much easier than in consumer markets. Whereas manufacturers of consumer products have target audiences that can be measured in millions, in business-to-business marketing your target audience can be measured in thousands, or even, in certain market sectors, in hundreds. For example, the market for zinc is worth £47 million, but less than 300 companies purchase zinc and the major purchasers can be counted on your fingers.

Computer databases enable you to identify companies that are likely to respond to you by matching your existing customer profile with Standard Industrial Classifications (SIC) and seeing which other companies fall into the same classifications.

UK Kompass, for example, have a massive database of over 165 000 companies that you can access by SIC, size, product, sales turnover, number of employees or location, and you can trace each company's activities right down to the products they make. There is plenty of published data, as well as the services of such companies as Market Location Ltd, to help you build a database of potential purchasers.

First find your buyer

Did we give the impression that this life was easy? Of course there's a catch. The major problem is that companies do not buy anything. People do. And this is where targeting becomes extremely difficult in business-to-business marketing. Unlike consumer marketing, where one person or a small family group makes the buying decision, in business-to-business marketing you need to establish a dialogue and influence a larger number of people within each company. It is very unlikely that less than five people will be involved and there are occasions when as many as 150 people will be involved in the decision-making unit.

The way that companies arrive at the final purchasing decision is complex, and will differ from company to company. It can involve the board as well as senior and middle management in a wide range of departments working to different disciplines within a company. It can be influenced by people outside the purchasing company. Often the key decision makers are not in management at all—they are people in the office and on the shopfloor who will be using your product or services. And once you have identified the key decision makers, the next problem is to reach them. Most companies have built an infrastructure to protect them from people who are trying to sell things.

Lead generation is the first step in a complex area of purchasing and this will vary if you are selling replacement equipment or if you are selling a totally new product or service. The Cranfield School of Management study for the Financial Times, *How British Industry Buys*, is helpful here—copies can be obtained from the Financial Times.

Direct response press advertising

Research on 800 business-to-business advertisers by MIL Research Ltd, found that 40.2 per cent of advertising costs was spent on press advertising, with 34.5 per cent in business publications. Brochures to support the sales leads accounted for 14.4 per cent. Exhibitions accounted for 14.1 per cent. Direct mail to existing customers and prospects accounted for 8.1 per cent. Thus the key medium for lead generation is press.

In this country, using press advertising we have the ability to target with a high degree of accuracy in different market sectors. There are over 3000 publications covering virtually all businesses and industrial, commercial, trade and professional markets. These give advertisers the opportunity to reach decision makers and people who can influence the decisions, using precise targeting.

'Horizontal' publications enable you to reach people by position or job function across a wide spectrum of industries. 'Vertical' publications enable you to reach specific industrial or business sectors. Virtually every sector of business has its own specialist publication—often several. The medical profession alone has over 200.

An in-depth knowledge of each publication and its individual characteristics is essential in planning press advertising. Some publications will build product awareness and establish product status but give low response rates. Other publications are better at generating low-cost response. Know your media and the role they can play in your overall marketing strategy. Some advertisers use one publication to project brand identity and another for response advertising. A number of publishers have recognised this and produced product card packs, designed purely to get response, which they mail to subscribers to their 'status' publication.

Considerable research has been carried out on businessmen, their areas of buying responsibility, their decision-making involvements and the publications they read. The Business Media Research Committee's *Business Survey* should be on the desk of anyone planning press media for business-to-business advertising.

Direct mail

While direct mail plays a lesser role than press advertising in sales lead generation in business-to-business, it is a medium that will grow—thanks to the business magazine publishers. They have now built up large databanks of subscribers. They can select by SIC, size, location, job title, areas of buying responsibility, and they are now in the list rental business. All the major publishers—AGB, Benn, EMAP, Maclean-Hunter, Morgan-Grampian, Patey-Doyle and Reed—can help you target mailings to reach key decision makers.

Exhibitions, as well as enabling you to reach new prospects and meet existing customers, also provide a direct mail opportunity, because many exhibition organisers rent the names of those who attend.

The message

If you get the media right, the next step is to get the advertising right. Put across an advertising message that people will respond to and you'll get the leads you are looking for.

Appraise your product or service, look at your competition, research your market, understand your customer, establish a creative brief—all of which are as important here as in other types of advertising.

Follow-up

Once you have a lead it is vital that this is followed up promptly and properly. The way you respond and the speed with which you respond are important if you are to convert that enquiry into a sale. There should be total synergy between the original advertising and the follow-up. All too often people invest too much in the advertising and pay too little attention to the follow-up needed to turn that expensive enquiry into a sale.

Any follow-up should remind people of the advertising they responded to in the first place. This should be designed to amplify and expand the information in the advertising, clearly and simply but in greater depth. Ideally, it should be capable of closing the sale or, in a more complex situation, to make the prospect want to see someone from your company.

With the cost of a sales call running at between £150 and £200, it is usually cheaper and faster to follow up the sales lead with a carefully constructed mailing pack, including a personal letter and your brochure. Naturally, if the lead is from someone within a company that you have already identified as a prime prospect, get the salesforce to *deliver* your follow-up pack, which now becomes the 'sales presenter'.

Telephone can also be used for immediate response to a sales lead. If you are sending out a follow-up pack, say so; if the prospect wants a sales visit, fix it. After you have sent out the follow-up pack, 'phone to see that it has arrived. Find out if your prospect, or his or her colleagues, needs further information. Every contact should be helping you to sell, to turn that lead into an order.

Do not forget that decisions in purchasing in business-to-business can take time. Sometimes as long as five years can elapse from enquiry to purchase. With sales calls getting more and more expensive, direct mail can play an increasingly important role in keeping your company to the forefront of the prospect's mind.

If you are using third parties to follow-up your sales leads, your dealers or your distributors, make certain that they do so properly. Those leads cost you money. If the enquirer isn't getting the follow-up that is expected, you, as the advertiser, get the blame, not your distributors.

Finally, one tip that will put your learning curve up with a vengeance. Put yourself in the place of a potential customer. Respond to your own advertising and that of your competitors and see how each one, including your own company, reacts to the sales lead. Then ask yourself: 'If I was the customer, whose company would I buy from?' Make sure it's yours.

Checklists
Business-to-business opportunities for direct marketing:

- off-the-page sales
- product and service enquiries
- qualified leads
- brand/product preference
- informed audiences—non-customers
                          —customers
- corporate awareness

Will the direct marketing strategy:

- have measurable effect?
- provide a good return on investment?
- enhance the company image?
- be consistent and synergetic with other marketing activities?
- offer value to the recipient?
- contain appropriate messages?
- yield data for future use?
- support and be acceptable to the salesforce?

Print media choices:

- insert and response advertising
- list mailing (external lists)
- dialogue programme (internal lists)
- personal mail (from named individual to named individual)
- catalogues
- customer magazines
- annual report

The opportunity base model
The willing buyer:

1 is aware that the product or service exists
2 recognises the need for the product or service
3 has a desire to satisfy that need
4 has prioritised that need above other competing or conflicting desires
5 is satisfied that the product or service will satisfy the need

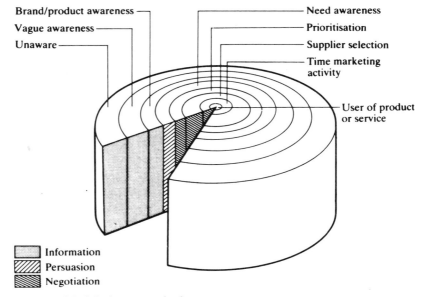

Figure 8.1 Model of opportunity base

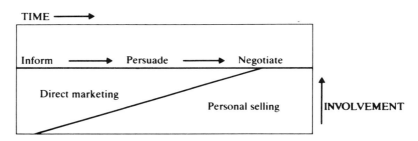

Figure 8.2 From information to negotiation

6 is assured that the seller can deliver and support the product or service
7 is satisfied that the price/contractual terms are as favourable as possible.

The process is concentric (see Figure 8.1), moving from informing through persuading to negotiating. In planning a direct marketing strategy to support a salesforce, the key question is: 'In which band is the individual we need to talk to situated?'

As we move through the sales process from information to negotiation, the need for personal selling increases. Striking the correct balance and cutover point is critical (see Figure 8.2).

If a lead does not justify the salesperson's time in following up, no action will be taken even if the lead has potential value. The result is a dissatisfied enquirer. The cutover point is too early. Leaving the customer contact too late is to invite an informed and potentially willing buyer to talk to your competitors.

A business-to-business action matrix

The first step in any business-to-business programme is to create a marketing plan to cover every stage of the campaign (Table 8.1). Answers to the following questions should be set out in a programme matrix and agreed before the programme starts.

1 *Who are the target audience for the product?*

They might be:
(a) an individual decision maker for a low or repeat purchase, so that a one-step sale is possible;
(b) an individual decision maker for a more expensive or less common product, who will need a number of approaches, e.g. a direct mail package followed by a questionnaire and then an order form;
(c) an individual decision maker with a complex or expensive product, when a variety of different approaches will be needed, e.g. direct mail followed by telephone appointment setting a sales call and product demonstration;
(d) a number of people because the purchase is very expensive or affects many parts of the company, e.g. group strategy controller, budget controller, technical controller, manager, end user.

2 *What list sources, internal and external, are available?*

(a) Start by creating a file of existing customers with their contact and purchasing history, as they will be the best prospects for new purchasers. In addition, put any companies you no longer wish to trade with in a suppression file.
(b) Add recent enquirers. Again, contact history should be listed, plus data on the source of their enquiry.
(c) Collate current sales leads and make a decision either to exclude them from the programme or to transfer them into some aspects of it.
(d) Only then should outside lists, directories and compiled files be considered. Base your selection on profiling the existing customer and enquiry bases and selecting similar companies in terms of factors such as industry type, number of employees and geographical location.

Table 8.1 A programme matrix

List sources	Total quantity	Contact 1	Quantity	Fulfilment	Contact 2	Contact 3
Existing customers	55 000	Mailing version 1A	25 000	Send product ⟶	Mail thank you	—
		Mailing version 1B	25 000	Sales visit ⟶	Send product ⟶	Mail thank you
					Arrange demo ⟶	Send product
		Telephone call script 1	5 000	If 'Yes' Send product ⟶	Mail thank you	—
					Tel. thank you	—
				If 'Maybe' Sales visit ⟶	Send product ⟶	Mail thank you
					Arrange demo ⟶	Send product
				If 'No' Information pack ⟶	Sales visit ⟶	Telephone
Recent enquirers	10 600	Mailing version 1C	10 600	Sales visit ⟶	Send product ⟶	Mail thank you
					Arrange demo ⟶	Send product
Old sales contacts	800	Telephone call script 2A	400	Information pack ⟶	Telephone call ⟶	Sales visit
						Arrange demo
		Telephone call script 2B	400	Questionnaire pack ⟶	Telephone call ⟶	Sales visit
						Arrange demo
Martin's customers	250	Letter from Martin	250	Sales visit ⟶	Send product ⟶	Mail thank you
					Arrange demo ⟶	Send product
Danny's customers	200	Letter from Danny	200	Information pack ⟶	Sales visit ⟶	Send product
						Arrange demo

Outside List 1 — 25 000 — Mailing version 3 — 25 000 — Information pack ⟶ Sales visit ⟶ Send product / Arrange demo

Outside List 2 — 15 000 — Mailing version 3 — 7 500 — Information pack ⟶ Sales visit ⟶ Send product / Arrange demo; ⟶ Telephone call ⟶ Send product / Arrange demo

Mailing version 4 — 7 500 — Questionnaire pack ⟶ Sales visit ⟶ Send product / Arrange demo; ⟶ Telephone call ⟶ Send product / Arrange demo

Outside List 3 — 30 000 — Mailing version 4 — 15 000 — Questionnaire pack ⟶ Sales visit ⟶ Arrange demo / Send product; ⟶ Telephone call ⟶ Sales visit

Mailing version 5 — 15 000 — Information pack ⟶ Telephone call ⟶ Sales visit

3 *What is the contact strategy with different groups of customers?*

A contact strategy needs to be set for different target groups based, where available, on previous successful contact experience. For example, direct mail can be used for lead generation, to create a response to a questionnaire, to sell immediately or in two stages. A telephone call can do the same job. Thus a decision needs to be made on what target group will be reached more cost-efficiently by direct mail than by telephone, and whether a number of different contacts need to be made during the selling process. Having decided on the methodology, timing and frequency of contacts need to be agreed.

4 *How will a response be fulfilled?*

For each target market define the necessary speed and complexity of response. In some cases there may be a legal requirement for a contract to be signed or a cooling-off period to occur. Fulfilment methods include:

(a) acknowledgement of order either with the delivery or separately
(b) information pack
(c) questionnaire pack to gain information on customer requirements
(d) application pack
(e) telephone call
(f) sales visit
   or any combination of the above.

5 *What is the follow-up strategy?*

Define the follow-up procedures for each group of prospects:

(a) buyers
(b) buyers who don't pay
(c) enquirers
(d) questionnaire responders
(e) receivers of application forms, telephone calls and sales visits who have not bought.

6 *How will monitoring and analysis of results be carried out and what are the criteria for success?*

At each stage a methodology must be agreed for monitoring and analysing the effectiveness of each action.

(a) How will results be collated, e.g. manually, or as part of the computerised fulfilment process? Who will be responsible for obtaining the results of, for example, a sales call?

(b) How will costs be allocated over a series of fulfilment letters which share common artwork or in terms of a salesperson's annual salary?

(c) What criteria for success will be used? Must each part of the contact strategy be profitable, or will it be acceptable if the programme as a whole makes a profit but an individual component only breaks even?

9

Financial services

RICHARD HILL

Personal financial services advertising has grown dramatically over the last 10 years and the direct response sector of personal financial services advertising even more so. In the last few years this dramatic growth has been fuelled not only by the Financial Services Act, the Building Societies Act and new pensions legislation but also by the fact that financial services companies have woken up to the dramatic impact marketing (and especially direct response) can have on their businesses. With 1992 just around the corner and Britain arguably the most free market in Europe for financial services, we can expect more of the same.

Growth and size
In 1987 financial services advertisers spent nearly £700 million out of a total of £6.3 billion on advertising all consumer products and services. This means that they account for 11 per cent of all promotional spend in 1987 compared with 6.5 per cent in 1981. Additionally, that growth in expenditure equates to a 48 per cent increase in real (inflation adjusted) terms. There are now over 800 companies, selling via nearly 1700 brands over 50 financial products or services.

In terms of direct response, personal financial service companies represent the largest spenders (at rate card) in the press (page space and inserts) (see Table 9.1).

When press and broadcast media are taken together, financial services represent 10 of the top spending 100 advertisers (see Table 9.2), 19 of the top spending 100 brands (Media Expenditure Analysis (MEAL)) and 83 of the top spending 500 brands (Media Register). The top 40 parent companies spent £233 million on these brands during 1989.

Table 9.1   Press advertising of personal financial products and services 1988

Total no. ads	Rate card expenditure £m	% of all press ads	% of all press spend (rate card)
19 984	116 021	15.8	23.0

Source: Nationwide Market Research.

Table 9.2   Top spending financial services companies 1989

Rank	Advertiser	Total (£000s)	TV (%)	Press (%)	Radio (%)
1	NatWest Bank	25 733	11 672	533	12 849
2	Halifax Building Society	24 161	10 304	68	13 188
3	Midland Bank	24 101	12 772	91	10 495
4	Abbey National Bank	22 839	11 470	226	10 476
5	Barclays plc	17 948	9 251	54	8 105
6	Nationwide Anglia Building Society	14 730	4 916	1 666	7 863
7	TSB Bank	12 065	6 903	460	4 300
8	Lloyds Bank	9 629	4 584	—	4 778
9	Guardian Royal Exchange Assurance	8 314	6 445	—	1 494
10	Royal Bank of Scotland	7 819	4 494	4	3 060

Source: MEAL.

Legislation

Marketers in financial services must ensure that they are familiar with increasingly complex legislation and regulations affecting their work, including bodies such as the Bank of England, the Department of Trade and Industry (DTI) or the Office of Fair Trading (OFT) and of self-regulatory authorities specific to their area of business (see Table 9.3 overleaf). These include:

1 Legislation, e.g:
   - Trades Descriptions Act
   - Fair Trading Act
   - Data Protection Act
   - Consumer Credit Act
   - Financial Services Act

2 Advertising codes and authorities, e.g:
   - BCAP   British Code of Advertising Practice
   - ASA   Advertising Standards Authority

Table 9.3 Regulation of financial services advertising

	Media and/or type of advertising			
	Non-broadcast media (excluding investment advertising as defined in Financial Services Act)	*Non-broadcast media* (all financial advertising defined in Financial Services Act)	*Broadcast media* (all financial advertising including investment advertising as defined in Financial Services Act)	*Cable* (all financial including investment advertising as defined in Financial Services Act)
Responsible government department	DTI	DTI	Home Office	Home Office
Administrative authority	OFT	SIB	SIB IBA	SIB Cable authority
Established means	ASA/CAP	5 SROs (AFBD; FIMBRA; IMRO; LAUTRO; ISRO)	(TV) ITCA (Radio) ICR	5 SROs Cable operators/providers
Major legislative and/or self-regulatory requirements	Financial Services Act Trade Descriptions Act Fair Trading Act Consumer Credit Act BCAP	Financial Services Act SIB's Rules SROs' Rules Take over panel BCAP	Financial Services Act Trade Descriptions Act Fair Trading Act Consumer Credit Act IBA Code	Financial Services Act Fair Trading Act Trade Descriptions Act Consumer Credit Act IBA Code or Cable Authority Guidelines SROs' Rules

Source: Advertising Association.

- ITVA   Independent Television Association
- CAA   Cinema Advertising Association
- BDMA   British Direct Marketing Association
- DMSSB   Direct Mail Services Standards Board

3 Self-regulatory organisations (SROs), e.g:
- LAUTRO   Life Assurance and Unit Trust Regulatory Organisation
- FIMBRO   Financial Intermediaries Managers & Brokers
              Regulatory Association
- IMRO   Investment Management Regulatory Organisation
- UTA   Unit Trust Association
- AFBD   Association of Future Brokers and Dealers
- ISRO   International Securities Regulatory Organisation
- SIB   Securities Investment Board

4 Trade associations
- ABI   Association of British Insurers
- FHA   Finance Houses Association
- CCTA   Consumer Credit Trade Association
- BIIBA   British Insurance and Investment Brokers Association

5 Ombudsmen
- Insurance
- Banking

Direct marketing in financial services

Most financial services are relatively intangible. The only form of 'product' that exists is a transaction methodology (e.g. cheque book, credit card) or a value certificate (e.g. bank statement, share certificate, insurance certificate/schedule/policy) that, in itself, may have little intrinsic worth being paper or plastic based, even though it represents something very valuable.

Clearly, this makes direct response marketing of the product or service potentially very attractive and profitable, as costs of fulfilment are relatively low even when high levels of security are required.

However, whereas most tangible consumer products have a distinct and discrete price for a distinct and discrete reward (e.g. clock-radio £19.99) with a standard margin for the product, the nature of consumer financial services frequently requires a quite different costing approach that combines input expenses-based costing with customer/portfolio costing. This is because:

   (i) Many financial services have to be underwritten and some have to be priced individual sale by individual sale. This allows, in turn, the potential profitability of each customer to be established and those that are believed to be unprofitable risks to be declined.

  (ii) This need to ensure profitability via underwriting control means that there can be substantial built-in wastage, as anything from 5 to 95 per cent of applicants may be rejected. This can increase the fully loaded cost per sale substantially over the basic recruitment cost per response.

 (iii) It is the lifetime value of the net income from the customer that is frequently important, as little revenue may be earned at sale time (e.g. a credit card customer with a nil balance at issue has cost money to acquire, will continue to cost money to service and will not become profitable until his or her individual balance is large enough to produce enough interest revenue to pay for the cost of the acquisition and servicing as well as the money he has borrowed).

Given these factors, detailed planning, targeting and costing of each campaign for each product are essential. Of course, this is also true of tangible, consumer products. However, with them the variables leading to a profitable share are likely to be somewhat fewer and more fixed as campaign profitability is not dependent on two variables, i.e. the response mix *and* the underwriting mix produced by that response mix. However, the planning stages for a campaign are the same as for any direct response campaign, with the possible exception that the test matrices are likely to be more complex.

   The design of direct response financial products for customer segments based on class, age, lifestyle, geographic or geodemographic variables makes sense *before* they are marketed. This means that database information can be a key building block for a successful campaign. With proper database usage it is possible for customers, for example, to be 'pre-screened' (i.e. underwritten before response), so that promises can be given that the product is 'guaranteed' to be available to *you*, Mr Customer, should you respond. Techniques of this type, when combined with a multi-media approach (e.g. direct mail combined with coupon and inbound telephone response plus outbound follow-up), can raise response/conversion rates as much as tenfold.

Summary
Direct response marketing of financial services is growing fast. It is complicated not only by the 'standard' legal and regulatory framework,

but also by legal and regulatory hurdles that can be specific to sectors of the financial service industry or even particular products. The nature of campaign planning is similar to that for other direct response campaigns except that the extra legal and regulatory burdens have to be taken into account. In addition, campaign planning should ensure that a customer/portfolio costing approach is combined with input expense-based costing to help to ensure profitability.

10

Direct marketing and packaged goods

BRYAN HALSEY

Direct, or targeted, marketing is slowly gaining recognition as a means of selling and/or promoting packaged and branded goods, including fast moving consumer goods (f.m.c.g.), although case studies are still few and far between. Nevertheless the dynamic nature of the direct marketing industry whose members are constantly exploring new applications for their techniques, coupled to problems being experienced by conventional marketers, will ensure its gradual acceptance.

Dramatic developments in consumer marketing over the past 10 years continue to cause serious problems for conventional marketers, presenting openings for the skilled and realistic direct marketer.

Changes in retailing The large multiple retailer is continuing to grow in influence, with ever fewer buying points, an even greater dependence on own labels, and a total disdain for point of sale promotion. At the same time there has been a re-emergence of the corner grocery, often under Asian control, whose numbers and locations are a major headache for the salesforce.

Changes in media The media scene is about to undergo further change with the opening of more broadcast channels, while recent years have seen the arrival of satellite and cable TV, falling audiences, rising costs and the widespread use of pre-recorded videos.

The changing consumer The typical consumer, much beloved of mass marketers, has all but disappeared. Women marry later, have fewer children, and often work as well as run a home. The birth rate has fallen. Ethnic groups are affecting consumer taste. Most homes today are occupied not by standard 'ITV families' of two parents and two children, but by single parents, empty nesters, senior citizens and, increasingly, by men and women of all ages living alone.

Changing goals Marketers are increasingly compelled to deliver short-term results, which has led to an on-going shift away from long-term brand development towards short-term tactical activity, much of it highly wasteful in terms of return on investment.

Amid this vast sea of change, direct marketing is beginning to be seen by many as a panacea, which, if used properly, it can be. It certainly holds the key to long-term relationships with expensively won customers, and to more efficient database-driven sales promotions. On the other hand, there are three major obstacles to the direct sale of goods from factory to consumer:

- The very real fear of disturbing established channels of distribution, e.g. salesforces, wholesalers, retailers.
- The high cost of direct marketing for single mass-marketed low-ticket lines.
- The logistical and practical problems of distribution.

The first essential, therefore, before embarking on a direct marketing programme, is to determine exactly WHY it is being considered. The existence of a simple customer list, or a fully-fledged database, in itself is not a sufficient reason. All too often expensive databases are set up without reference to how they will ultimately be deployed.

Is DM for me?

Any conventional marketer who can tick one or more of the following statements should investigate both the strategic and tactical potential of direct marketing:

I've introduced some great new products but I can't persuade retailers to give them shelf space. ☐

Every year my company introduces more new lines than we can find, or afford, mass media to promote. ☐

I know that 90 per cent of my traditional sales promotion activity is wasted but there doesn't seem to be an alternative. ☐

I can persuade my customers to try my products but I need to improve on their loyalty to the brand. ☐

Some products we could introduce are not suited to our normal retail network; I would like to try selling them direct to the consumer. ☐

The problem with our advertising is that there is so much about our product that we would like to tell people, but we can't for one reason or another. ☐

Much of the profit in my business comes from incremental add-on sales. ☐

We can promote our product to the public but the trouble is that shop assistants can't answer customers' questions. ☐

We're losing touch with our customers and what they think; if we received more feedback, including complaints, we could provide a better service. ☐

All the main contenders in our market offer very similar products and terms; we're looking for a way to gain an edge over the competition. ☐

What can direct marketing do for my brand?
The following list, condensed from case histories in four continents, suggests some of the specific uses to which direct marketing can be put by packaged and branded goods manufacturers:

- Reinforcing brand loyalty, customer retention (e.g. a collection and reward scheme directed specifically at prospects and frequent users instead of at the public as a whole).
- Database sales promotion (reducing waste and improving efficiency by targeting known non-user prospects).
- Identifying and serving niche markets (using couponed or telephone response advertising to identify prospects who are then promoted by direct mail or telephone).
- Direct sale of products that cannot be delivered conventionally.
- Promoting products for which media advertising is not possible or cannot be afforded.
- Cross-selling from major to minor product lines (e.g. using packs or guarantee cards to obtain the names of buyers who then receive offers of ancillary or related products).
- Augmenting product information to consumers and prospects. (Retail-

ers and their staffs can seldom explain a product's technical benefits well, whereas direct methods can do it comprehensively and expertly.)

- Training and motivating dealers and staff.
- Promoting new and unconventional uses for established products. (A branded product rarely dares to veer from its chosen image to advocate an alternative use for itself, but a directly addressed message may do so with less risk of detriment to the brand's overall standing.)
- Feedback and research from 'live' users. (The ultimate goal of direct marketing is an on-going dialogue.)
- Overcoming weak geographical areas of distribution, by direct marketing to localities having likely customer profiles.
- Putting customers in touch with specific stockists, and vice versa.
- Adding value to a product or service (e.g. a personal information service to update customers with new product features).
- Supplementing salesforce calls cycle. (Direct mail or telephone can contact a retailer for a fraction of the cost of a visit.)
- Creating leads for salesforce and dealers. (Research shows that customers who have identified themselves are always the best prospects.)
- Liquidating advertising costs through direct sales of related goods (the classic double-duty theory: advertising that sells can also be effective as brand image advertising—for example, selling clothing with a well-known logo).
- Maintaining long-term links with customers; maximising the lifetime value of a customer. (As the car companies do, staying in touch with a customer to monitor and satisfy changing tastes and needs.)

A cursory study of the foregoing demonstrates how demarcation lines between advertising, distribution, sales promotion, customer service, product development, market research, etc., are being eroded in response to new needs.

Entry into direct marketing demands a careful study of sales promotion practice and its rules and regulations, which are detailed in the British Code of Advertising Practice (see Appendix 2) and the British Code of Sales Promotion Practice, available from CAP Committee, Brook House, 2–16 Torrington Place, London WC1E 7HN. It also requires familiarisation with the specialisms of direct marketing, including database and list management, direct mail print and production, telephone marketing, direct response advertising, household distribution, fulfilment, geodemographics and psychographics, and statistical analysis. Fortunately each of these specialisms has its own practitioners, textbooks, symposia, etc.

A company considering the use of direct marketing for packaged goods must ultimately make a decision on its organisation. There are three broad choices, dependent, of course, on the objectives:

1 *Total marketing* (or maxi-marketing)   A far-reaching decision to adopt strategic direct marketing for all of an organisation's marketing activity. While it is rare for established organisations to switch to this route, many new companies have already adopted it, often using a direct marketing agency to implement or orchestrate their total marketing programme. Total marketing is increasingly deployed by the financial institutions.

2 *Integrated marketing*   The various disciplines (e.g. brand advertising, direct marketing, sales promotion and PR) work together to ensure a consistency of objectives and image throughout an organisation's entire marketing effort.

3 *Parallel marketing*   Brand awareness, sales promotion, and direct marketing work in splendid isolation. The benefit of this approach is almost certainly political or logistical rather than enhanced efficiency, but it has its adherents.

However, before embarking on direct marketing for conventionally distributed goods, an early discussion with a firm of experienced multi-discipline practitioners is advisable.

11

Charities

DAVID STRICKLAND-EALES

The title of one of Dale Carnegie's best-known books *How to Win Friends and Influence People* is in the minds of most charities when they are considering, or are already using, direct marketing. And, in the main, it is seen as a highly efficient, non labour-intensive means of fundraising.

Uses of direct marketing

Charities use direct marketing for many applications, but principally for:

- donor recruitment and fundraising
- membership
- sponsorship (e.g. Third World children)
- mail order catalogue selling
- legacy income generation
- campaigning/lobbying
- general communications
- research

As the competition between charities intensifies—fuelled by an ever-growing demand for income to finance the services or aid provided by charities—so the importance of the contribution made by direct response fundraising grows, and it is now recognised as a significant source of revenue.

Direct marketing media

Like other market sectors, charities use a range of direct marketing media:

- *Direct mail*: probably the most successful, cost-effective and universally relevant medium.

- *Press advertising*: effectiveness (i.e. money raised off-the-page) has declined over recent years other than for major disaster appeals, e.g. Bhopal, Ethiopia. Its application is now focused more on two-stage tactics (or lead generation), membership or appeals with a topical dimension.
- *Loose inserts*: increasingly used, chiefly for 'high ticket' fundraising like child sponsorship or long-term giving programmes—usually in the Third World.
- *Television and radio*: since restrictions were lifted in 1989, a number of charities have experimented with TV fundraising but it has yet to prove its cost-effectiveness.
- *Household distribution, telephone and outdoor media*: relatively undeveloped.

The profit margin

Like all other applications of direct marketing, there are both successes and failures in the charity market—some of them spectacular. In the main, the failures can be attributed to one or more of the following:

- inappropriate goals/expectations
- poor execution
- lack of attention to detail

What return can a charity expect from any investment in direct response fundraising? As in all other market sectors, response rates, expected return-on-investment (ROI) rates and so on are bandied about constantly. The truth is, *there is no single level of across-the-market* expectation. It is all a function of the equation based on cost, volume, organisation, audience, proposition and profile.

However, as a rule of thumb, only very rarely does a charity's initial investment in direct marketing—that is to say, its first campaign (irrespective of media)—yield a profit (excess of revenue over total costs). It is unwise, other than in exceptional circumstances, to expect an immediate net return. Fundraising is like most other businesses: the real profit comes from the on-going relationship with the donor/supporter through the continued use of direct marketing and, in particular, direct mail. Here, it is not uncommon to find ROI levels at well in excess of 500 per cent and, exceptionally, above 1000 per cent.

Motivation to respond

Direct response fundraising differs from all other applications of direct marketing in the motivational rationale of the respondent. Giving to charity is all about appealing to self-esteem, not greed or fear or security or any of the other more basic human needs. There is no 'need to buy' rationale of the kind that can be created with, say, financial services or consumer goods. And it is the ability to really understand this behavioural difference and to know how to apply the techniques of direct marketing effectively which distinguishes the good from the bad and the successes from the failures.

The uplifting effect of long copy letters, premium gifts, involvement devices and so on, which work so well in other direct marketing applications, sometimes work for charities, but not always. Surprises (failures) lie in wait. The key, as in all uses of direct marketing, is to test—but test intelligently.

The use of premium gifts as a reward for a response to a charity does work, but there is a much greater need for the premium to have direct relevance to the subject/cause. A premium of 'perceived' or notional/intrinsic value rather than real value often works just as well. The development of devices such as 'Rolls of Honour', 'Friends', Donor Hierarchies/Clubs are good examples of this.

As with most other consumer markets, research is critical. Many charities make use of research to measure interest in their work, the relevance of their tactical approach and the targeting of their direct mail.

Reciprocal mailings

One of the most successful of all forms of direct mail fundraising has been through the operation of 'reciprocal mailings'—that is, where one charity mails another charity's list of donors/members and vice versa. For further guidance on this, the Institute of Charity Fundraising Managers (ICFM) has produced a Code of Practice for Reciprocal Mailings as a guide and basis of agreement for all interested parties. The ICFM also provides excellent basic and advanced training/workshops in the application of direct marketing for charities.

Key points

To make the best use of a direct marketing programme, bear in mind the following 10 key points:

1 Tell a positive story—people need to feel there is hope in sight to encourage them to give.
2 Create a real human need—because people give to people, not organisations.
3 Tell real stories—human interest is the best motivation.

4   Use responsibly the tricks of the trade—lift letters, clever formats and so on can work.
5   Make it easy for people to respond—the donation form must be 'user friendly'.
6   Tell them why you need their help—creating the 'rationale to give'.
7   Make the donors feel good—don't make them feel guilty about not giving.
8   Find an interesting way to tell your story—copy is very important.
9   Involve the donors in the story/the project—make them feel that their gifts will do something positive.
10 Say 'thank you' afterwards—consider the 'thank you' as part of the relationship building, not as an administration cost.

12

Retail sector

NEIL STEVENS

The use of direct marketing by a retail company is potentially full of contradictions.

The shopkeeper's culture, expertise and investment are all focused on operating and selling through stores and people. So how can a marketing tool specifically designed to bypass the salesperson and shop find a place in that business?

In fact, once these contradictions have been resolved, direct marketing can be a very powerful part of the retailer's marketing tool-kit.

Many retailers collect names and addresses of their customers in the ordinary course of business, e.g.:

- in-house credit cards
- other in-house credit arrangements
- home delivery service
- service agreements
- guarantee cards.

And these lists can often provide the basis for setting up an active direct marketing operation.

Strategy
The first step is to be clear about the strategic implications of this approach. Direct marketing will offer two possibilities:

1 to generate more store traffic; and
2 to sell goods direct.

Before embarking on direct marketing to generate store traffic, ask yourself:

1 Will the mechanics allow its effectiveness to be measured? You must have a method of comparing it with traditional above-the-line advertising.
2 How is the database actually going to be used? It is easy to be enthused by the very idea of all these potential marketing opportunities without subjecting them to a cold bucket of reality.

If your prime purpose is to use direct marketing to sell direct, ask:

1 Will they be additional sales or will they merely replace shop sales and at a lower margin?
2 What range of products should be offered for direct sale? If it is distinctive and separate from that on offer in your stores it can solve the problem of 1 above. On the other hand the catalogue then ceases to function as a store guide.
3 Have I recognised the potential cultural conflicts that may arise when the disciplines of direct marketing are introduced to a retail business? Generally retailers do not make good direct sellers, and vice versa.

Once the strategic issues have been resolved the tactics and techniques become clearer.

Increasing store traffic

For the retailer using direct marketing to encourage store traffic, many of the techniques designed to maximise mail order response do not apply. By definition, his customers are not 'mail order responsive': they buy from stores. So make copy short and to the point. Keep the mailing pack simple. Ten separate pieces may work for the dedicated home shopper, but probably won't for the retail charge cardholder. In fact, a postcard mailing, in which you squander those extra grams allowed by the Royal Mail, will probably work better than the heavyweight pack.

Some form of incentive, though, is essential: a privileged customer evening with 10 per cent off all purchases; a prize draw on the night as an additional attraction to a store opening; a £5 voucher when you spend £50 accompanying an advance notice of the sale. And usually the incentive can be the reason for the outgoing name and address to be returned so that the performance of the promotion can be measured.

What is crucial to all the above is the backing and cooperation of the stores sales staff. And this can be enhanced if the sales from your promotion can be presented as incremental, thus adding to the retail staff's incentive scheme payments.

Once the value of the direct approach has been demonstrated, ways of expanding the customer database soon arise. For example, if you are offering money off vouchers in the press, ask for the name and address to be completed before presentation at the counter; the request can only add value to the offer. But don't forget to source key the vouchers and ask your stores to return them to you. Lists generated this way are not refreshed so don't keep mailing them unless you are measuring the response; 18 months is probably the maximum life of such a list.

Direct selling

Retailers often start selling direct as an additional service to the store customer. If a catalogue or leaflet is being produced as a store guide, then it is a short step to add an order form and ship direct to the customer's home.

Merely doing this can produce substantial mail order turnover—but not a genuine mail order business, because new customers are generated through the stores at no cost to the mail order business. There is a temptation to extend the distribution of the catalogue outside the store, incurring advertising and postage costs to do so.

It is essential in this mixed type of business to keep track of the source of orders coming into the mail order division, and to allocate promotion costs to these sources so that their effectiveness can be judged. You need to know if the orders coming in at no cost from the stores may be concealing an unprofitable two-step advertising campaign.

The stores themselves can be used as a medium for the mail order business, housing, for example:

- a catalogue shop-in-shop where samples of products only available through mail order are displayed;
- a laser disc display unit which allows customers to browse through illustrations of products and through which in-house cardholders can order;
- a stand fitting into a metre of shelf space which advertises the catalogue and invites orders;
- a point-of-sale dispenser for mail order leaflets;
- bag-stuffing of mail order leaflets.

But in all cases there must be confidence that the direct sell offering does not clash with the main business of the store.

Potential problems

The mixed retail/mail order business gives rise to a number of potential problems:

1 Where the ranges offered by the mail order and retail businesses overlap, pricing can be a point of conflict. The direct seller will want high prices so that he has room to incentivise response and increase order value. The shopkeeper will favour low prices that are competitive in the High Street.

2 Prices are always best printed in the catalogue/store guide rather than on a loose insert. But if it has a life of six months or more, it can inhibit the needs of the retail business to raise prices.

3 The catalogue/store guide can also inhibit ranging in the store. If the products illustrated are not stocked by the stores, customer frustration can result. But maintaining them throughout the life of the catalogue reduces the flexibility of buyers seeking to refresh mid-season ranges.

13

Mail order catalogues

GEORGE SMITH

Operating through a catalogue is a high-risk, high-reward operation. It depends on large numbers to make sense of the inevitably high promotional cost. You will need lots of potential customers, then you will need lots of active customers, then you will need lots of repeat customers. At which point you may have built a profitable business.

The best tool with which to start a catalogue is a sizeable list of your own customers. Start to worry if you haven't got one, for this is not an area of direct marketing that can thrive on cold lists, no matter how apposite they appear to be. And, of course, building a catalogue operation is usually a long-term exercise. It has been said that it takes a first year to develop the right mix of product, a second year to attract 'first time' buyers, and a third year to see how many buy again.

Perhaps this exaggerates the problem, and I've yet to meet a catalogue operator who is willing to invest over a three-year period. But the main point is a good one: if you can get a catalogue right and profitable first time, you have achieved a minor trading miracle. And the direct marketing field is littered with the corpses of entrepreneurs who had a great catalogue idea but thought they would get their money back in a year. It doesn't work like that.

Part of the trouble is the sheer cost of the exercise. If you take what has become recognised as the standard module for a specialised mail order catalogue—32 pages of A5—you are going to need more than a hundred products to spread the risk. You are going to need sophisticated fulfilment capacity to deal not just with the actual orders but with the queries and the 'returns' (they can be up to 60 per cent in some fashion categories). And you may well have spent £40 000 in getting the catalogue to print.

It also takes time. The gestation period for a catalogue, involving price negotiation on a wide variety of products, a considerable photographic assignment and creative work on a scale that dwarfs anything else you're likely to produce—all this and four-colour print cycles—will mean that your catalogue planning period will be measured in months, not weeks. And usually lots of months, which denies you the tactical short-term advantages of other forms of direct marketing. In terms of sales forecasting, it can become a nightmare. Remember the plight of buyers with the large mail order houses who have to predict fashion taste in 12 months' time.

These are the pitfalls and they are often covered by sheer professionalism and a respectable budget. And, obviously, catalogues can be made to work and generate significant profit.

Before going further, it is worth pointing out the three main types of mail order catalogue: agency, direct and specialogue. The agency catalogue is the traditional multi-product catalogue often offering instalment payment facilities, run by an agent who receives a discount on purchases or a commission on sales. There has been a move away from ordering through agents, with customers now ordering direct using credit cards to stagger payments. Specialogues are the tightly targeted niche market catalogues that first made their appearance in the early 1980s.

Factors for success
The two key factors for success are probably intelligent product choice and worldly creative presentation.

PRODUCT CHOICE
'Product choice' means profitable product choice and not an aesthetic one. If a catalogue costs more than one pound to produce and distribute (and this can easily happen) it can only be underpinned by large order values and high margins. Certainly the average order value from a catalogue has soared in the last few years and it is probable that margins have not been reduced.

To operate a successful catalogue, you must take your business needs and attempt to approximate them to the customer's needs. Assuming, then, that you have the right product mix in fiscal terms, how do you make that mix attractive to customers? What, in other words, makes an objectively successful catalogue product? These truths will almost always apply:

- a product that's difficult to find elsewhere
- a product that's perceived to be unique

- a product that photographs well
- a product with a story behind it
- a product that offers a price advantage
- a product that you're confident to buy by mail order.

You should reconcile yourself to the idea that many products will fail. In a high-ticket catalogue, you may find that one-third are winners, one-third break even, and one-third are outright losers. Somewhere in the midst of this unpredictable arithmetic lies a viable catalogue operation!

These basic business points are being laboured because they put catalogue creativity into context. Bright and intelligent creativity can help a catalogue perform but not if that catalogue contains the wrong products.

CREATIVE PRESENTATION

The following are crucial in creating a catalogue:

1 Never underestimate the importance of copy. Tell a story. The old tradition of copy-as-caption is stone dead.
2 Never skimp on photography. The most mundane product can be helped with good photographic technique.
3 Plan in spreads. It's how the customer reads your catalogue and that makes it the best way to visualise it.
4 Mix products up. An unexpected product mix aids readership and helps build order value.
5 Be sensible about typography. This is no place for typographic fashion. The copy must be read and understood. So must the prices.
6 Vary squared-up and cut-out pictures.
7 Play games with actual sizes. An exciting close-up of one feature can be better than a diligent shot of the whole product.
8 Change the pace by varying the number of products per page.

The catalogue

Hard-won experience indicates that a smaller format is usually more profitable than a larger format; that best-selling products will probably be found on back covers or on the order form; and that you'll usually be wasting your time with anything less than four colours. And you will certainly need the assistance of a specialist in this area, for the dynamics and culture of a catalogue are markedly different from any other kind of direct marketing promotion.

Let me summarise by offering you the RADER formula for catalogue success:

- R FOR RELEVANCE   Is your catalogue relevant to the target audience?
- A FOR AUTHORITY   A catalogue should create trust between marketer and customer. Indeed, its very size helps do that. Are you optimising that authority?
- D FOR DISTINCTIVENESS   Every catalogue should have a personality. All products should aim to be distinctive in some way. If your catalogue looks just like someone else's, it's probably stone dead.
- E FOR ENTERTAINMENT   Any piece of print should aim to entertain. In the home, the catalogue is vying with the newspaper and the TV for attention. Bored customers don't buy.
- R FOR RETENTION   The biggest factor of all. It must be good enough to keep and to look through more than once. Catalogue response is measured in months, not weeks.

Apply the RADER formula to any catalogue you're producing and you'll know that you are at least reducing the area of risk.

14

Travel and leisure

JOHN McKENZIE

The travel and leisure industry is made up of a myriad of different operational and distribution methods. This is due to the unique ways in which the various sectors of this industry have grown up and developed.

The consumer need and desire to be well informed, before making what is, in many cases, a major expenditure, has in most cases resulted in a tradition of face-to-face selling via intermediaries and agents. This feature has remained throughout the massive growth phases of the 1960s, 1970s and 1980s, even though much of this industry is now dealing in more easily understood mass market 'packages'.

During this period of volume growth, profit margins have been steadily eroded, with profitability in the mass market often totally dependent on ever-increasing volume. When there have been setbacks in the past, as we have now, many companies have collapsed as expected business levels suddenly diminished and operating commitments strangled cash flow.

Only those operators with robust customer bases, or who were providing niche products and services with reasonable margins, have remained relatively immune. These have tended to be either the smaller, more flexible companies who have built up an exact knowledge of why, when, where, and what their clients are looking for, or else the larger players.

While direct mail and direct response advertising have been used extensively to sell travel and leisure, much of this activity is still rudimentary. Most companies have not invested sufficiently to harness, or harvest, the long-term benefits that modern information technology and direct marketing offers. This is partly a reflection of the poor profitability of many of the participants in this industry.

Relatively low-cost technology does now exist for all companies to understand precisely their customer dynamics and profitably employ direct marketing to appeal to distinct segments within their customer bases—through personalisation of their communications and basic individualisation of their mass product/services—this leap forward has, however, still to be taken by many.

Most companies are still a hostage to their history, afraid to upset their traditional intermediaries and unable to grasp that taking control of their own destinies will help them to optimise all their distribution channels, if planned and executed properly.

Direct marketing is flexible enough to enhance *all* these channels.

Consumers—business or pleasure—at all levels are becoming more sophisticated and demanding. This does not bode well for those marketers who do not have the resources to innovate, develop and adapt to meet the changing needs of the customers they gained and developed in the 'good times'.

Looking at a few of the business areas that make up this industry sector, there are some companies who realise the importance of these trends and who are hard at work creating the foundations of tomorrow's business.

Airlines

Programmes have been in place for many years now that try to lock in the most profitable consumer in this area—the business traveller.

The American carriers TWA, PanAm, and many others, introduced Frequent Flyer Programmes at the beginning of the 1980s that were specifically designed to identify their most frequent business travellers and reward them with points for each flight they took. These points could then be exchanged for air miles that became free flights when certain point ceilings were reached.

While they were very successful at locking travellers in, they were also instrumental in mortgaging tomorrow's profits. This resulted in the programmes having to be modified and restricted via a device called 'black holes' to avoid sending aircraft full of free-flyers out during peak holiday periods!

Our own BA has taken information technology to a far more sophisticated level and used it to target all aspects of its business. It has also invested, and continues to invest, significant sums of money in adding value to all of its customer offerings. This programme of innovation is not accidental but the result of being able to look in-depth at its business and customer dynamics and then create the 'branded' products to suit. Once they could only aim to be 'The World's Favourite Airline', now they are doing their utmost to own it. And, in the main, they are succeeding because they are able to take a 'holistic' view of what each customer segment wants out of a BA flight.

But it is not only the large players that can do this, as another British airline, Virgin, has proved. Its business class has a worldwide reputation far in excess of the routes offered and the secondary air terminal it operates from. Why? Because it has also invested in finding out and providing precisely what the business traveller wants, and competing hard for that business.

Both of these companies use direct marketing extensively to communicate their benefits to their customers.

Car rental

The car rental business is highly dependent on business travellers in Northern Europe, the leisure market in the South, and much of the overall business volume comes from outside the EC—mainly the United States. As such, it is probably the sector whose distribution channels are the most complex and intricate as well as being the most integrated with other parts of the travel and leisure industry.

Most car rental companies are extensive users of direct marketing, particularly joint 'affinity' activity with airlines, hotels, travel agents, and through agreements with other renters, i.e. Europcar, with National in the United States, and Nippon in Japan. They are also heavy users of frequency/passport-type programmes that offer renters discounts, car group upgrades, even free rentals, based upon rental usage levels.

Database building is fairly easy for such companies as the customer has to provide so much information at rental. Then, under the promise of service, express card schemes are used as bait for recruitment of frequent renters. The card is 'swiped' at each rental so each customer transaction can be logged onto the database. These schemes do, however, benefit customers with simplified billing and ensuring that contract rates negotiated with large corporate clients are delivered. They also considerably reduce the renter's administration costs.

However, in a business where the bulk of profits has traditionally come from the buying of new cars at massive discounts and then re-selling them after a short period at a profit, rather than from rental income, it is hardly surprising that reducing costs, making more money out of rentals, and locking customers in, has become such a high priority.

Hotels

Nearly all the major hotel groups are users of direct marketing to build loyalty and repeat business from their clientele. Like car rental companies, much of their efforts are concentrated on the business market both at the individual and corporate level.

Again, the opportunity for collecting data easily at the point of purchase presents itself. Hotels have been quick to offer privilege cards, so the frequent user obtains the individual services he or she needs, either through previous visits or the hotel's proactivity. By collecting and storing this type of individual data, then making it available at each location, the hotel can use it to pander to and recognise frequent users with excellent service to keep their loyalty.

More relevantly, this data can then also be used to communicate with the customer directly to increase dialogue, cross-sell leisure, and use the relationship built up to gain recommendations and new customers.

Tour operators

Within this extremely eclectic sector, our references are the companies that sell leisure holidays, activities and travel to the consumer.

In the United Kingdom many of the major companies are now subsidiaries of larger leisure groups, i.e. Butlins/Haven/Warners/Shearings all belong to the Rank Leisure Group.

There are, however, many independents like Crystal Holidays, Kuoni, Abercrombie & Kent, and Saga Holidays who have thrived and grown through their specialisations, i.e. skiing holidays, long haul trips, leisure for the over 50s. There are also the cruise companies and ferry operators.

Most companies in this area use direct marketing, the most common usage being direct response advertisements in the press, and occasionally on TV, to generate brochure requests. A few are solely direct-sell operations with no travel agent distributors.

In this area you would expect information technology to have reached a highly developed level. While this may be true of companies' booking and reservation systems, sadly it isn't when it comes to marketing. Most have developed their ability to control and monitor basic direct marketing, but not the individual profiling, research and product development tools to help them guide future service and product innovation.

Conclusions

In this brief, and therefore very incomplete, look at the travel and leisure industry, it is clear that some of the participants have progressed a long way while many others have far to go.

Continued success will accrue to those who fulfil the needs of their increasingly fragmented and discriminating markets, and understand all their customers as individuals.

The technology to put together the information to help companies capitalise needn't be costly, or implemented overnight, but failure to do so will cost in the long term. To quote an old cliché, 'In the land of the blind, the one-eyed man is King'.

Although price and value for money will always be important, increasingly profit is going to go to those who put customers' needs, suitability of product, and service first. Customer information is the start of not just doing this once, but repeatedly over time.

Direct marketing in itself is obviously not the complete answer, but it is the unique strategic resource best suited to gathering, managing and maintaining the information that will be key to many travel and leisure companies' profitable futures.

15

Club membership

JENNY PIZER

The range, size and scope of clubs varies widely—from the local tennis club to the major motoring organisation with many millions of members. Here, we concentrate on those clubs where a membership fee is required—not those, such as book and record clubs, where the purchase of a product is sufficient to gain 'membership'. Although there are many similarities between the two types of operation, membership clubs have certain characteristics.

1 *Raison d'être*: normally they are created from the need of a group of individuals to get together to progress a common interest or objective.
2 Membership applications are subject to acceptance, usually by a membership committee.
3 Members are required to pay a membership fee and, in return, receive a membership card as proof of entitlement to certain benefits or services.

New member recruitment
The following are suggestions for new member recruitment. Costs will vary, and the list begins with the most cost-effective. Remember, the medium, the offer and promotion should always be *tested* before mainscale roll-out.

1 *Member-get-member* Usually the best proponents of any club are existing members. Invite them to introduce friends and offer an incentive for each new enrolment.
2 *Lapsed members* This sounds simple, but many will have forgotten to renew. By re-approaching them after a suitable interval (perhaps three months), some will resume membership. It is worth looking at the cost-

effectiveness of a series of efforts over the period 6–15 months after lapsing.

3 *Gift membership*   Members are invited to give membership as a gift to a relative or friend. This variation on member-get-member is particularly successful during the period before Christmas. Policy on renewal needs to be established: should the *donor* or the *recipient* be approached to continue the membership at the end of Year 1?

4 *Self-submitted enquiries*   All clubs generate a number of enquiries about membership during the course of the year. A system needs to be established for the speedy and effective follow-up of such enquiries; a membership brochure and application form should be ready for prompt despatch.

5 *Space*   Advertisements in national and local press or special interest magazines. Be sure to test a one-stage versus two-stage offer early on (the former can generate leads cost-effectively from a small space).

6 *Inserts*   Although they are more expensive than space, inserts in national, local and specialist media are normally very cost-effective. You should test as wide a range of media as possible, including product despatches, credit card statements, utility bills, etc.

7 *Direct mail*   Potentially the most cost-effective of all selling opportunities; its success will depend on getting the right offer to the right audience at the right time.

8 *Radio or TV direct response*   These are both expensive media, and difficult to target accurately. Be sure to test carefully before committing substantial budgets.

Recruitment offers

The club's membership fee may be set by committee, but this should not prevent you from testing recruitment offers. For example, against a control of 12 months at full price consider:

- first three months free
- premium for joining
- payment by instalments
- two years for the price of one
- free entry in a prize draw for prompt response
- incentive for signing a direct debit mandate, or credit card continuous authority (see Figure 15.1 below)
- renewal at birth (renewal immediately after initial joining)

Whichever recruitment offer is tried, test results must be evaluated over a period of more than one year and preferably of three to five years.

RECRUITMENT COSTS

Establishing the target cost per recruit requires a full understanding of the value of new members over time. Thus new members are bought in at a cost greater than revenue generated in Year 1 on the basis that they will become profitable in the future.

Many organisations, however, do not take a long-term view and expect revenue to cover all membership costs during the initial year.

Retention

The overall objective of any club is to retain as many members as possible, for as long as possible, at the optimum revenue per head. It is important to keep accurate records of renewal performance so that business forecasts may be prepared. Analyses of performance should include:

1 *Retention by year of enrolment* The renewal rate will increase sharply during the first five years of membership, after which it will begin to level.
2 *Retention by payment method* Members who agree to pay for membership by direct debit, or credit card continuous authority, will always renew better than those paying by cash (cheque, bank or post office giro, etc.). It therefore pays to invest in incentivising members to upgrade to direct debit as retention levels will be increased and, over time, the costs will be more than recovered (see Figure 15.1).
3 *Retention by source of recruitment* This is often ignored, but renewal rates can vary widely, dependent on the source of the initial response.
4 *Retention by recruitment offer* Any special offers, discounts, incentives, etc., should be monitored carefully at renewal as performance will vary.

Communication with members

Renewal performance is directly related to whether members believe their club provides real benefits and value for money. Cash payers are particularly vulnerable at renewal—the simple act of writing a cheque dramatises the cost of membership and provides the opportunity to reconsider its value.

Thus some form of communication with members during the year is vital. It might be a direct mail offer, a club meeting, a simple one-colour newsletter, or a glossy four-colour magazine. The costs can be high, and it is often difficult to demonstrate the value without monitoring retention rates, and carefully testing, over time.

As a rule, you should aim to correspond with your members at least once a month and opportunities should be created to invite members to

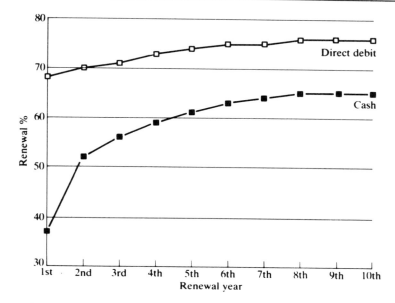

Figure 15.1 Retention rates (%) by length of membership in a typical club

enhance the quality of membership (e.g. by signing a direct debit mandate) whenever possible—either at renewal, or during the year. Wherever possible, the approaches should be interactive—members should have the opportunity to respond to you, either by writing or by ordering a product or service.

Remember, too, the value of a membership card—preferably plastic.

However sophisticated the communications with members, it is essential that the club management never fails to deliver the basic service or product. Without it the club becomes only a commercial enterprise, and justification for the membership fee dwindles.

16

Politics

GLENMORE TRENEAR-HARVEY

Following the June 1987 General Election, the Social Democratic Party split into two main factions. The division was painful, and, as is not uncommon in such a divorce, there was a bitter fight over the 'joint property'.

What was it that the factions thought to be of greatest value, to be fought over so vigorously? It was the party's *membership database*. Without question, direct marketing had arrived in British politics. In fact, the 1987 General Election was the first in which all major parties used direct marketing extensively.

By discovering direct marketing somewhat late, the British political parties have benefited from the current advanced state of the art. They have been able to embrace the traditional applications of political direct marketing and have added the best of contemporary commercial practice.

The changing scene

In recent years the main thrust of political electioneering had been the broadscale approach of mass propaganda. To ensure that the entire electorate was covered, political parties used mass media to spread, promote and explain their positions and beliefs. In the United Kingdom, this mass national approach was supported by the party faithful at the constituency level. Door-to-door canvassing, the leafleting of households and local political meetings were the order of the day.

Inevitably with such a general approach, usually only the central themes of a party platform were conveyed. As a result, the electorate tended to vote along fairly well-defined party lines rather than for specific policies.

Political life was either that of active involvement, *for a few*, at local level—or a rather detached remoteness for most as they observed the goings-on at Westminster.

Things have now changed, radically and quite dramatically. The key to this change is *direct marketing*.

Because of its largely covert nature, direct marketing is a difficult process to observe—unless, of course, you have been targeted by all the political parties! That is why, although evolutionary in its gradual impact on the electorate, the reality of the adoption of direct marketing by the political parties is actually revolutionary.

Politics is now being 'brought to the people'.

The personal approach

The parties have found that informative, detailed and persuasive material is best delivered to those who have a real or potential interest in an issue. This requires research, targeting, testing and, often, the building of a dialogue. These are prime roles for direct marketing.

From being a mass of anonymous voters, people are now being recognised as individuals. People with judgement; susceptible to persuasion. People with vocational, regional, ethnic and historical needs. Now, with direct marketing, it is possible to consider the individual's requirements and address those needs.

Such a statement, of course, is fundamental to all modern-day marketing. It is not surprising that the changing process of political persuasion has close parallels with the changes in commercial consumer marketing.

Commercial marketing has switched from the blanket cover provided by mass marketing to the accuracy and relevance of segmented, 'niche' marketing. In the same way, political persuasion has shifted from the general to the particular.

The political parties, like their commercial counterparts, have sought out information about their 'customers' and have come to know them better.

LISTS AND DATABASES
Rather than allow party supporters to show their interest once and disappear, untracked until the next election, the parties have realised how important it is to record the names and addresses of supporters.

Historically the main political parties in Britain are, in effect, a federation of local constituency parties. Lists of party members were usually held at a local level, not centrally. This has been an impediment to the development of political direct marketing, but it is being overcome. Now parties are gradually building central lists of supporters, often in parallel with, but distinct from, the constituency-held lists of party members.

Such central lists usually carry more information than names and addresses, and are being developed as proper databases. They have been built largely as a result of fundraising promotion—fundraising still being the major task of most political direct marketing activity. But, in addition to fund-raising, the database makes possible a wide spread of direct marketing activities: recruitment of members and workers; influencing political thinking; identifying marginal voters or key decision makers.

The existence of these databases has provided the parties with their most potent weapon. The affordability of contact allowed by low-cost computing power is ensuring their continued growth and use.

As the parties recognise their ability to target geographically and on special interest groups, they have used direct mail in particular to develop a dialogue with sectors of the electorate. They often address them with a relevance and a continuity that was once found only in the best of commercial customer relations.

In the United Kingdom direct marketing has been used now by every Member of Parliament, though most would probably fail to recognise the term and would be surprised to hear that its use is enshrined in statute (Representation of the Peoples Act). As thousands of prospective parliamentary candidates have found, they receive free postage for one mailing to every elector in the constituency in return for their electoral deposit. A generous and handsome way to discover the effectiveness of direct mail!*

The key to electoral success?

Will direct marketing prove to be the key to success in future general elections? Certainly it will play a bigger role than at elections in the past. As a fundraising tool, its effect has been dramatic. As a means of involving voters in the political process, it has embraced millions. It has proved remarkably effective in by-election campaigning, where low-cost personal computers and laser printers are bringing affordable computer power to every constituency, and direct marketing to the masses.

What we have yet to see is direct marketing being used on a massive scale to bring out the vote, other than the statutory right of each parliamentary candidate to have free postage for one mailing to every

---

* All other costs associated with the mailing, however, have to be declared as part of the candidates' total electioneering expenses.

elector in the constituency. But as pressure groups, politicians and their parties continue to recognise how direct mail, telemarketing, direct response advertising and database-building can help their cause, the place of direct marketing in British politics is ensured.

17

Collectibles

TERRY FORSHAW

'Collectibles' are products that are created and marketed on the strength of their *collectability*. Although the promotion of such products often focuses primarily on the aesthetic qualities and the scarcity value, the key quality is the product's strength as a collector's item.

Who buys collectibles?

The 'typical' collectibles buyer is usually considered to be an older (35–55), married female in the fairly broad BC1C2 socio-economic grouping. Furthermore, buyers of collectibles can be broadly split into three categories: *collectors, home enhancers* and *investors*. Collectors are likely to be the core market, committed as they are to collecting and repeat purchase. Home enhancers represent a larger, if less committed, group of collectors, buying less frequently, often on impulse, and primarily to enhance the decor of the home. Investors appear to buy collectibles for their scarcity value, being concerned with the investment possibilities of the collection as much as the collection itself.

Why do people buy collectibles?

Although some collectors do seek out limited editions and concern themselves with the investment potential of the product, aesthetic factors, such as the *style, design* and *appearance* of the product, are generally much more important to the purchaser. The investment potential is more likely to act as a *rationalisation* for what is largely an emotive purchase of a luxury item.

The following summary suggests some of the main reasons why people buy collectibles:

- to enhance the decor of their home
- to own attractive luxury items
- for personal status reasons—as a reflection of their personal taste
- strong liking for, or affinity with, the subject matter
- the impulse of the moment
- exclusivity—the product is not widely available
- for investment reasons—more as a justification of purchase
- the product's affordability
- a liking for a particular artist or manufacturer
- sympathy or empathy with a sponsor.

Choosing the right product

The following products can easily be presented as collections, series or sets and are typically offered by the major UK collectibles companies: *thimbles, plates, figurines, small sculptures, porcelain dolls, pewter models* and *jewellery items*.

As well as the type of product, the *subject matter* is of fundamental importance when choosing products. The following regularly appear in the Sunday supplements and loose inserts: *royalty, landscapes, flowers, oriental art, birds, animals, elegant ladies, children* and *pets*.

Ultimately the choice of product will depend upon the *marketing objectives*. Do we want to expand our customer base or do we want to maximise sales from existing customers? Thus, should the product have broad appeal to the wider audience or should it build on known customer affinities? Alternatively, do we want to create *new* markets or chase a known competitor's market? Therefore, should the product be innovative and break new ground, or should it closely reflect the characteristics of successful competitors' products?

Pricing the product

The price should not be set too low. It should reflect the quality and the perceived value of the product. Where the aesthetic qualities, the uniqueness and the scarcity of a product are highlighted, it does not make sense to present the product as a low-priced bargain buy.

Indeed, in accordance with classic pricing theory, 'superior' collectibles can actually have a higher demand at a higher price due to snobbery motivations.

The price need not simply be regarded as the *total* price of the product. For example, whereas a prospective customer may be reluctant to pay £195.00 for a porcelain figurine, this suddenly becomes acceptable if the price is presented as ten easy, interest-free monthly payments of only £19.50.

Where a series or set is on offer with a display case, shelf or stand it is better to build the cost of the latter into the individual product price and to offer the complementary accessory *free*. This, then, does not detract from the value and importance of individual items in the collection, but rather provides a tempting incentive and encourages greater commitment to the series (by providing a 'home' for each piece in the collection and a gap for each missing piece).

Finally, any pricing decision should consider whether the price is to be *inclusive* or *exclusive* of postage and packing charges. For lower priced products (say £15–£30) postage is usually shown as an additional charge. However, premium priced products can 'lose' the postage costs in the price and also present inclusion of postage as an additional benefit.

Promoting collectibles

If we are to persuade people to part with comparatively large sums of money for what are essentially 'luxury' items, it is important that the promotional thrust exudes *quality* and *credibility*. Whether the medium be off-the-page, inserts or direct mail, it is important to remember that the *product* is the 'hero' and should dominate the promotion.

A strong *guarantee* is essential—the stronger the better. A guarantee to refund *all* monies paid *and* return postage for any reason at any time within a 12-month period is much stronger than a 28-day money-back guarantee which does not cover return postage. And the difference in returns will be minimal. Of course, whereas such a strong guarantee is essential for operations that ask for money up front, for companies that supply goods on approval the guarantee would cover the approval period only.

As with all direct marketing promotions *ease of ordering* and *ease of payment* are important. Most collectibles companies offer telephone ordering facilities with credit card payments as an option. And a free 0800 number and a FREEPOST address further encourage the impulse purchase. Customers should be permitted to pay by whatever method suits them (cheque, postal order, credit card, direct debit). The following options are commonly used:

- SEND NO MONEY NOW—Invoice for product (or first instalment) will be sent *prior* to despatch of product.
- SEND NO MONEY NOW—Invoice will be sent *with* product to be paid after period of home approval.
- Send cash for product, or first instalment, with the order.

The first option is the easiest for the prospective customer, but the projected increase in response naturally needs to be traded off against the bad debt risk. Consider also the level of *initial commitment*. Where the first in a collection is sold with *no obligation* to buy subsequent issues, there is obviously less commitment to the series and attrition rates will be high. Alternatively, where the *series* is sold up front there may be a lower initial response, but there will be a greater commitment to purchase further issues.

With most collectibles promotions, the *offer* itself is rarely complex. The *product* is king. Use of premiums, discounts, competitions, prize draws, etc., is very restrained. Although display accessories are occasionally offered free as an integral part of the product—and sometimes the first (or last) of a series is offered free—there is little else. Nothing should detract from the *importance* of the product and the *credibility* of the main offer.

Finally, a 'return by' date, as well as increasing *urgency*, can support the idea of limited supply. The latter can be enhanced further by limiting all orders or subscriptions to one per household (or two to preferred customers).

Legal guidelines

As well as the usual legal and regulatory restrictions for mail order companies, there are areas of special concern to marketers of collectibles. Advertisements and promotional material must:

- state the delivery time clearly—for collectibles, lead times are invariably longer than the preferred 28-day period specified in the Code of Advertising Practice, often being 6 to 12 weeks;
- where commencement of manufacture is dependent on a minimum level of response, state so clearly.

In case of limited editions, advertisements must:

- avoid misleading prospects about scarcity and future value of limited editions;
- make clear the nature of the limitation—by number, by application or subscription within a stated period, or by other production-related methods;
- offer to inform all interested purchasers of the total number of items eventually produced world wide, where a finite quantity is not stated because of the broader nature of limitation;

- spell out the exact limitation period and final close date, where an offer is made in more than one stage.

Deciding whether to offer limited editions needs considerable thought. Although the limiting of an edition can add credibility to the offer, it can also restrict sales opportunities if demand is underestimated. Since a product's aesthetic appeal is a more significant motivation to purchase, most broad appeal products should not be offered as a limited edition. This in turn adds credibility to the concept of limited editions, whose use can then be restricted to specialist-appeal, high-ticket collector's pieces aimed at niche markets.

Checklist
1 Should I choose a product that can be presented as a *series* or *collection*, or a single-sell specialist appeal item?
2 More specifically, what *type* of product should I choose—a figurine, a plate, thimbles, or perhaps something totally new?
3 What *subject matter* would have the most appeal?
4 Should the product be presented as a *limited edition*?
5 What are my *marketing objectives*? Do I want to build or expand my client file, or do I want to maximise sales from existing customers? Does the product I've chosen fit these objectives?
6 Have I priced the product low enough to attract a wide audience, but not so low as to detract from the aesthetic qualities of the product and the credibility of the offer? Alternatively, have I priced the product high enough to maximise my margins and to appeal to specialist niche markets?
7 Should I present the price as a one-off payment, or should I offer a series of easy, interest-free monthly instalments?
8 Does the product lend itself to the addition of a complementary display accessory? If so, how should the cost of this item be built into the price of the product?
9 Should the price be *inclusive* or *exclusive* of postage and packing?
10 Does my advertising have a *quality* feel to it? Is the standard of photography excellent and the copy compelling?
11 Does the *product* itself dominate the promotion?
12 Should I offer the product on a cash-up-front basis, or should I offer home approval? If payment is not requested up front, should the invoice be sent *prior* to despatch of the product or *with* the product?
13 Have I included a strong *guarantee* of complete satisfaction?
14 Is it easy for the prospect or customer to order and pay for the product?

Should credit card payments be accepted and telephone ordering facilities offered? Do we have the staff and systems to cope with both? Should we offer a free 0800 number and a Freepost address?

15 Should the customer be committed to the *series* initially, or should the first in the collection be sold with *no obligation* to buy subsequent pieces?

16 Would the promotion benefit from careful use of an incentive, a discount, a competition or a free draw?

17 Have I included a *return-by date*?

18 What is the delivery period? Have I clearly specified this in the promotional material?

19 If the product is a limited edition, is the *exact* nature of the limitation clear in the advertising?

20 Does the promotional piece satisfy the requirements of the Code of Advertising Practice? Would I be wise to get Advertising Standards Authority approval for the copy?

18

Subscription publishing

HELEN ALEXANDER

Direct marketing is essential for building circulation for paid-for and controlled circulation magazines and newspapers. This chapter will deal with the direct marketing of a paid-for weekly magazine, but the principles hold true for newspapers, or for controlled circulation publications. The marketing of books direct by publishers is still very under-exploited in this country.

The aim of direct marketing in publishing is to build circulation in the most efficient way possible in order to maximise overall profitability. This means, if there is advertising revenue in the magazine, that in order to deliver a specific readership to the advertiser it may be efficient to spend more money to reach a target audience, in order to get more return from advertising revenue.

Modelling

Selling circulation involves a degree of science. Planning and modelling of the market help enormously in deciding what resources are needed, and allow what-if scenarios to be tried out. It is essential for building circulation, and a good model must be regarded as the most important tool to have in place.

There are few sophisticated circulation models on the market. The most practical comes from the Lighthouse Corporation in the US. The range of models is large (monthly or weekly; over three or five years; with five or ten sources). Do not over-complicate your plans: it is dangerous to get into the situation where feeding your circulation model becomes an end in itself.

Planning the year

Only the broad outline of the process of building circulation is given here, as the modelling will probably be done on a computer.

1 Outline the number of subscribers (if any) who have a long-term subscription, e.g. two years, which keeps them on your file for the year.
2 Calculate the number of subscriptions that are due to expire over the year, and when. It may be convenient to indicate this by month. You also need to know whether they are expiring for the first, second, or third (etc.) time.
3 Apply to these cohorts of subscribers your historical renewal rates, with any adjustments you feel confident to make. You will then be building up a picture of the numbers of subscribers you will have if you do not search for any new business (i.e. those who are on your file all year, plus the percentages of those who do renew, by month).
4 Assuming that you want to raise your circulation with new business, you have to estimate response rates to new promotions, using all available sources. It is the balance of these sources that is the delicate secret to maximising the profitability of circulation.
5 The testing programme must be outlined as a timetable for the year:

- When are you going to mail? How many?
- What lists will you use?
- Which creative material?
- Which renewal tests can you implement and how can you take action on the results?
- What new sources will you test?

Renewal business

It is much less expensive to induce someone to renew (repeat) than it is to get them to start (trial). *Delivery* and *service* are aspects of your product which make a huge difference to the level of subscriber satisfaction, and thus their propensity to renew. In addition, *price* will play a major part— both in its absolute level and in its relationship to the price paid for the first year of subscription. Over time it is possible to build up a picture of price sensitivity, by offering different prices to discrete groups (e.g. in a different country, or in the same group—information is fast shared and some potentially loyal customers will be upset by differential treatment).

Similar tests are possible to ascertain sensitivity to different strategies:

- all subscription years at same price
- increased discount for loyalty
- reduced discount as time progresses and habit is formed.

The balance between response rate for first year, renewal years and the overall revenue received should dictate which pricing strategy you follow.

Premiums and all kinds of gifts should also be tested and tested again on renewals. They can be very effective, but the danger is that the cycle continues: a premium one year leads to expectations of premiums in another.

The other variable that can affect renewal rate is the timing, number and appearance of reminders to renew. Creative work has a significant effect and is easy to test on an A/B split of subscribers over a given period.

The number of reminders sent can also affect the renewal rate, but you have to test where, for your magazine, the return diminishes. The timing of reminders must be sufficient to allow one to be received, replied to, and for your fulfilment system to acknowledge receipt in order not to exacerbate the problem of having a reminder cross in the post with a renewal request.

Test in your market which is the best moment to begin sending reminders in order to maximise response. Is it six months, four months, three months or even one month before expiry?

New business

The quest for new sources of subscribers continues. This is simply a checklist of some of those that should not be forgotten.

1 *Expires:* a cheap list to mail; they are already familiar with the product, and are often an excellent source.
2 *White mail:* all the unsolicited requests to subscribe (or rather, all those not using a coded order form).
3 *Coupons in the magazine:* as above, but there can be much variety between loose inserts, bound-in inserts, those in the copies sent to subscribers, those in the copies available at news-stands, or in any other group's copies into which it is practical and economic to insert.
4 *Telephone:* the higher costs involved here need to be tested to see if they are outweighed by higher response. This source can also be used for renewal business.
5 *Off-the-page advertising and 'piggy-back' mailing:* useful sources to test, but the acquisition costs tend to be high.
6 *Direct mail:* mailings can be the most highly focused direct marketing activity, but the costs of a solus mailing can be high. The choice of lists is the most important variable in this activity. The best response is usually from lists of subscribers to other publications—the targets are already responders and are accustomed to receiving a publication on

subscription. Advice about clean lists, merge-purging and adherence to Data Protection Acts applies in publishing as in other markets.

How much can I afford?
The answer to this lies in the publishing strategy of your magazine (i.e. how much contribution do subscriptions have to make?). However, it is essential to make sure that you are using an average life of a subscription when calculating its overall worth. Thus, you will need to know, for any one subscription:

- first-year revenue
- second-year revenue
- subsequent years' revenue
- average subscription life
- promotion cost of gaining the sub (including lists, production of material, inserting, post, merge/purge)
- promotion cost of renewing the sub
- production and distribution cost of the sub.

The original source by which a subscriber joined may tell a lot about its subsequent behaviour. Patterns emerge. It is a tough and detailed task to know the average life, renewal rate, costs, etc., for each source, but it is essential if you are to evaluate the effectiveness of one source against another over time using a measure more subtle than response rate or acquisition cost.

Is everything else in order?
The service elements to the marketing must be in place. The whole marketing mix is important. Customer service, delivery, advertising, information systems and the product itself all are sensitive areas affecting your long-term business.

Testing conclusion
Direct marketing techniques in publishing can only make sense if they are put through the general direct marketing maxim: test, test and test again. Price, list, offer, product, package and every other variable must all be subject to that discipline. Likewise, the information systems backing needed for success in publishing have their counterparts in other fields.

The major differentiating feature of the publishing industry is the presence of a potential second revenue stream from advertising, which can alter profit contribution dramatically if circulation marketing produces a readership of interest to advertisers. It is the beauty of direct marketing that it allows the focus on specific targets, when sold to an advertiser, to maximise the overall profitability of the publishing venture.

PART **III**

Services

19

Direct marketing agencies

DRAYTON BIRD

A few years ago, choosing a direct marketing agency was much easier than it is now. The reason is simple. There were very few around that were any good. Now, there is a much wider selection—and they vary considerably in the way they operate, and in some other important respects. Moreover, if there is confusion about precisely what constitutes *direct marketing*—and there is—perhaps there is even more on what direct marketing agencies are and how they operate.

Most direct marketing agencies are organised in much the same way as an advertising agency—with creative, account handling, production, print and media departments—and, in addition, can usually advise you on mailing lists, on the peculiar demands which direct mail print calls for and, in the larger agencies, on database development, management and exploitation. In some cases, they will even advise you on the mysteries of telephone marketing.

Your direct marketing agency will fulfil the same function for you within the realm of direct marketing as your advertising agency does within the realm of advertising. The agency will advise you, work with you to plan better, help you meet your objectives, evaluate your results and, last but not least, bring some impartial perspective to the way you view your activities.

Strategic or tactical?

Some agencies are little more than creative consultancies—and none the worse for that. They will produce creative work to order for your projects as they come up. Their involvement is not strategic. If you are perfectly happy to handle all your own marketing planning, they may well be the right people for you.

Other agencies are 'full service', handling everything from planning through to evaluating the results of your plans.

A few large agencies are also multinational. You may benefit from what they have learned in other markets about similar businesses to yours— quite apart from what they have learned in the UK market about other clients whose experiences may be of value to you. However, such agencies do not come cheaply.

And finally, some agencies go beyond what one would normally imagine to be the function of an agency. They will not merely buy print for you and arrange for its handling, but they may even have their own in-house printing facilities. Indeed, some agencies are in fact the progeny of printing organisations; others are the progeny of mailing companies; and yet others are subsidiaries of sales promotion houses.

The origins of your agency are quite important. The majority of the larger agencies, for instance, are advertising agency subsidiaries. If you wish your direct marketing to be handled in tandem with your advertising, that might be an important consideration.

Do you need a direct marketing agency?

Do you need an agency at all? If so, do you need a *specialist* agency, or should you give it to an ordinary advertising agency?

First of all, unless you have worthwhile money to spend, you'll find it hard to get really good service from any agency. The income you have to offer will not entice the agency to employ their best people. Equally, if your business is very complex or technical, it may be difficult for an agency to understand.

In either case, it is probably best to handle the marketing yourself, possibly with the help of freelance copy and art teams and consultants who have low overheads to meet. You will undoubtedly make mistakes—but so would the inexperienced people an agency would put on your account, if they got it.

Even some very large and successful businesses find it pays to do their own marketing to a large extent. The Reader's Digest, for example, produce all their mailings in-house, though their advertising is generally handled by agencies.

Another typical 'in-house' example would be a technical publisher with a great many books to sell and a relatively limited budget for each book. No agency can afford to spend the time necessary to understand each of these books and do a decent job. Certainly not for the kind of fees such a publisher can afford.

How to choose your agency

If you *do* have a reasonable budget and your business will benefit from the help of an agency, an obvious first step is to look for creative work you like and—perhaps even more important—which appears repeatedly. That means it works. Find out who did this work, and put them on your list of possibles as a future agency.

Comb through the publications about direct marketing; attend the seminars and conferences; look out for people you find impressive.

Your final source is the most obvious one: ask people you know who work in direct marketing or with direct marketing agencies, and consult the British Direct Marketing Association.

Now compile your short list. It would be unwise to select more than five agencies in total. More than that, and they begin to merge into one smiling face when you see them. Then ask:

1. WHO ARE THEIR CLIENTS?

Good companies gravitate to good agencies. Ask if the agency minds you contacting existing clients to ask their opinions.

All their clients may not be happy with them *all* the time. But most should be happy most of the time if the agency is good.

2. WHAT CASE-HISTORIES CAN THEY SHOW?

Ask them to show you examples of their ability to turn disaster into triumph. And explain why they succeeded.

Also, a few examples of failure. Nobody's perfect! But good people can tell you what went wrong because they learn from their mistakes.

3. WHO WORKS FOR THEM?

Ask them how many of their people have had to face your problems? How many have had to deal with the problems of the business as *clients*?

Is their work done by them, or by outside freelancers? It's more difficult to exert quality control over people who aren't actually in the office.

(Make sure, by the way, that you go to their offices. You won't learn nearly as much by asking them to come to you.)

4. WHAT SHOULD YOU ASK THEM TO DO?

If you ask them to comment on your business, they have to understand its peculiarities first. That takes time—and money. If you pay peanuts, you get monkeys.

If you want carefully considered proposals, then expect to pay—unless your business is so big the agency is willing to speculate. More on this in the next point.

5. WHAT ABOUT CREATIVE IDEAS?

Everybody likes to try before they buy. In our business this means speculative creative work. Should you ask your potential agencies to put up some work so you can see whether you like the way they approach things?

If your account is very small, they won't bother. If it's potentially enormously lucrative, they probably will.

But however large your account, consider paying a sum which may not be enormous, may even be nominal, but demonstrates that you are willing to pay *something* to get the agency to take their eyes off their most important business—their existing clients.

6. WILL YOU BE COMPATIBLE?

The client/agency relationship is in some ways rather like marriage. Opposites attract, and a very dull client may be attracted by a zany, wildly creative agency. Unfortunately, opposites often have tremendous rows after that initial thrill, and the marriages end in divorce.

In fact, long-term relationships seem to subsist much better amongst people who are really quite similar. So, in my experience, small clients do best with small agencies; large clients do best with large ones.

7. MEET THE PEOPLE

Most agencies put their hot shots onto new business. It is important that you find out who precisely is going to work on your business day to day. It may even be that the agency doesn't actually know yet. In that case, you should probe and find out who they have in mind, or what kind of people.

At the very least, it is vital that you know who at the top level of the agency is going to be personally involved in your account. Unless there is somebody right at the top committed to your business, then the relationship will fail.

Costs

Charges obviously relate to what the client wants done, which will vary enormously. There are three methods of charging work for most clients.

1 Charging by the hour, with a different rate for each person working on the account. After careful discussion of requirements the agency should

give the client a rough estimate of the expected monthly cost. It is also wise to agree in advance for a regular review of the fee structure.

2 Commission plus relevant fees. There will always be hard bargaining about this. When a lot of money is being spent, 15 per cent commission is sometimes a high figure, but an account cannot really be well handled by an agency on less than 10 per cent. If the agency does extra jobs, such as preparing mailings, an additional hourly fee should be negotiated in advance.

3 An agreed monthly fee based on the estimated amount of work to be done. Once again this figure can be reviewed regularly, but it gives the agency the certainty of knowing its probable revenue over a period, enabling it to plan better for business. Consequently, the client should get the best possible deal on this basis.

How to get the most out of your agency

Understanding and *sympathy* are, in my view, the key to a successful relationship. There are few businesses in which more things can go wrong than in direct marketing. It is a business concerned not only with grand strategies (e.g. isolating your customers as individuals and building a relationship with them over time), but also with minutiae (e.g. making sure the order form fits the envelope and that people's initials are correct on that envelope).

And because so many things can go wrong, it's necessary to understand the process. But few clients do. Therefore, I think it's a good idea for you, or whoever will handle the direct marketing, to spend some time in the agency. You will then understand the trials and tribulations involved and this understanding will build a better relationship.

By sympathy, I suppose I imply that old-fashioned Christian idea of treating other people as you would like to be treated yourself. It may be an old idea, but it works tremendously well in business. Try being a 'nice guy' to your agency.

On the other hand, when things go wrong, don't do what most clients do—pretend that it was all the agency's fault and you never agreed to it in the first place. Take your share of the blame. They will be so astonished at this that you will be a friend for life.

It is extremely important, if you must have an agency, that you choose the right one. Direct marketing is growing so fast that talent is in short supply. This doesn't stop people claiming expertise they don't possess—in fact it encourages it. But it does mean you can't afford mistakes.

20

Consultancies

PETER TOMKINS

The word *consultant* is one of the most misused and misunderstood within the direct marketing sector. It is sometimes used to refer to management, marketing, telephone, creative, catalogue, list, database, recruitment/ appointment, acquisitions or systems—in other words, a *specialist* in a technique or discipline within the direct marketing environment.

However, the more generic, high-level definition as used within this chapter is of a free-standing direct marketing professional who is *independent* and *objective* with solid broad-based skills and experience. These will probably include:

- earlier responsibility as a senior manager within a direct marketing profit centre
- sound core direct marketing management/marketing/financial skills as well as appropriate qualifications
- proven ability to both challenge and create business and marketing plans for client needs
- wide experience across the UK and international client/service/supplier scene
- up-to-dateness as to resources and techniques available within the industry
- professional independent status (i.e. membership of the Institute of Management Consultants, Institute of Marketing Accredited).

The importance of specific briefs

The number of consultants of this calibre within the UK is extremely limited—probably less than 20. Hence, any user of consultancy resources should be very clear as to the real needs and expectations. Hence, if a large traditional non-user of direct marketing channels (for example, an fmcg company) wants objective and independent advice on the appropriate use of direct marketing, including the pitfalls and opportunities as well as possible methodology for market entry, a high-level free-standing consultant is likely to be the ideal choice.

On the other hand, if a company needs highly specific, detailed guidance on a particular technique or facet of direct marketing, these skills may or may not be found within the free-standing consultancy. A more specific consultancy would be a better option, or possibly one of the large direct marketing service companies (i.e. computer bureaux and direct response agencies). In the latter case, remember that the independent, detached factor no longer prevails and other considerations may possibly influence direction and recommendations.

All too often a specialist consultancy (for example, a creative consultant) carries out part of the tasks of a direct response agency (such as a test/trial campaign) or vice versa. Client companies engaging such consultancies or agencies should state their needs, roles and expectations very clearly.

Neither of the two types of consultancy outlined in this chapter is usually retained on an open-ended basis. It is usual for their work to be carried out against *specifically* agreed briefs. These client-written briefs should include the scope, output expectations, general direction and payment basis. A consultant should *never* be 'around-for-ever'. A good consultant will always complete a task as quickly as possible and, hopefully, be used again when there is a similar need.

A good consultancy should also be prepared to turn down work for which it is *not* fully qualified, equipped or experienced, and indicate other more appropriate sources! The only time a consultant should hold a longer term tenure is on a retained hand-holding/watching brief for a specific developing area of a client's business. (Even here, perhaps, client management or a non-executive director should ideally provide this.)

Fees

Prevailing practice on fees for consultancy is driven by marketplace needs and by supply and demand. For both free-standing and specialist consultants the fees are usually based on a time rate (hourly or daily) plus VAT and expenses (recharged at cost). Daily rates in 1990 ranged from £300 for a new and relatively inexperienced specialist to around £1250 for a top-flight UK specialist or free-standing high-level practitioner. Sometimes inclusive project fees are quoted, yet these should always be justifiable on the basis of time, etc.

When should a consultancy be used?

There is obviously no absolute answer to the question of when to use a consultancy. Basically their use depends upon a specifically identified need, which might arise from:

- market entry intentions
- key management change
- reorganisation of a company
- upgrading of technology and systems
- takeover or diversification circumstances.

Such use of an *appropriate* consultancy resource can ensure that expensive mistakes are not made and that options have been fully explored and evaluated, through a personal, confidential appraisal of all the salient factors.

Do's and don'ts

When selecting and using consultants:

1 Ensure that a comprehensive brief is developed and agreed, including duration, costings and output requirements *before* the assignment commences.
2 Don't ask a direct response agency to undertake an objective independent consultancy assignment.
3 If the client company is totally new to the use of direct marketing channels, get a truly independent assessment of the implications and difficulties.
4 Ask what kind of consultant is needed—in-depth specialist or free-standing broad-based practitioner.
5 Find out what skills and resources the consultancy has. It's a people business: only pay for people and needed resources, not overheads.
6 Always try to obtain two or more *comparative* quotations for an assignment.
7 Always see the consultant who will actually undertake the work and make sure that that person will be around for the duration of the project.
8 Check the credentials, references and similar work of the consultancy to ascertain that no conflict of interest would occur. Ensure that the consultancy has been in business for a reasonable time, yet not too long to have become stale or detached from current reality. (The trade bodies, i.e. BDMA, can provide these data.)

9 Make sure that the assignment is not open-ended—unless that is what is wanted!

10 Use a clear thinking consultant with good analytical skills who can provide well thought through solutions and options. Don't hire a parrot unless that is what management wants!

21

Computer bureaux

RUSSELL LOGAN

In the direct marketing industry, computer bureaux are frequently used by companies that already possess large computers. Why do they pay to use bureau facilities?

Direct marketing campaigns place sudden strains on conventional administration systems. They create huge volumes of *output* (a million address labels, perhaps, or half a million laser letters) and cause surges of *input* (thousands of responses in a fortnight). They need *specialist services* (de-duplication, address improvement, geodemographic analysis).

So when direct marketers approach computer bureaux, it is not for conventional bureaux products. They want specific direct marketing services. Those services fall into three categories: input, output and specialist.

Input

Response handling is often contracted out to a fulfilment house—a specialist company dealing with orders or enquiries from receipt to delivery. It needs to be able to cope with sharp peaks in incoming mail, process these peaks quickly and efficiently, and have replies swiftly in the mail. The fulfilment house may create the first computer file of raw response, ready for analysis and addition to the mailing database. You have to decide whether to integrate this response data immediately into your mailing database, or whether to let the fulfilment house handle immediate response, and have the file updated later. Generally, this second approach is cheaper, and is often perfectly adequate. It allows the costly updating of the mailing database to be performed less often, at lower overall cost.

Output

If an outgoing mailing requires only labels from names on the company's own file, there is little need for a bureau. Any computer can print. But *large* mailings usually demand more mail-specific facilities. Well-targeted mailings may need complex selection software to analyse and find the best prospects. Effective mail shot techniques may need clever personalisation and laser-formatting. Inclusion of rented lists in the mailing will require efficient merge/purge systems. High-volume output will need automatic Mailsort procedures.

It is normal practice for direct marketers to look outside for these facilities. Good address-manipulation software is very difficult to develop in-house, and there is no need for everyone to re-invent the wheel.

Fortunately, these facilities are in such frequent demand that you do not need to scour the country to find the best bureaux to provide them. Address manipulation should be part of the service offered by whoever controls your outgoing mailing. To have one bureau de-dupe the files, another print the output, and a third control the physical mail-out simply adds to the overall production time. It also makes it easy for suppliers to pass the buck.

Specialist

Direct marketers often look outside for any of these services:

- file maintenance
- address improvement
- database analysis.

FILE MAINTENANCE

Many companies use bureaux to maintain their mailing files. The company processes the orders and handles day-to-day administration itself, and its bureau holds the file. What really matters in these cases is that the bureau can de-duplicate efficiently. De-duplication software varies. Some bureaux are much better at it than others. Some can handle domestic but not business addresses; others cannot 'clean' poorly created addresses. If de-duplication is crucial, you must *test* the services offered. Offer each bureau the same file, and see what each makes of it.

ADDRESS IMPROVEMENT

If your addresses are carefully captured in the first place, you will have little need for clever improvement services. But if your initial capture is poor, you must find a bureau that can improve the quality (correct the spelling, ensure towns and counties agree, etc.). Many addresses are poorly captured—because of small newspaper coupons, or carbon copies, or unmotivated staff. The best bureaux can clean these addresses up. Most can't. Unclean addresses give customers a poor impression of your company, de-duplicate less efficiently, and earn less postal discount. If you need this service, buy the best.

Whatever the quality of the addresses themselves, they will have to be postcoded and processed for Mailsort if you are to earn the substantial discounts available. Generally, postcoding and Mailsort services are available only via specialist suppliers.

DATABASE ANALYSIS

Modern marketing methods from time to time require files to be subject to geodemographic profiling or multivariate analysis. Again, these services almost always involve the use of specialist bureaux. But the bureaux do not have to be a part of your day-to-day list management procedures. You use these bureaux as an adjunct to your normal operation, sending them an extract of your file for processing separately.

If you decide that you do need a specialist direct marketing computer bureau, how do you choose which one to use?

Concentrate on the *service* you require. You will not be choosing your bureau by the criteria used by conventional bureau clients. You will want specific services, coordinated as far as possible into the rest of your direct marketing campaign. Define exactly what it is that you want the bureau to do. Draw up a thorough brief.

What do you want?

Bureaux offer a wide range of skills, but how many are relevant to the project in hand? Don't choose a bureau for its expertise in areas you won't use. But *do* ensure the bureau can handle all the things you want done.

1 Get quotes *and descriptions* for the features you know you're going to need. They may include keypunching, address correction, postcoding, geodemographics, regression or multivariate analysis, 'bespoke' system design, consultancy, laser printing.
2 Make very clear to the bureau how big your files may be, and exactly what you want held in them (specify every field).
3 Ask (and seek evidence) about their turnaround time, lead time and security procedures. Phone some of their existing clients and ask them (privately) for their opinion.
4 Decide the kind of price you want to pay: cheapest you can get, or best

value? Make sure you learn *all* the costs, not just the main production charges. Don't forget charges for set-up, account management, file storage, special software. Is there a minimum charge per run? And when comparing different bureaux, don't just compare price lists, compare their charges for doing a particular job—the one they may be doing for *you*.

Don't put price at the top of your list. Yes, it may cost you £100 per thousand to create a list, or £200 per thousand to install a marketing database. But to select and print labels thereafter may cost a mere £20 per thousand—where the cost of the total mail shot is £400 per thousand. Computer costs really are not a significant part of the overall budget. So don't get hung up over them. Buy yourself something decent.

22

Mailing houses

JOHN HUGHES

Direct mail users often employ a mailing house to send out their material, because of the specialist equipment and staff needed to despatch ten thousand or a million letters at one time.

To ensure that the mailing side of direct mail production runs smoothly, bear the following points in mind:

- pay attention to detail throughout
- put detailed instructions on paper
- involve production and mailing at an early stage, along with creative and the client.

Briefs

Two sets of written instructions will be needed: a mailing plan, and a materials summary.

MAILING PLAN
The plan should contain the following details:

- quantities to be mailed
- the precise mailing date
- postage tariff: Mailsort 1, 2 or 3, or Mailsort 4 (PPA)
- description of:
  inserts
  address carrier
  outerwrapper/envelope
  the code given to each piece of material
  size of each item
  weight of each item

- inserting sequence, i.e. the order items are enclosed in the envelope
- the direction that inserts face in the envelope.

It must list separately the number to be mailed in each test segment (allowing a small number for 'overs'). Codes are also essential for effective processing. Each personalised item should carry its own unique reference number, and a code can also be used to indicate the type of insert, list or test.

MATERIALS SUMMARY

This lists all components required in a campaign, summarising each by code, quantity and type. Other information such as date of delivery to the warehouse, supplier and packing details can also be useful. The summary serves as a warehouse guide to the total number of items available by type/code. Stock can be drawn off as required for each mailing segment.

Warehousing

More problems occur in the warehouse than are usually acknowledged. It is vital to keep tight control, knowing exactly how much of each item is in stock and when it was received. This is more difficult than is often assumed, and the warehouse manager must have the relevant information, i.e. both the mailing plan and the materials summary.

Samples of each item received should be examined to check that folding, size, weight, quality and quantity tally with the advice note and instructions. At the end of each mailing campaign, detailed mailing figures should be provided.

A problem area for many mailing houses is 'overs' left in the warehouse. Overs should be counted, packed and coded, reported to the client on an 'overs' report, and placed safely in the warehouse awaiting disposal instructions. More often than not they wait and wait. It is normal practice after a reasonable period of time to charge for storage. It is better to deal with them promptly otherwise they clog up space and interfere with the efficient function of the house.

Execution and despatch

Monitoring of each process at all stages is absolutely essential and accurate records must be kept, especially regarding quantities. Each machine or packer should keep a log of work done by code, date and quantity, noting any problems experienced during the process.

Samples should always be taken off the production line at the start and passed to the client to check and approve, even if time constraints mean inserting continues.

Remember to get details right. The figures are indicators of potential problems, so be suspicious if they do not add up. Check and double-check at each stage—addressing, computer finishing, folding and enclosing. The consecutive numbering of personalised stationery needs a particularly careful check.

Mailing-house production cannot be left without mention of the ongoing debate between hand enclosing/packing and machine processing. It is a myth that hand inserting is less capable of producing a quality product against machine, but the key is control and checking.

Costs

The mailing house suffers from being at the sharp end of the business and too often the most sensitive to price cutting. It does not pay in the end to cut corners at this point. Too much money is at stake by then in terms of material and personalisation costs.

It is important to ensure that all details are thought of and included in the original costing, to avoid later haggling over bills.

Samples

A sample of the mailing can prevent many errors. It should show the inserting order, size and folds of inserts and the direction they face in the envelope. The best is a 'live' package prepared by the client; second best is a dummy package.

If a sample using actual printed components is available, it enables other factors to be covered, serving as a benchmark for the job:

- If a window envelope is used, the position of the addressed material in relation to the window can be checked before computer finishing, labelling/ink jetting or folding. Always check that it shows through the window *at time of set-up*.
- Tolerances of size, weight, type of folding, etc., can be checked against machine specifications.
- A package can be weighted to ensure that it falls in the projected tariff band under Mailsort and costs what the client has budgeted.

Fulfilment

Some mailing houses also offer a fulfilment service, dealing with the response to the direct marketing campaign. Its brief might encompass

- enquiry or order reception and processing
- data capture via hard copy or telephone
- a relational database
- on-line enquiry access
- high-quality, fast turnround printing system for invoices, despatch notes, quotations, acknowledgement letters, lead generation information
- accurate reporting (sales, media, stock, geographic, etc.) to enable the client to evaluate performance and plan new campaigns
- pick-and-pack capability
- well-organised warehouse.

Fulfilment needs to be fast, efficient and totally accountable, with procedure controls and quality checks at every stage providing a full audit trail.

The links between mailing house and client should be virtually transparent, so that the respondent is unaware that the response handling team is not part of the client company.

Standards

At all stages, build in quality control checks and written reports. Set standards—they must be high—and insist on their being met. Quality usually costs money, tempered only by the quest for efficiency.

There is no substitute for dogged, relentless commitment to standards. Everyone involved must clearly understand the goals required: an accurate mailing, delivered on time.

To clients, the best advice is to work with a mailing house you like, which shares your goals and which you know has the physical potential to provide the service.

To the mailing house, remember your reputation is everything. Be honest and hardworking. Charge enough to make a profit or you will have no business. Enjoy the challenges and reap the benefit of your efforts.

23

Third party mailing lists

RUTH NAYLOR-SMITH

The list of people to whom your promotion is mailed is without doubt the single most important factor affecting response. The most wonderful creative pack and offer, mailed to the wrong list, will fail but even a mediocre pack, targeted to the right people, stands a reasonable chance of success.

So why is list selection so frequently left until the last minute? It should form an integral part of campaign planning, following hot on the heels of the strategic considerations. This simple step of upgrading the decision-making process about your target reader will instantly uplift response—if only because the creative thinkers will then be able to direct their concepts and design to the recipients.

Planning list usage

Before you even start to consider which specific lists, or segments of lists, to use, bear in mind three basic and obvious rules:

1 Your own customer list will always give you better results than any other list that you might use—often by as great a ratio as 3:1.
2 The best mailing lists to rent—or buy—are those which demonstrate characteristics most similar to your own list. Strictly vertical lists—e.g. lists of wine buyers to whom you wish to promote your own wine offer—will most likely not be available to you on competitive grounds, so selection needs to be based on matching customer profiles.
3 A mailing list of individuals who have shown a previous willingess to buy by mail will almost always pull better than a non-responder list, however accurate the target market may be in the latter case.

Types of list
In consumer, business-to-business and international markets, lists fall quite neatly into three levels of responsiveness:

1 *Mail order purchasers*: people who have taken the ultimate step of parting with money through the post. These include buyers of items from space advertisements, inserts, direct mail shots and catalogues—household objects, fashion, gardening items, gifts, books, computer software, business equipment, etc. Paid subscribers to publications and purchasers of insurance offers would also fall into this prime category.
2 *Responder lists*: individuals who have made an enquiry or replied to a 'free' offer but who have not been required to make any payment. Into this category would fall controlled requested circulation magazine lists, enquirers in a two stage sale and lifestyle databases.
3 *Compiled lists*: usually built from published sources, association listings, shareholder records or the electoral roll. These lists are very useful when trying to reach the full universe of people available within a particular sector, but they do not have the advantage of demonstrating the key element of 'mail-responsiveness'.

Lifestyle databases
It is worth making special mention of one of the newer developments in the list rental market—that of lifestyle databases. These unique files are developed from completed questionnaires and have the significant benefit of giving an enormous amount of *factual* information about individuals, from the type of house they live in, their income, the number of children they have living at home and the type of car they own, to their hobbies and pastimes, TV viewing habits, and their concerns about the environment. The combination of psychographic (intangible) information and demographic data (hard facts) makes these files—if used correctly—equally as effective as proven mail order responders; sometimes more so.

Sources of lists
There are currently three to four thousand mailing lists available on the UK rental market, selectable in a whole host of ways to permit finer definition. This is 10–12 times more than in the early 1980s but there are still major gaps in the marketplace which may necessitate detailed research for highly specific target groups. Lists can be sourced through:

1 *Other list owners*: it is not uncommon for competitive companies to exchange lists, or arrange reciprocal rentals.
2 *Directories* can be useful as a source of low-cost, well-defined lists. Bear

in mind that they have no proven mail responsiveness, and directories cannot be as accurately maintained as a list which is held on-line on a computer system and regularly updated.

3 *List brokers* generally offer the most convenient means of access to a range of suitable lists. Their stock-in-trade is the ability to propose the best selections from all lists available to match your target market.

The British List Brokers' Association exists to determine and maintain standards, so do check that the broker you wish to use is a member of this association.

HOW TO GET WHAT YOU REALLY WANT

To ensure that you actually mail the people you want to reach, it is important to brief a list broker and to know what details to ask about lists suggested to you. By following this checklist, you will get prompt and accurate information:

Market profile
- Give your broker as many details as you can about your target prospect.
- Provide sample mailing pieces (if available) together with other background material on your offer.
- Itemise lists that have already given good results—and those that have not.
- Allow your broker to interpret your needs creatively in the light of his or her expert knowledge—this may lead to some surprises that may well be worth testing.

List make-up
- Does the list represent active customers, expires or prospects? Can each be selected out?
- Is it possible to take recent names only?
- Is the list made up of home or business addresses?
- What products or services have customers bought? For what price? Were they sold by mail, coupon ads or catalogues? Are they credit buyers?
- If the list is compiled, what sources were used? When was it last updated and cleaned?
- If it is a consumer list, when was it last cleaned against the Mailing Preference Service file?
- Was the data 'fairly' collected and is it accurately registered under the Data Protection Act 1984?

Performance data

- Ask list suppliers how their lists work for other rental users. They will not be able to give details of percentages but may be able to indicate the products or offers for which it has been successful.
- Check the supplier's policy on undeliverables. The industry norm is reimbursement of rental costs on all gone-aways if over 4 per cent of names rented are returned.

Addressing/postal requirements

- Can the list be delivered in the format you need? This is usually cheshire labels, self-adhesive labels or IBM compatible magnetic tape.
- What percentage of the list is postcoded? Can it be supplied in 'Mailsort' sequence?
- Can the list owner provide an accurate cross-section or 'nth name' for testing?
- If you are using labels, can key-codes be printed on them and are they the right size for your order form or envelope?

Timing

- Allow at least three weeks between order date and required delivery date; longer if lists need to be ordered from overseas. Inform the supplier of your mailing dates so that competitive clashes can be avoided.

Price and conditions

- Ask list suppliers to spell out their conditions of usage clearly. Normally lists are provided for one-time rental use only; responders can be added to your own file, non-responders cannot. If you are buying a list, is it just for your own unlimited use or can you rent it to others?
- Get a firm quotation for all the charges involved—basic rental price, selection charges, extra charges for labels, magnetic tape deposits, styling, country name, key-coding, etc.
- Check that the owner will deliver to your chosen destination. Some will only supply to a recognised computer bureau or mailing house; others may even insist on owner mailing.
- Be prepared to supply sample mailing pieces—the owner has the ultimate right to decide whether or not the list will be released for your offer.
- Expect to sign detailed terms and conditions. List warranties, which were introduced with the Data Protection Act, will also need to be signed, by both the owner and the user.

- Remember that list security is paramount, and that owners insert check names, known as seeds or sleepers, into the list.
- When you finally order your lists, don't forget to stipulate the quantity of names required!

These golden rules form the key to successful list acquisition. Follow them and your mailing will go through the doors of the people who want to buy from you.

24

Print

JOY ROBINSON

Organising print for direct marketing applications requires a substantial amount of planning and coordination. It is also important to get the cooperation of designers at the earliest possible stage in their creative process to ask such questions as:

- Is the item part of a mailing?
- Is it to be personalised, and if so by which medium?
- If a mailing pack, what size is the envelope?
- Do all the items fit into the envelope?
- Are there any weight constraints?
- Is the item folded, or can it be refolded, in such a way as to make it suitable for machine enclosing?
- Does the reply device fit into the reply envelope?

Most companies employ an outside bureau to assist with the data-processing side of direct marketing production, and specialist advertising agencies advise their clients on all items relating to direct marketing, including print. However, there is no reason why a company cannot produce print for direct marketing, subsequent to some careful research.

Personalisation

There are five main methods in which you can personalise your mailing. In order of quality, they are: sheet fed laser; web fed laser; ion deposition; ink jet; and impact.

The most widely used machine is the Xerox 9700 or 9790 laser printer which personalises A4 sheets of paper. It is very versatile in terms of scheduling, or getting your job done quickly, mainly because there are so many machines available at laser bureaux around the country (see Table

Table 24.1   Summary of machines and costs for personalising printed mailings

Machine	Max size of paper acceptable	Approx. cost per thousand	Maximum paper weight acceptable	Dot/ resolution
Xerox 9700/9790	A4	£14	240 gsm	300/300
Siemens ND3	Any length × 406 mm	£13	160 gsm	240/240
IBM 3800	305 × 378 mm	£14	120 gsm	240/240
NBS 7500	610 × 210 mm	£18	300 gsm	240/240
Variojet 2800 (ink jet)	Print area any length × 270 mm	£16	Suitable for various substrates	120/120
Impact	305 × 450 mm	£1.80 per line	200 gsm	Ribbon

24.1). However, the formats that are available are limited. The continuous machines (Siemens and Variojet) are able to process a larger size piece of paper for the same cost as the smaller Xerox machines and can thus save you money.

The Xerox machines can print on both sides of the paper, which is useful if you wish to personalise both sides of a letter. The Variojet and Siemens ND3 can print in more than one colour.

Note that with the IBM 3800 you should avoid highly coated papers and ink coverage of more than 240 per cent.

The paper you supply for use with Xerox 9700 and 9790 should be long grain A4, not heavily coated, trimmed to size very accurately and packed in tight boxes, not loose on pallets. Otherwise the sheets can become distorted and will be unsuitable for use in the laser printer.

Envelopes
You can buy these to order (bespoke), or off the shelf. Most envelope-making machines also have flexo printing units 'in-line', enabling one pass printing and make-up. Litho printing 'in-line' is not so common, and most litho printed jobs are either printed in flat sheets or reels prior to manufacture or overprinted after manufacture.

The most commonly used fast-running litho overprinting machine is called a Jet. You'll find that quantities up to 100 000 can be cost-effectively overprinted from stock.

Bespoke envelopes can have multiple windows, in various shapes and sizes, and even tear out panels to reveal text or illustrations from your sales literature inside. The creative mind can run riot as long as you remember that the envelope should have enough substance to prevent its falling apart in the post.

Instead of paper envelopes you can use plain plastic and plastic metalised envelopes. These can be extremely effective visually and are cost-efficient. Their light weight often enables you insert more items in the envelope if you are almost on a Post Office weight band.

Specialist finishing

Two basic sizes of printing press with 'in-line' finishing are available in the UK: 630 × 965 mm and 451 × 670 mm. These machines have attachments to add gum, fragrance burst, coin rub inks or silver latex, and to perforate, number or die-cut. Plow-fold towers and rotary blades enable the printer to produce inserts or one-piece mailers folded, gummed, sealed and ready to mail in one operation. The machines can also be used for more conventional work such as 16-page booklets, again produced in one operation, from blank reel to finished piece.

In addition to the production of inserts and one-piece mailers, these machines can be used to print game pieces and promotional cards. Some printers have ink-jet systems in-line, which can be utilised either for adding basic codes or for fully addressing a one-piece mailer ready for posting. The minimum order quantity for either machine is approximately 100 000 impressions. Make-ready times for some of the more involved pieces can be as long as 24 hours, therefore the minimum quantities will vary according to the complexity of your design. You'll be charged for 'make ready', so it sometimes pays to keep the design simple.

There are 'off-line' finishing systems such as the Hunkeler, which can process reels of paper that have already been personalised or printed. The reel-fed Hunkeler machine generally available in the UK can process three separate reels of paper, two of which can be pre-personalised. The system will diecut, perforate, fold, glue, apply plastic cards and tip on self-adhesive labels.

Sheet-fed finishing machines can produce very similar pieces as the reel-fed but, generally, they are more suitable for smaller quantity print-runs.

Weights

Weight is a very important factor in direct marketing—and not only in relation to postage costs. Loose inserts placed in newspapers and magazines are also priced on weight if they weigh over 10–12 grams.

The calculation to determine the weight of a piece is as follows: length × width × grammage × numbers of sheets, divided by 1 000 000. For example, an A4 sheet of 100 gsm would weigh:

$$297 \times 210 \times 100 \times 1 \div 1\ 000\ 000 = 6.24\ g$$

As ink makes up a very small portion of the overall weight of a pack it does not need to be taken into your calculations.

An example of a typical mailing pack

C5 window envelope 90 gsm	8.36 g
A4 letter 100 gsm	6.24 g
4 page A5 leaflet 160 gsm	10.00 g
A5 flyer 115 gsm	3.60 g
C6 reply paid envelope 80 gsm	3.32 g
	31.52 g

An example of a typical magazine insert

142 × 440 on 90 gsm	5.62 g
142 × 440 on 115 gsm	7.20 g

SIZES

The following envelope sizes are useful to remember. Note that DL is the size most commonly used.

Minimum Post Office size of reply cards: 70 × 100 mm
114 × 229 mm = oversize DL
102 × 216 mm = undersize DL

These envelope sizes are ideal for packs in which the reply device should not be folded. Envelopes should be 8 mm wider than the largest insert and 4 mm higher. Remember to keep the reply portion of an insert to less than 25 per cent of the total size to avoid paying VAT. Envelopes, letterheadings and reply cards attract VAT; leaflets, booklets, brochures and catalogues do not. A good rule of thumb would be that anything that would normally be used for written or typed correspondence is likely to attract VAT. If in doubt contact your local VAT office.

Timetables

In an ideal world, a mailing pack should take four weeks to produce, from approval by the client to having artwork completed. Then allow two weeks to litho print, one week to laser print and one week to enclose.

When large quantities are involved it is obviously necessary to order paper in advance and schedule in production with relevant suppliers.

Typical packs/inserts

The following examples illustrate typical packs and inserts and their production requirements.

A 500 000 copies of a direct mail pack.

Components:

1 Personalised letter/application form, two colours
2 Business reply envelope, one colour
3 Outer window envelope, two colours outside, special opaque inside
4 Colour leaflet, 210 × 396 mm folded to 210 × 99 mm.

Production techniques used:

1 Printed continuous and personalised on Siemens. Letter becomes address medium, showing through window aperture, A4 width; application form size 170 mm wide (max. size possible)
2 Printed flexo, special making, 102 × 216 mm
3 Printed flexo, special making, 114 × 229 mm, made up and printed in one pass
4 Printed mini web on special reels—420 mm wide. Weight of pack: 30.2 g. Cost: £80 per thousand including lasering but not artwork or design.

B 10 000 of a direct mail pack.

Components:

1 Personalised letter and application form
2 Business reply envelope, C6
3 Outer envelope in four colours, 220 × 220 mm
4 Colour leaflet, 210 × 525 mm (160 gsm) folded to 210 × 210 mm
5 Gift flyer, 210 × 210 mm.

Production technique used:

1 Print sheet fed, 355 × 210 mm (max. length to fit Xerox 4050 sheet fed laser)
2 C6 printed litho on stock envelopes
3 Stock envelope overprinted in four colours
4 Printed sheet fed on SRA2 machine

5 As above. Weight: 47 g. Cost: £415 per thousand including lasering but not artwork or design.

PROBLEM

To produce 1 500 000 inserts at no more than £16.50 per thousand, including artwork, colour separation and one four-colour plate change.

Solution

Budget cost for artwork and films, £3000. Size decided at 142 × 440 mm, folded to 142 × 88 mm in-line on 90 gsm woodfree matt-coated papers. Produce three images from one set of plates and one revolution of the machine special reels. (Could have been produced four out running against the web and folded off line.) Cost £21 021 = £16.01 per thousand total.

Conclusion

The most effective way to ensure the smooth execution of any direct marketing print piece or pack is to consult all interested parties as early in the design stage as possible.

25

Training

DEREK HOLDER

The range of skills and functions outlined in the matrix (Table 25.1) indicates that training in direct marketing is:

- crucial to effective management performance;
- continuous throughout the direct marketing career of an individual;
- ubiquitous, i.e. it must be carried to all sections in the organisation;
- similar to general marketing training in principle, but different in important aspects. The rest of this chapter develops that point.

Specific features of direct marketing training

All marketers need to understand customer needs. This requirement is greater in direct marketing however, because direct marketers are *closer* to their customers. Both have quick and easy access to each other. If direct marketers misjudge customer needs, they know immediately— either through response or non-response. Direct marketers must therefore be trained to be much more sensitive to customer needs. They must understand the 'private' nature of every relationship and, technically, must be able to use a range of personal communication media skilfully.

Much of the work of a direct marketer is task, project, campaign based. The execution of several relatively small-scale projects simultaneously is commonplace. This requires organisational skills of a high order. People and projects require highly active management. The direct marketer needs to be skilful in getting the best out of others (colleagues and suppliers of a range of products and services) and in scheduling and controlling campaigns. Time management, people management and financial resource management skills are at a premium in such an environment. Training has a vital role to play here.

Table 25.1   The skills/functions matrix

SKILLS	FUNCTIONS					
	PLANNING		EXECUTION		MONITORING	
	Knowledge of	Ability to	Knowledge of	Ability to	Knowledge of	Ability to
CONCEPTUAL	Long-range planning Short-range planning Objectives, missions Strategies Environmental circumstances	Think long term Think short term Conceptualise objectives, etc., and express clearly abstract key environmental issues	Scheduling and appropriate techniques: e.g. GANTT charts, PERT Key budgeting concepts: e.g. cash flow, lifetime values	Think laterally and sequentially Think graphically React quickly and flexibly to market developments	Principles underpinning control and evaluation techniques	Think analytically
HUMAN	Organisation's human resources Leadership skills most likely to be effective Motivation Communication Creative	Plan and organise DM personnel Plan and organise project teams Plan incentive programmes Communicate effectively (writing) Generate ideas	Practical problems in DM Campaign management Problems faced by suppliers	Manage project teams (lead and motivate in a hectic environment) Communicate with and manage suppliers—computer personnel, printers, executives, etc.	The data culture attitudes and ways of working in that culture Problems faced by data analysts	Empathise with data analysts Communicate with, lead and motivate analysts
TECHNICAL	Planning techniques Environmental analysis Budgetary control and financial analysis Database marketing	Prepare and write short- and long-term plans Understand and interpret data Budget, prepare statements, etc. Plan database	Technical aspects of scheduling Organising and budgeting (too detailed to enter here but include management and development and response handling)	Perform technical tasks efficiently, quickly, accurately and under severe time pressures	Control and evaluation techniques	Apply control techniques efficiently and flexibly

The defining quality of direct marketing is its measurability. Every penny spent can be accounted for and related back to results. Consequently, direct marketers must be analytical in outlook and in their execution and monitoring of campaigns. They need to be numerate—with a grasp of statistical techniques and financial control techniques. They must be able to track the performance of a campaign and quickly analyse results, feeding them back into the marketing plan. This demands mental flexibility as well as technical know-how. Again, training has an important part to play.

Direct marketing media are highly technical. The main medium is print. Here direct marketers need to understand creative processes, technical processes and how they interrelate. They must be able to brief creative people, understand print production techniques and know how to contain the processes involved within strict budgetary limits. This places a premium both on technical knowledge and on interpersonal skills.

The skills audit

The skills shortage and technical change in the industry mean that things are changing fast in direct marketing. People need to be trained to adapt, to cope and to manage; to be both reactive and proactive. But first we need to diagnose our training needs. Everyone in direct marketing has a responsibility here. The individual, the line manager and the training department should all be actively involved. And outsiders can be brought in—specialists in direct marketing training can be particularly useful adjuncts to the internal direct marketing skills appraisal process.

Where to go

Training providers come under the following headings:

1 Institute or trade associations
2 Independent training organisations
3 Academic institutions
4 Commercial seminar/conference organisations.

Having assessed your training needs internally, by using the skills audit, it is recommended that you approach your specific trade association or institution for advice. In the case of direct marketing, the main trade body is the British Direct Marketing Association which, together with the Direct Marketing Centre, maintains lists of suppliers.

Tailored versus public training

Tailored in-company training which fits into the existing internal training programmes offers a high level of specific relevance to companies. This is the most expensive option and one that should be viewed in the context of training needs over time. It is most suitable for larger companies with higher numbers of staff to absorb the costs.

Training through public seminars and conferences offers the benefit of broad market exposure and the bright idea and techniques, but does not provide specific training on how to implement direct marketing concepts and techniques.

Qualification versus non-qualification training

Personnel interested in progressing their careers are concerned to achieve higher qualifications. Business school courses from HNC to MBA can be relevant in broad managerial terms, but specific qualifications may be more practical in cutting a person's learning curve and enhancing a manager's job performance. Relevant qualifications are:

- Chartered Institute of Marketing Certificate and Diploma
- CAM Certificate and Diploma
- Relevant modules of the Open University Business School programme (e.g. Marketing)
- BDMA Diploma in Direct Marketing, run by the Direct Marketing Centre.

CAM (The Communication, Advertising and Marketing Education Foundation) can be contacted at Abford House, 15 Wilton Road, London SW1V 1NJ, telephone 071–828 7506. The address of the Direct Marketing Centre is 1 Park Road, Teddington, Middx TW11 0AR, telephone 081–977 5705.

Conclusions

Training is not a panacea, nor is it a short-term solution. A professional training programme, whether administered by the personnel department or by line management, should be viewed as a corporate investment. Well-organised individual training programmes motivate staff. The excellent companies are those which neither regard training as an after-thought nor are too busy to bother, but which budget sensibly for it in monetary and time allocations. Be warned by the quote from Peter Drucker: 'If you think education is expensive, try ignorance.'

26

Royal Mail

GRAHAM HUGHES

The Royal Mail offers a wide range of postal services to users of direct mail. These cover the three main parts of a direct mail campaign:

- outward mailing (mail shots/door-to-door deliveries)
- incoming responses
- fulfilment.

They include inland and international services.

A basic outline of all the relevant services is given below, and a list of useful Royal Mail publications and details of who to contact for further help is at the end of the chapter.

Outward mailing

METHODS OF STAMPING

If you are doing a large mailing, then you will probably want an alternative to affixing postage stamps to each item. There are several time-saving options:

Prepayment in money

Minimum mailing: 500 letters/packets or 20 parcels. Many main Post Offices will accept prepaid mail—your local counter will tell you the location of your nearest accepting office. You pay the standard postage for each item, hand the unstamped items over and the Royal Mail will frank them for you with a postmark.

For further information see the *Technical Mailing Manual* or ask at your nearest Post Office.

Franking machines

Postage is paid in advance. The letters are fed through a franking machine, which prints a postmark on each one. The machine records the amount of postage used and when your prepaid amount expires you can top it up again. Machines can be leased or purchased from a number of companies that have been authorised by Royal Mail.

For further information see the *Technical Mailing Manual* or contact your Letters Business Customer Care Unit for a list of authorised suppliers and service conditions.

Printed postage impressions (PPI)

Minimum mailing: 4000 letters, 1000 packets or 100 parcels in one posting. An identifying serial number is allocated to your company which you can print on envelopes, labels or wrappers as a PPI. Payment is made when the items are handed over to Royal Mail, either in cash or through an account.

For further information see the *Printed Postage Impressions* brochure.

DISCOUNT SERVICES—MAILSORT

Mailsort is the name of the Royal Mail customer-sorted discount services. For mailing of more than 4000 letters or 1000 packets, of the same size and weight, which can be presorted by postcode (or 2000 letters for local postings). Mailsort consists of three delivery options:

- Mailsort 1—delivery the next working day
- Mailsort 2—delivery within 3 working days
- Mailsort 3—delivery within 7 working days.

The Royal Mail offers a free Mailsort database which contains the sortation plan and a user's guide to help you plan the computer programming and handling operations necessary for Mailsort. Discounts range from 13 to 32 per cent, depending on the service chosen and the degree to which you can presort the items.

For further information contact your Letters Business Customer Care Unit.

HOUSEHOLD DELIVERY SERVICES (HDS)

This is the Royal Mail's door-to-door leaflet distribution service, which offers delivery of unaddressed promotional material to all areas of the UK. Deliveries can be as small as a postcode sector (approximately 2000 delivery points), or as large as the entire country. The items in a distribution must be identical in size and weight and weigh less than 60 g.

Each item will be delivered by a Royal Mail postman, along with the regular mail, during a specified two-week period.

For further information see the *Household Delivery Service* booklet, or phone 0865–780400.

Incoming responses

BUSINESS REPLY AND FREQUENT SERVICES
Both services enable your customers to reply to you without having to pay postage. Reply cards and envelopes are printed under licence with a reply-paid design approved by the Royal Mail (first and second class available).

Freepost offers an additional feature enabling your customers to reply to you, on their own stationery, without having to pay postage (only second class available).

The charges for both services are an annual licence fee, the first or second class postage plus a small handling charge for every item received. Discounts are available for licence holders receiving more than 50 000 items per year.

For further information see Business Reply/Freepost application forms, available from your Royal Mail Business Centre.

ADMAIL
Admail is a contractual redirection service. It enables you to quote a response address local to the area of your advertisement but to have the replies redirected by Royal Mail to another address within the UK (e.g. your fulfilment house). It can also be combined with the Freepost service.

For further information contact your Letters Business Customer Care Unit.

PRIVATE BOXES
These are sometimes known as PO boxes. The service enables you to quote a PO box number instead of your address and enables you to call and collect your mail from the local Royal Mail delivery office.

There is an annual fee, which varies according to the combination of services you require: letters only, parcels only, or letters and parcels collected or delivered to your address.

For further information see the *Inland Letter Rates* compendium. A Private Box application form is obtainable from your Royal Mail Business Centre.

Fulfilment

PARCELFORCE STANDARD
- Delivery normally in 2–3 working days
- Items up to 30 kg
- Size limits up to 1.5 m length and 3 m length and girth combined
- Around 20 000 acceptance points.

A range of special facilities are available for contract customers. These include:

- individually tailored pricing and special collection services
- TRAKBACK—optional proof of delivery service for parcels
- return Paid Parcels—this facility is useful for offering your customers the opportunity of returning unwanted goods, which you have sent to them on approval, without their having to pay postage. (Your customer is given a label which, when used, is invoiced to you by Parcelforce.)
- cash on delivery—for payment of a fee, Parcelforce will deliver your parcel and collect the payment from your customer, which you will then receive within two weeks of delivery.

PARCELFORCE 24 AND PARCELFORCE 48
These are contractual services with individually negotiated prices. They offer a guaranteed next day and two day delivery to 95 per cent of all UK business addresses. The services offer several all-inclusive features, e.g. money-back guarantee, insurance up to £1000, delivery confirmation by telephone.

The services accept items up to 30 kg, 1.5 m in length and 3 m length and girth combined. Special arrangements can be made for the acceptance of heavier and larger loads. Service features include: flexible collection arrangements, computerised consignment tracking and a weekly data service report.

PARCELFORCE DATAPOST
By this method contract and non-contract terms are both available, with guaranteed delivery by 10 am next day to almost any major UK destination, and by noon next day almost everywhere else in the UK.

A money-back guarantee and insurance (including consequential loss) are provided and items up to 30 kg are accepted.

Sameday Delivery is available within Central London and between selected Business Centres in the UK.

For further information on all Royal Mail Parcelforce services, please call 0800 22 44 66.

Royal Mail International Services

INTERNATIONAL DIRECT MARKETING

Royal Mail International offers a range of distribution and fulfilment services, plus an International Direct Marketing information pack and Business Travel Guide to help UK businesses compete effectively abroad. Please contact Royal Mail International, FREEPOST, Room 320 (IDM), 52 Grosvenor Gardens, London, SW1W OYA.

ACCOUNT AND CONTRACT SERVICES

A number of account and contract services are available for customers with regular or large volumes of mailings.

Airstream

Royal Mail International's service for large volume senders of business mail speeds your personalised direct mail and other correspondence to its destination with a global, door to door service. Fast and reliable, Airstream is simple to use and has account facilities, making it the first choice international airmail service for senders of business mail.

Printflow

Printflow—a menu of services for printed matter—is ideal for companies sending non-personalised mail shots, information packs and brochures. A complete range of worldwide print distribution services offers you the opportunity to choose your desired combination of speed and economy.

Airmail Packet Contract

Offers you an economic and quick way of despatching lightweight goods by air using simple customs documentation. Account facilities are available and the pricing structure is straightforward.

International Business Reply Service (IBRS)

IBRS makes it easy for customers and prospects to respond to you at no cost to themselves; they simply return your pre-paid envelope or reply card. This service includes all EC countries, the USA and most other major UK trading partners. A one-off fee covers the cost of your annual licence and the first 1000 replies in that year.

Swiftair

Swiftair is the worldwide express letter service that gives important mail the 'VIP Treatment'. Swiftair items receive priority handling and separate sorting to ensure a service that is faster than Airmail, yet far more economical than couriers. Pre-paid Swiftpacks offer an even more convenient service. Available at post office counters, or via your firm's collection.

GENERAL SERVICES

Royal Mail International offers a range of general services for sending letters, small packets and printed papers. You can choose between airmail for speed, or surface mail for added economy. The following services are also available at Post Office Counters: Swiftair—the express airmail service; Advice of Delivery; Registration; and Insurance. For more information, consult *Royal Mail International's Comprehensive Mailing Guide for Business Users*, available at your local main post office counter.

Further information and advice on any Royal Mail International service can always be obtained from your local Royal Mail Business Centre listed in the telephone directory.

Parcelforce International Services

INTERNATIONAL STANDARD SERVICE

Items receive priority handling at every stage. The service is available to virtually every destination around the world. These are daily scheduled outlets to key destinations.

INTERNATIONAL ECONOMY SERVICE

This is a service for non-urgent parcels with longer delivery times compensated for by very low prices. It is available to almost every destination in over 200 countries and territories.

Extra services available with both Standard and Economy services include:

- Insurance
- Express delivery
- Cash on delivery
- Prepayment of Customs fees
- Free collections
- Generous size and weight allowances.

DATAPOST
Contract and non-contract terms are both available. The system gives a guaranteed timetabled delivery of goods and documents to over 120 countries and territories around the world, including next day delivery of documents to New York and most European destinations. It also provides a free money-back guarantee and insurance (including consequential loss) with generous size and weight limits up to 30 kg.

For further information on any Royal Mail Parcelforce International Services, please call free on 0800 22 44 66.

Inland and/or International Parcelforce services

Call 0800 22 44 66 for any enquiries regarding Parcelforce services, customer care, contract benefits, or for obtaining copies of service guides.

Useful Royal Mail publications

COMPENDIA
Information on Royal Mail services and prices, available from Post Office Counters, is given in four booklets:

- Inland Letters
- Royal Mail International's Comprehensive Mailing Guide for Business Users
- Inland Parcels
- International Parcels.

'TECHNICAL MAILING MANUAL'
This manual gives details of standard requirements when using Royal Mail services—e.g. weights and sizes, method of address, envelope designs— and is available from:
Room 221
Royal Mail Marketing
148–166 Old Street
London EC1V 9HQ

'PRINTED POSTAGE IMPRESSIONS'
This brochure, which provides a users' guide and PPI design instructions, is available from your Letters Business Customer Care Unit.

'HOUSEHOLD DELIVERY SERVICE'
This booklet, which tells you how to use the service and how the service works, is available from the HDS National Booking Centre.

'INTERNATIONAL BUSINESS REPLY SERVICE'
This is a leaflet that gives more details about the service and the countries to which the service is available.

For further information

INLAND AND/OR ROYAL MAIL INTERNATIONAL SERVICES
Contact your nearest Royal Mail Business Centre, which is based at your District Head Post Office. The address and telephone number can be obtained from your nearest Post Office, the local telephone directory or directory enquiries.

INLAND AND/OR INTERNATIONAL PARCELS SERVICES
Contact your nearest Parcels District sales office. The address and telephone number can be obtained from your nearest Post Office, the local telephone directory or directory enquiries.

There is also a Royal Mail Parcels general enquiry number which you can call free on 0800 300 363.

HOUSEHOLD DELIVERY SERVICE
For information and booking, contact:
  HDS Booking Centre
  PO Box 1000
  Oxford
  OX4 5XA
  Tel: 0865 780400

PART **IV**

Controls and regulations

27

Direct marketing and the law

COLIN FRICKER

The practice of direct marketing is subject to controls and regulations which are derived from three main sources:

- the general law relating to business operations, and to advertising in particular
- the nature of the product or service being advertised by direct marketing
- the specific features characterising direct marketing.

General law

It is vital to remember that the law of contract applies to purchases generated by direct marketing, just as it does to contracts brought about in other ways. The following points—which apply equally to business-to-business contracts—should be noted as essential ingredients of a contract:

1 There must be an intention to be legally bound by the contract. It is not enough for it to be binding in honour only, as with, say, the Football Pools.
2 An offer has to be made and acceptance (unconditional) given. It is not always obvious when an *offer* is being made, as opposed to an 'inducement to buy'. For example, the display of items for sale in a shop window is not an offer to sell them so much as an 'invitation to treat', or inducement to a potential customer to enter the shop and make an offer. Because the first step in the 'offer and acceptance' nexus is therefore made by the customer, it is for the shopkeeper to accept the offer or refuse it. The shopkeeper may, at Common Law, refuse such an offer even if the price of the goods has been displayed and the customer offers that price; however, if, in such a case, the shopkeeper

asked for a higher price, he or she would be liable to prosecution under section 20 of the Consumer Protection Act 1987, for giving a false indication as to the price of goods on sale.

The importance of this concept to direct marketers is that mail shots and off-the-page advertisements normally amount to 'invitations to treat' rather than to legal offers. So it is the customer who makes the first legal move to enter into a contract by replying to the invitation. In sales promotion schemes, however, if a member of the public fulfils whatever is required to qualify for a gift, the contract comes into existence there and then (even if entry to the promotion is free). This is because it is not an inducement to buy, as such.

It is also interesting to note that, whereas, to be legal, an offer has to be communicated—i.e. it has actually to reach the person who may wish to accept it—the acceptance of the offer need not do so where, by tacit or express agreement, it is sent to the offerer through the Royal Mail. (This applies in England and Wales but not under Scottish law.) In such cases the offer is deemed to have been accepted the moment it is put into the letter box and post-marked. (The interesting practical consequence of this exception is that an offer cannot be legally withdrawn after the acceptance has been posted in such circumstances even though the offeror is unaware that acceptance has been made and even though he or she may not actually receive it until days later.)

3 There must be real, legal consideration which has value. This is usually goods or services in return for money, but it can include the doing of some act (such as in sales promotions when compliance with a condition, e.g. collection and despatch of labels, creates a binding contract).

4 The parties to the contract must have legal capacity. Minors (persons under 18) have certain legal incapacities, as have those for whom others have been appointed to act (under Mental Health Legislation, for example). Companies can act only in accordance with their Memorandum and Articles of Association; otherwise their acts, such as entering into a particular contract, may be *ultra vires*.

5 There must be no mistake as to the identity of the other party or as to the nature of the contract, e.g. what is being sold.

6 The contract must not be for an illegal or unenforceable purpose—e.g. a wager or lottery—or for the commission of a crime.

7 It must be in whatever form the contract in question has to be in. In practice, unless the conveyance of land is involved, ordinary writing (or even spoken words or conduct) are adequate.

Further obligations
Other essential points to remember, when considering legal obligations between two parties, include the following:

Discharge   The best way to discharge a contract is to fulfil it but the obligations of one party may be discharged if the other party breaks the contract.

Express and implied terms   While express terms are those that are stated in the agreement, or documentation of which the agreement is comprised, Parliament has laid down a number of terms which apply whether or not either party expresses them or even realises that they do apply. These are:

1 *The Sale of Goods Act 1979* (replacing the Act of 1893 of the same name) creates implied warranties as to title, description, merchantable quality and fitness for purpose in contracts for the sale of goods.
2 *The Supply of Goods and Services Act 1982* applies similar warranties to contracts for hire of goods and to contracts for goods and services together.

Prior to *The Supply of Goods (Implied Terms) Act 1973*, implied terms as to description, merchantability and fitness in sales to consumers could be 'struck out' by incorporating an exclusion clause in the contract, but the 1973 Act prohibited this. *The Unfair Contract Terms Act 1977* went further; it provides particular protection for the consumer by outlawing any attempt to exclude the implied undertakings mentioned above in any contract for sale of goods, for hire of goods or for sale of goods and hire of services together.

The protection for businesses, however, is qualified—such implied undertakings are excludable if the exclusion satisfies a test of reasonableness.

Further, a party to a contract for sale of goods, etc., cannot exclude liability for breach of contract where that party imposes standard terms of contract on the other party or where, in any case, the other party is a consumer, *unless* the test of reasonableness is satisfied.

Note should also be taken of the Consumer Transactions (Restrictions on Statements) Order 1976, which makes it a criminal offence to display a notice or advertisement purporting to take away rights conferred by Sale of Goods Acts (e.g. by saying 'no refunds', 'credit notes only', 'sold as seen and inspected') or to reproduce a manufacturer's guarantee without a further statement that the consumer's statutory rights are not affected thereby.

1. *Misrepresentation Act 1967.* This provides legal remedies for a buyer who can show he or she was misled as to a fact on which he or she relied. But for a statement or representation by the seller to give rise to legal effects it must be more than opinion and must not be merely advertiser's puff.

A fraudulent misrepresentation—difficult to prove—results in rescission, indemnity and damages for deceit. Honest but negligent misrepresentation can result in damages and or rescission, while misrepresentation without negligence can entitle the buyer to rescission.

2. *Unsolicited Goods and Services Acts 1971 and 1975.* These are intended to counter 'inertia selling'. If unsolicited goods are sent to a potential customer—not to another business—and the sender does not try to get them back either within the next six months or within 30 days after the recipient has given notice that the goods are regarded as unsolicited, the recipient may keep them.

But, more significantly, it is made a criminal offence to demand payment for unsolicited goods or to threaten legal proceedings, or to demand payment for unsolicited entries in a trade directory.

3. *Trade Descriptions Act 1968.* Although the main purpose of this Act is to protect the public, it also extends to transactions between businesses. Basically it makes it a criminal offence, in the course of a trade or business, to apply a false trade description to any goods, or to supply or offer to supply any goods to which a false trade description is applied. Those who publish mail order catalogues have to be careful to describe the goods accurately since, although they may not be offering them for sale (see earlier), they are exposing them for supply and are therefore deemed by Section 6 to be offering to supply them.

Furthermore, since 'supply' is wider than 'sale', free gifts appear to be covered if the supply is made in the course of a trade or business.

The Act also applies to misleading indications as to prices of goods, but the relevant Section 11 was replaced by Part III of the Consumer Protection Act 1987, which extends controls to prices for services, but which applies only to the protection of consumers, not businesses.

There are a number of defences to charges under the Act. These are:

(a) that the offence was due to mistake, or reliance on information supplied, or act or default of another person, or an accident or some other cause beyond his or her control; and

(b) that he or she took all reasonable precautions and exercised all diligence to avoid committing the offence—this means that he or she had set up an efficient system of training and monitoring;

(c) that he or she did not know and could not have found out with reasonable diligence that the goods did not conform to the description applied to the goods;

(d) in the case of an advertisement committing an offence, that it was published in the course of such a business and the publisher did not know and had no reason to suspect that its publication would amount to an offence.

4. *Consumer Protection Act 1987.* As has been seen, Part III replaces, insofar as consumers are concerned, and extends Section 11 of the Trade Descriptions Act on prices. The new Act creates a general offence of giving to a consumer, in the course of any business, misleading indication as to the price at which any goods or services are available.

Price indications that are correct at the time given may subsequently become misleading and give rise to an offence. So if prices in a catalogue become out of date during the 'life' of the catalogue—say, because of a change in the level of VAT—they would become misleading until replaced by a catalogue with the new prices. In such cases, the new prices would have to be drawn to the attention of anyone ordering from the original catalogue before supplying the goods ordered.

Part III repeals the unworkable Bargain Offers regulations and empowers the Secretary of State to approve a code of practice. This has been done and the Price Indications Code of Practice sets down the way in which traders should indicate prices in a clear and acceptable way.

The defences under the Act are similar to those under the 1968 Act, including the 'innocent publication' defence available to publishers. There is, however, a refinement to the 'due diligence' defence in that the accused has to show that it was reasonable, in all the circumstances, to have relied on information supplied, with particular regard to the steps taken to verify the information.

5. *Control of Misleading Advertisements Regulations 1988.* These new regulations are aimed at protecting the interests of consumers, traders and the general public from the effects of misleading advertisements.

The term 'advertisement' means any form of representation made in connection with a trade, business, craft or profession in order to promote the supply or transfer of goods or services, immovable property, rights or obligations.

To be misleading an advertisement must in some way deceive, or be likely to deceive, the persons at whom it is aimed or whom it reaches and must thereby be likely to affect their economic behaviour or must injure, or be likely to injure, a competitor.

The bulk of complaints will continue to be handled through existing channels—which, in the case of direct marketing and of advertising in general, means the Advertising Standards Authority (ASA).

The Director General of Fair Trading, however, is given power to react to complaints that the ASA has not been able to resolve. After taking into account the gravity of a complaint and also the public interest, the Director General can decide to take court action if no immediate undertaking is given to discontinue the advertisement. The court can grant an injunction (interdict in Scotland) preventing further publication. The Director General of Fair Trading therefore acts as a 'long-stop' to the ASA, which has been strengthened in its position by the Regulations.

6. *Consumer Credit Act 1974*. This comprehensive Act created 35 new offences. It provides for the Director General of Fair Trading to administer a licensing system to control organisations which operate a consumer credit or hire business where the agreements are regulated.

A regulated agreement is one that is not exempt. In practice this means, in the case of consumer credit agreements, personal credit agreements by which the creditor provides the debtor with credit not exceeding £15 000. The debtor must be an 'individual', which can include sole traders and partnerships.

A regulated consumer hire agreement is one made by a person with a hirer for the bailment of goods to the hirer, which is not a hire-purchase agreement, is capable of subsisting for more than three months, and does not require the hirer to make payments exceeding £15 000.

Small agreements for credit or hire payments not exceeding £50 are not exposed to some of the Act's requirements relating to form and content, withdrawal and cancellation.

It is a criminal offence to engage in regulated agreements without a licence. Furthermore, any such unlicensed agreements are unenforceable at law.

The Act controls the documentation, withdrawal and cancellation of such agreements, aimed at protecting the individual. But of particular significance to direct marketers are those provisions governing advertisements for credit or rental facilities. The *Consumer Credit (Advertisement) Regulations 1989* lay down the minimum information that such an advertisement must contain, including, in the case of 'full' advertisements, a note of the annual percentage rate of charge (APR). It is a criminal offence to issue an advertisement other than in accordance with the Regulations.

7. *Theft Act 1968*. Perhaps the main practical influence of this Act on direct marketers relates to lists. A person who dishonestly by deception

obtains property belonging to another with the intention of permanently depriving the other of it—such as by renting a mailing list from a list owner and dishonestly using it more than the number of times agreed without paying for such extra uses—is *prima facie* committing an offence under the Act.

8. *Lotteries and Amusements Act 1976.* This covers lotteries and prize draws. The following points should be remembered:

(a) a lottery is a distribution of *prizes by chance*;
(b) as such, it is illegal unless *entry is free*;
(c) if any skill or judgement is required *it is not a lottery—it is a prize competition*;
(d) a prize competition involving the use of skill to make a LEGAL FORECAST is lawful, as is a competition involving a substantial degree of skill;
(e) a legal forecast is one not relating to a future event, or to a past event, the results of which are not yet ascertained or generally known.

Let us look at a few examples.

A promotion where everybody wins will generally eradicate the element of chance and it will not therefore be an illegal lottery. But if there is some uncertainty as to what or when participants may win, chance comes into it in the promotion. Note also that the word 'prize' should not be used in an 'everybody wins' campaign.

Free entry promotions are not illegal lotteries even where prizes are distributed purely by chance. This is because the law's aim was to prevent 'the poor'—who possessed only enough to feed their children—from losing that money on lotteries, and clearly no money can be lost if entry is free.

But free entry may be combined with an inducement to make a purchase and still prevent a lottery being illegal, so long as it is *possible* for every leaflet, coupon, card, etc., to be available *without charge*. If, however, the entry form is available only in a magazine or periodical—which the potential entrant has to buy so as to get hold of the form—the competition is not likely to be seen as a 'free draw'.

If the competition involves skill or judgement it is a prize competition. To be safe, the competition should be based wholly on skill. In two-stage promotions neither stage must involve chance if it is to be a prize competition, so that skill testing followed by a random draw would result in an unlawful lottery.

The British Code of Sales Promotion Practice lays down a number of rules about prize draws, etc., as do the Codes of Practice of the BDMA (see Appendix 3) and of the Association of Mail Order Publishers. One important point can be mentioned here. In a prize competition it is vital to indicate the criteria by which entries will be judged. If the winning entry is to be the one nearest to the view of a panel on a given problem, the criteria used by the panel have to be clearly stated. Otherwise the entry nearest to the judgement of the panel will have got there solely by chance or luck.

9. *Copyright, Designs and Patents Act 1988.* Copyright exists in all original literary works. 'Original' does not mean that the work is new; it means that the work is the product of independent effort by the author. And it need not have 'literary' or 'artistic' merit in the commonly accepted meanings of those words. So directories, timetables, fixture lists and mailing lists can be 'original' as well as the normal product of the advertising copywriter's skills and generally accepted literary and artistic works such as books, articles, recorded performances, films, paintings, photographs, architectural designs, etc.

The 'first author' is the author with one major exception: if work is produced in the course of employment, the employer of the author of that work is the copyright owner; the copyright owner is *not* the employee. Under the previous law (Copyright Act 1968) there was another exception to the 'first owner' principle whereby the copyright in artistic work, e.g. photography, commissioned by someone, vested in the person commissioning. Now, however, it vests in the artist, although as copyright is assignable the artist may agree to assign it to the agency giving him or her the commission.

So it is essential for anybody who wishes to incorporate in promotional material or advertising something in which someone else holds copyright to obtain that person's permission beforehand. This includes testimonials.

The Act also creates 'moral' rights:

- The right of paternity: to be identified as author or director—to have identification clearly displayed on the work in a reasonably prominent position. This lasts for the life of the author plus 50 years.
- The right of integrity: to object to the way in which work is treated if such treatment is derogatory. This lasts for 20 years after the person's death.
- The right to object to the false attribution of a work. This ends 20 years after the person's death.
- The right to privacy of certain photographs and films, subject to certain exceptions. This lasts for the life of the author plus 50 years.

These rights protect authors of copyright literary, dramatic, musical or artistic works, directors of copyright films, and architects.

Unlike the right of paternity, the right of integrity and the right to object to false attribution are automatic. The right of paternity is only effective once the author has asserted it and third parties are not bound by it unless the assertion has been brought to their attention.

Anyone who, in the course of business, possesses or deals in a falsely attributed work, knowing or believing it to be false, infringes the right not to have a work falsely attributed.

For treatment to be regarded as derogatory—under the right of integrity—it must involve the addition, deletion, alteration or adaptation of the whole or part of the work and either amount to a distortion or mutilation or be otherwise prejudicial to the honour or reputation of the author or director.

'Moral' rights cannot be assigned but can be waived by the person with the right, as long as the waiver is in writing. Naturally these new rights must be taken into account by any organisation likely to commission, publish, release or display copyright works.

10. *Infringement of trade marks.* The unauthorised use of a registered trade mark amounts to an infringement and its owner will be entitled to claim damages or seek an injunction.

Unauthorised use would include the incorporation in a mail shot of the reproduction of an item which itself incorporated a registered trade mark without authority.

11. *Libel.* This is defamation by the written or broadcast word. There are a number of key elements:

- the defamation must refer to the person bringing the action
- it must be false
- it must be 'published' to someone other than the person being defamed.

To be defamatory the published statement has to be such as to lower the victim's reputation in the estimation of right-thinking people. Unfortunately, as it is not necessary to show that the person making the statement intended to defame or even knew that the statement was defamatory, 'innocent' defamation can be actionable.

Thus, the incorporation of someone's photograph without his or her permission, where this suggests that the subject of the photograph was in some way not what he or she professed to be—such as the use of a sportsperson's photograph to endorse an advertiser's product when the sportsperson claimed to be of amateur status—would be actionable.

It is therefore vital that if the name and/or photograph of an identifiable person is used in a mail shot the prior consent of such a person should be obtained.

12. *Data Protection Act 1984.* This Act is a novel and far-reaching piece of legislation with implications in every sphere of activity where computers are employed to hold and use the names, addresses, or other personal data of living persons.

For this reason it is vitally relevant to the direct marketing industry. It covers the use of automatically processed information relating to individuals and the provision of services in respect of such information.

For the purpose of this summary, the word 'data' is regarded—accurately—as in the plural.

All 'data users'—those who maintain computer records of individuals—must register with the Data Protection Registrar and give the types of persons on whom they hold data, the nature of the personal data held, the purposes for which they are held, the sources from which they are derived, and the classes of people to whom they will be disclosed.

All 'data users' must comply with eight data protection principles:

(a) The information to be contained in personal data shall be obtained, and personal data shall be processed, fairly and lawfully.
(b) Personal data shall be held only for one or more specified and lawful purposes.
(c) Personal data held for any purpose or purposes shall not be used or disclosed in any manner incompatible with that purpose or those purposes.
(d) Personal data held for any purpose or purposes shall be adequate, relevant and not excessive in relation to that purpose or those purposes.
(e) Personal data shall be accurate and, where necessary kept up-to-date.
(f) Personal data held for any purpose or purposes shall not be kept for longer than is necessary for that purpose or those purposes.
(g) An individual shall be entitled:
    (i) at reasonable intervals and without undue delay or expense:
        • to be informed by any data user whether he or she holds personal data of which that individual is the subject; and
        • to have access to any such data held by a data user; and
    (ii) where appropriate, to have such data corrected or erased.
(h) Appropriate security measures shall be taken against unauthorised access to, or alteration, disclosure or destruction of, personal data and against accidental loss or destruction of personal data. (This also applies to personal data in respect of which services are provided by computer bureaux.)

The Act gives significant new rights to data subjects. They have the right to have a copy of the information about themselves which is held in computers; the right to claim compensation for damage and associated distress arising from the loss or unauthorised destruction or disclosure of personal data or from the inaccuracy of such data; and the right to challenge the accuracy of the information about them held on computers and, where appropriate, to have it corrected or erased.

The Advertising Association has prepared a Code of Practice covering the use of personal data for advertising and direct marketing purposes which incorporates a foreword from the Data Protection Registrar. A revised and amended edition was published in June 1990.

The general effect of the Act, as currently interpreted by the Data Protection Registrar, is that, unless the identity of a data user and the intended uses and disclosures are clear to the data subject from the context in which the information is being supplied, the data user must give some notification of such unanticipated uses, etc., to the data subject at the time of collection. Put another way, if the identity of the data user and the intended uses and disclosures are clear, then no further explanation is necessary; but where uses such as list rental or exchange are intended or some other substantially different use, some explanation has to be given to the data subject.

Therefore, if the personal data collected from a completed off-the-page coupon is intended to be used for list rental purposes, the advertisement should include a statement on the following lines:

'We may pass your name and address to other companies so that they may mail you with offers that they think would interest you. [Please tick this box if you do not want us to pass your name on in this way.]'

The words in the square brackets are recommended as good commercial practice although they may not be strictly required by the Act.

There is currently a difference of opinion between the Data Protection Registrar and the Advertising Association as to the appropriate time at which any notification that may be required is actually given. Both agree that this notification, if required, should be given at the time data are collected, e.g. by inclusion on a newspaper advertisement, on the question-naire, etc.

The Registrar feels that this should apply in every case come what may, whereas the Advertising Association (AA) feels there are some particular circumstances where it may be virtually impossible or highly impracticable to give such notice at the time of collection. In such cases the AA feels the notification should be given at the earliest subsequent opportunity, such as at fulfilment, but certainly prior to the intended use giving rise to the need to notify so that the data subject has time to object if he or she wishes. The legal position on this score is therefore the subject of confusion and only a court can decide the correct interpretation. Advice should be sought, from the BDMA or the AA, on the latest developments on this subject, and on the forthcoming EC directive on data protection.

Laws specific to the product or service being advertised

Certain specific legislation—specific, that is, to the type of product being advertised—must be noted. This includes:

- Medicines Act 1968, for medicinal products
- Food Labelling Regulations 1984, for food
- Medicines (Labelling and Advertising to the Public) Regulations 1978, for medicinal products for which no prescription is necessary
- Hallmarking Act 1973, for precious metals
- The Forgery and Counterfeiting Act 1981—prohibiting the reproduction of bank notes and coins; consent can be obtained from the Bank of England for promotional purposes, subject to certain conditions.

But the major piece of specific legislation is the Financial Services Act 1986, which affects everyone who runs an investment business in the United Kingdom.

THE FINANCIAL SERVICES ACT 1986

'Investment business', for the purposes of this Act, means:

- the buying and selling of investments
- arranging for others to buy and sell investments
- managing of investments belonging to others
- giving advice to others on their investments
- the operation of a collective investment scheme.

Unless a person carrying on such a business is exempted under the Act, it is an offence so to do without authorisation from the Securities and Investments Board (SIB), one of the self-regulating organisations (SROs) or a recognised professional body (RPB) who each police the investment business activities of their members. The criminal penalties for breaches of the Act, or of rules or regulations thereunder, are severe. (An interesting effect of the definition of 'investment business' is that an apparently innocent practice, such as the endorsement by a non-investment firm of another's investment services product, could probably involve the non-investment firm in carrying on an activity for which authorisation is needed under the Act. Charities, mail order companies and affinity group organisations could be particularly vulnerable.)

The Act lays down rules for the advertising of financial services and products to the public. These can be summarised thus:

1 Advertisements relating to financial products/services must be either:
   (a) exempt (a very narrow category); or
   (b) approved by an authorised person before issue.
2 They must conform to the general principles of being true, fair, clear and not misleading
3 Every form of advertisement is covered 'whether in a publication, by the display of notices, signs, labels or showcards, by means of circulars, catalogues, price lists or other documents, by an exhibition of pictures or photographic or cinematographic films, by way of sound broadcasting or television, by the distribution of recordings, or in any other manner'.

The 'Know Your Customer' rule

This rule says that a firm must not perform any investment services for a person unless the firm has taken reasonable steps to ascertain from that person such facts about his (or her) personal and financial situation as may be expected to be relevant to the proper performance of those services (as laid down by the SIB or SRO). (This rule does not apply to transactions resulting from off-the-page advertising or to execution-only customers. Execution-only customers are those who come to the firm of their own accord for the execution of a specific piece of business and who do not rely on the firm's advice in making up their minds what to do.)

The effect of this rule and of the 'Best Advice' rule (which says that no other financial service must be thought to meet the desired objectives more advantageously than that which is being offered) on direct mail is that the nature of the offers by this medium must be more generalised. The offers in mail shots must *not* suggest a greater degree of knowledge of the recipients' financial status and needs than is in fact the case.

This means that no personal recommendation can be given in mail shots, such as 'Dear Mr Smith, this offer is strongly recommended to you Mr Smith, because you Mr Smith, etc., etc.'. The result of this restriction is that mail shots have become more accurately targeted—the recipients must be more closely selected so that the mailed offer, generalised though it may be, is likely to be that much more relevant to them.

Off-the-page advertising The substance of an off-the-page (OTP) advertisement is that an investor can respond by making an immediate commitment (in the form either of an offer to contract or of acceptance of an offer). An advertisement is not OTP if a positive response from the investor cannot be converted into an investment agreement without further literature being sent or a discussion entered into.

OTP advertisements can be used for life policies and units in regulated collective investment schemes such as unit trusts, and for certain types of PEPs. However, OTP adverts for certain investment agreements fall outside the OTP advertising regime altogether, such as those for public offers of shares.

Financial services or products   Where these are involved, mailing houses and advertising agencies should always ensure that:

- their client has been authorised, under the Act, to carry on that business;
- the advertisement, mail shot, etc., conforms to the rules laid down in or by the Act, relevant SROs' rules, and the British Code of Advertising Practice;
- the final version of the advertising copy and artwork is 'signed off' by the authorised client (who has to appoint someone in the firm to give such approval).

Telephone marketing agencies   The position of such agencies under the Act is unclear and is under review by the SIB. The uncertainty stems from the fact that unless a telephone marketing agency is itself authorised under the Act—which it would not normally be—it cannot carry out marketing calls except where it has been made an 'appointed representative' of an authorised client. Since, however, an appointed representative may represent only one such client at one time, telephone marketing agencies are placed in a difficult position.

Unsolicited calls   These are banned under the Act except where the SIB permits them, i.e. where the products being sold are unit trusts or life assurance policies—both products being subject to a 14-day cooling-off period. A call even remains unsolicited if it is a response to an *implicit* invitation to call, such as the supply of one's telephone number in a tear-off request to an advertiser for further information.

Conclusion
Complicated though compliance with the Act may be, it is essential that the rules—of which this chapter can give only an indication—are under-

stood. Indeed it is generally agreed within the direct marketing industry that the discipline imposed on the marketing of financial services will result in

- an end to poorly targeted 'junk mail'
- better list/product selection and matching
- better analysis
- smaller campaigns, better results, better offers and better consumer benefits.

The specific features characterising direct marketing

Apart from the *Mail Order Transactions (Information) Order 1976*, the controls on direct marketing are those provided by self-regulatory, and generally voluntary, measures.

Self-regulation has developed so as to complement the basic legal controls; it sometimes goes further than the law requires, it is flexible and informal and can be adapted speedily to meet changing circumstances.

Furthermore, such a system is followed in spirit as well as to the letter because it is the product of the very people who have agreed to be regulated by it and whose representatives developed it.

There are three main bodies of self-regulatory rules.

1. *The British Code of Advertising Practice (BCAP)*. This is policed by the Advertising Standards Authority (ASA), which deals with complaints made by members of the public, and by the Committee of Advertising Practice (CAP) which handles complaints from commercially interested parties. Both are funded by a surcharge on advertising expenditure collected by the Advertising Standards Board of Finance (ASBOF).

The central concern of the BCAP is with the *content* of advertisements. Apart from a handful of cases, such as where the consumer's health or safety may be adversely affected, the Code does not concern itself with matters other than the lawfulness, honesty, fairness and decency of the advertisement itself.

BCAP applies to advertisements in newspapers, magazines and other printed publications; indoor and outdoor posters; aerial advertisements; cinema and video cassette commercials; advertisements on viewdata services; and to advertising material such as brochures and leaflets, whether these are mailed or delivered directly, or reach their public as inserts in newspapers or other publications, through distribution in shops or at exhibitions, or in other ways.

The four principles which underlie the BCAP are that all advertisements should be:

(a) legal;
(b) decent—i.e. they should contain nothing likely to cause grave or widespread offence;
(c) honest—i.e. there should be no attempt to exploit consumers' credulity or lack of experience or knowledge in any manner detrimental to their interests;
(d) truthful—i.e. no advertisement, whether by inaccuracy, ambiguity, exaggeration, omission or otherwise should mislead consumers about any matter likely to influence their attitude to the advertised product.

Certain categories of advertisements, as well as being covered by the main body of the Code's rules, have additional rules including mail order and direct response; financial services and products; limited editions and children. The rules on mail order and direct response are being extended to include list and database practice.

The sanctions for contraventions of the Code are as follows:

(a) If a recalcitrant advertiser refuses to withdraw or correct an advertisement, the media owners are informed and that advertiser will thereafter find few who are prepared to publish any more of his or her advertisements.
(b) Adverse publicity in ASA or CAP reports are often picked up by the media as news items, and this serves to warn the public.
(c) In the case of direct mail, 'commission' that would otherwise be payable to 'recognised' mailing houses will be withdrawn from a firm that has handled the offending advertising material.
(d) Withdrawal by the Royal Mail of volume discounts under Mailsort contracts for presorted mail.

2. *The British Code of Sales Promotion Practice (BCSPP)*. This is aimed at regulating, primarily in the interests of the consumer, the nature and administration of those marketing techniques that are used to make goods and services more attractive to the consumer by providing some additional benefit, whether in cash or kind. These include premium offers; reduced price and free offers; distribution of vouchers, coupons and samples; personality promotions; charity-linked promotions; and prize promotions of all types. It also applies to sales and trade incentive promotions, to editorial promotional offers and to some aspects of sponsorship. This Code is regulated by the ASA and CAP, as in the case of the BCAP.

All the trade associations in the direct marketing industry make compliance with BCAP and BCSPP conditions of membership, and incorporate them in their own Codes of Practice. Some of these association codes cover areas not covered by the two national codes; the British Direct Marketing Association's code, for example, includes guidelines on telephone marketing.

3. *The BDMA Telephone Marketing Guidelines* provide principles of ethical and professional conduct for members who make use of telephone marketing to both consumers and businesses. They were drawn up in consultation with the Director General of Fair Trading and cover areas such as disclosure of name and purpose of caller, honesty of statements, the hours during which calls should be made, courtesy and procedures, restriction of contacts—e.g. no consumer calls to individuals at their place of work unless expressly invited—and so on.

Mention must also be made of three further mechanisms set up to protect the consumer.

- *The Mailing Preference Service (MPS)* This allows members of the public to have their names and addresses removed from—or added to—mailing lists controlled or used by MPS subscribing companies.
- *The Telephone Preference Service (TPS)* This is scheduled to be set up in 1991 in conjunction with the Office of Telecommunications (OFTEL), and has a similar objective to that of MPS, but in relation to telephone marketing calls.
- *The Mail Order Protection Scheme (MOPS)* This protects a consumer who buys off-the-page from a national newspaper—other than through a classified advertisement—and who loses money because of the failure of the advertiser to supply goods ordered or to refund money when goods are returned. The consumer is reimbursed from a central fund set up by the newspapers.

The direct marketing industry is expanding as more and more organisations appreciate the benefits of this logical, cost-effective, selective and responsive selling medium. As it grows, so does the representational and watchdog role of the bodies set up to regulate the practitioners.

PART **V**

APPENDICES

1

Direct marketing campaign checklist*

1. What do I want to achieve?
   - sell a product/service?
   - maintain client relationship?
   - pre-dispose through information?
   - build brand loyalty, trial?
   - switch-sell?

2. Is the offer relevant to the target audience?
   - do they appreciate/understand it?
   - do they want/need it?
   - how often would they buy it?
   - is it easily bought?
   - would they buy it now, and why?

3. Is there an obvious gap I'm filling?
   - in product/service terms?
   - in distribution terms?

4. How should I use direct marketing?
   - alone?
   - in combination with other methods?
   - is it appropriate?

5. If my answers to question 4 were 'yes' or 'no', then:
   - why 'no'?
   - why 'yes'?

6. Is the target audience prepared to:
   - accept a direct marketing approach?

* Acknowledgement: McCann Direct.

    – respond positively?
    – react adversely?

7. Do I have sufficient expertise to use direct marketing effectively in this situation?
    – if 'yes'—how detailed?
    – if 'no'—why, WHAT DO I NEED?

8. What would be the most cost-effective direct marketing method(s)?
    – inserts?
    – direct response advertisements?
    – direct mail?
    – telemarketing?
    – affinity marketing?
    – point-of-sale take-ones?
    – TV response?
    – radio response?
    – other?

9. What revenue/profit do I need to generate from my budget?
    – what is the potential?
    – what return should I expect?
    – what if I don't reach my target?

10. What list development/life time value has a new customer?

11. What is an enquiry worth to me from someone who didn't buy?
    – through resolicitation?
    – future cross-sales?

12. How do I best identify, reach and test the segments in my target market?

13. Is the timing right?
    – right time to purchase?
    – right time to plan for purchase?
    – right time for consumer to act?
    – right time for need fulfilment?

14. Can I fulfil everything I'm promising in terms of
    – timing?
    – quality?
    – price?
    – distribution and accessibility?

15. Does the campaign/programme fit into my overall medium- or long-term strategy in terms of
    - brand building and awareness?
    - positioning in the marketplace?
    - competitive offerings?

16. Are there any legal implications I have to consider for the target audience I am addressing in terms of
    - the product or service offer?
    - the pricing and timing?
    - the creative and copy treatment?

17. Have I discussed all this with my agency?

2

British Code of Advertising Practice

The following extracts from the British Code of Advertising Practice (8th edition) include: Part A (Preliminary), pp. 19–22; Part B (General rules), pp. 23–37; and relevant sections from Part C (Particular categories)—Sections VI–VII, pp. 60–68, and Sections IX–XII, pp. 71–79. The full text is available from the Committee of Advertising Practice, Brook House, 2–16 Torrington Place, London WC1E 7HN.

Part A

PRELIMINARY

Scope

1.1   The Code's rules apply to
- advertisements in newspapers, magazines and other printed publications;
- indoor and outdoor posters and other outdoor advertisements, including aerial advertisements;
- cinema and video-cassette commercials;
- advertisements on viewdata services; and to
- advertising material such as brochures and leaflets, whether these are mailed or delivered directly, or reach their public as inserts in newspapers or other publications, through distribution in shops or at exhibitions, or in other ways.

1.2   The Code's rules do not apply to
- broadcast commercials;
  (Television and radio commercials are subject to a similar, but statutorily based, Code administered by the Independent Broadcasting Authority (IBA). IBA works closely with the Independent Television Association (ITVA) and with the Association of Independent Radio Contractors (AIRC). These two bodies, both of which are member organisations of CAP, are responsible for much of the work entailed in the pre-clearance of commercials. In a similar way, commercials carried by cable services are subject to a statutory form of control exercised by the Cable Authority.)
- advertisements in media which are principally intended for circulation outside the United Kingdom; or to
- advertisements addressed, either directly or in their professional journals, to members of the medical and allied professions in their professional capacities. (Most advertisements in this last category are subject to statutory controls, notably under the Medicines Act 1968, and to the Code of Practice administered by the Association of the British Pharmaceutical Industry.)

1.3   Communications and material of the following kinds are not regarded as advertisements for the purposes of this Code:
- statutory, public, police and other official notices;
- material published as a matter of record only;

- non-advertising matter (e.g. works of art) exhibited on billboards or other advertising sites used primarily for advertisements;
- private correspondence, as distinguished from personalised or individually addressed circulars;
- oral communications, including telephone calls;
- press releases and other public relations material;
- the contents of books and the contents of the editorial columns of the press, even if either of these has the outward semblance of advertising material;
- packages, wrappers, labels, tickets and the like, except to the extent that either
  a) they advertise a sales promotion, or a product other than the one they contain, or are attached to; or
  b) they are depicted in an advertisement; in which case any words, pictures etc. which are reproduced in a legible or otherwise comprehensible manner are subject to the Code on the same basis as the other contents of the advertisement. Material which is *not* shown (e.g. because it is on the opposite side of a pack to that depicted) is not subject to this Code, though it may entail obligations under the British Code of Sales Promotion Practice.

1.4 The application of BCAP to advertisements within the scope of the code on tobacco products, reproduced as an appendix to BCAP, is set out on page 81.

Definitions

2. For the purposes of the Code
   - a **product** is anything that is capable of forming the subject matter of an advertisement. It is most often a tangible object of trade, but may also be, for example, a service or facility, an idea, a cause or an opportunity;

     (Because products are so various, much of the Code is expressed, for the sake of clarity, in terms most apt in relation to goods. Wherever this is the case, the principles embodied in the rules concerned are to be understood as applying, in all appropriate circumstances, equally to other kinds of product.)
   - a **consumer** means any person likely to be reached by a given advertisement (and not only a member of the general public, or one of those directly addressed);
   - except in the case of the Cigarette Code (App. 1) references to the **United Kingdom** are to be understood as relating also to the Isle of Man and the Channel Islands;

       –   **claim** is to be understood as applying to both express and
           implied claims.

(Other definitions of limited application are explained at appropriate
points throughout the Code.)

Interpretation

3.1   The opinion of the Advertising Standards Authority on any matter
        concerning the interpretation of the Code is final.

3.2   Conformity with the Code is assessed in the light of an
        advertisement's probable effect when taken as whole, and in context.
        In applying these criteria, particular attention is paid to
        –   the characteristics of the likely audience for the advertisement;
        –   the medium by means of which the advertisement is
           communicated;
        –   the nature of the advertised product; and
        –   the nature and content of any associated material made available
           contemporaneously to consumers by the advertiser.

3.3   The Code is interpreted in the spirit, as well as in the letter.

3.4   The Code does not claim either legal force or legal authority; it is thus
        inappropriate for its provisions to be construed in the fashion in
        which a statute or legal document would be construed.

3.5   For the sake of clarity and brevity, many rules in the Code use only
        masculine and singular forms of words. This is not to be understood
        as implying the exclusion of women, legal persons or groups of
        whatever kind from the scope of such rules, to the extent that it is
        appropriate they be included.

3.6   Advertisements published in languages other than English may
        present difficulties. Steps have been taken to produce abbreviated
        versions of the Code in others of the languages spoken in the United
        Kingdom. None the less it may be impossible in some cases, at
        present, for ASA or CAP to judge the extent to which an advertisement
        not in English conforms to the Code.

3.7   There are many statutory rules governing advertising. These are
        often complicated and professional advice should be sought when in
        doubt about their application. References in this edition of the Code
        to statutes and other legislation are believed to be correct at the time
        of going to print; they should be read in the light of any subsequent
        modifications, repeals or re-enactments.

References to the Code

4.1 The Code is divided into four parts (an *Introduction* and *Parts A, B and C*). Each Part is divided into *paragraphs*, each distinguished by a different arabic numeral. These paragraphs, in turn, may be further divided into *sub-paragraphs*, distinguished from each other either by further arabic numerals (1.3; 4.2, etc.), or, occasionally, by letters. Part C comprises twelve *sections*, each of which is identified by a roman numeral. These sections are sub-divided into paragraphs and sub-paragraphs as described above. References to the Code should identify the Part referred to, and quote as appropriate, the section, paragraph and sub-paragraph number(s) and letter(s), thus: B.6; C.VIII.1(a) etc. References made outside the Code should be preceded by 'BCAP'.

4.2 References to Appendix 1 should conform, as appropriate, to the guidance in the preceding sub-paragraph.

Commencement

5. This edition of the Code comes into force on publication. It replaces all previous editions.

Part B

GENERAL RULES

The obligations of the advertiser

1.1 Primary responsibility for observance of this Code falls upon the advertiser, and remains with him even when delegated, for practical purposes, to an advertising agency or other intermediary.*

Substantiation

1.2 Before offering an advertisement for publication, the advertiser should have in his hands all documentary and other evidence necessary to demonstrate the advertisement's conformity to the Code. This material, together, as necessary, with a statement outlining its relevance, should be made available without delay if requested by either the Advertising Standards Authority or the Committee of Advertising Practice.

1.3 Whenever conformity with the Code is a matter of judgement rather than evidence, the advertiser should be prepared to explain without delay, when requested to do so, why he believes his advertisement conforms to the Code.

1.4 An advertisement may be found to be in contravention of the Code if the advertiser does not respond, or delays his response, to such requests from the Authority or the Committee.

Confidentiality

1.5 Subject to their overriding duties to the Courts and to officials with statutory powers to compel disclosure, the Authority and the Committee will always respect any request that genuinely private or secret information supplied in support of an advertisement should be treated in confidence.

ALL ADVERTISEMENTS SHOULD BE LEGAL, DECENT, HONEST AND TRUTHFUL

Legality

2.1 Advertisements should contain nothing which is in breach of the law, nor omit anything which the law requires.

---

* This provision in no way affects the responsibility of advertising agencies, which contract as principals, in their relations with publishers.

2.2   Advertisements should contain nothing which is likely to bring the law into disrepute.

(As to the treatment of advertisements apparently in conflict with the law, see Introduction, paragraph 16 above.)

Decency

3.1   No advertisement should contain any matter that is likely to cause grave or widespread offence. Whether offence is likely to be caused and, if so, of what gravity will be assessed in each case in the light of the provisions of A.3.2 above and of the standards of decency and propriety that are generally accepted at present in the United Kingdom.

3.2   Some advertisements, which do not conflict with the preceding sub-paragraph, may none the less be found distasteful because they reflect or give expression to attitudes or opinions about which society is divided. Where this is the case, advertisers should carefully consider the effect that any apparent disregard of the sensitivities involved may have upon their reputation and that of their product, and upon the acceptability, and hence usefulness, of advertising generally.

3.3   The fact that a product may be found offensive by some people is not, in itself, a sufficient basis under the Code for objecting to an advertisement for it. Advertisers are urged, however, to avoid unnecessary offence when they advertise any product which may reasonably be expected to be found objectionable by a significant number of those who are likely to see their advertisement.

Honesty

4.1   No advertiser should seek to take improper advantage of any characteristic or circumstance which may make consumers vulnerable; as, for example, by exploiting their credulity or their lack of experience or knowledge in any manner detrimental to their interests.

4.2   The design and presentation of advertisements should be such as to allow each part of the advertiser's case to be easily grasped and clearly understood.

Truthful presentation: general

5.1   No advertisement, whether by inaccuracy, ambiguity, exaggeration, omission or otherwise, should mislead consumers about any matter likely to influence their attitude to the advertised product.

Matters of fact

5.2   1. Whenever an advertisement is likely to be understood as dealing with matters capable of objective assessment upon a generally agreed basis, it should be backed by substantiation as required by B.1.2 above. The adequacy of such substantiation will be gauged by the extent to which it provides satisfactory evidence that the advertisement is both accurate in its material details and truthful in the general impression it creates.

2. No advertisement should claim that the account it gives of any facts is generally accepted, or universally true, if there exists a significant division of informed opinion as to how either the accuracy or the truthfulness of that account may properly be assessed.

3. When a factual claim in an advertisement is said to be supported by the results of independent research, the advertiser should be able to show that those responsible for the research accept as accurate his account of it.

4. Advertisements which contain material of the kinds described below are not to be regarded, for that reason alone, as in conflict with the Code's rules on truthful presentation:

a) obvious untruths, exaggerations and the like, the evident purpose of which is to attract attention or to cause amusement and which there is no likelihood of consumers misunderstanding;

b) incidental minor inaccuracies, unorthodox spellings and the like which do not affect the accuracy or truthfulness of the advertisement in any material respect;

c) accurate descriptions of the contents of books and other media of communication in circumstances in which some of the matter so described cannot itself be substantiated. (Publishers are urged, none the less, to consider carefully the possibility of harm or distress resulting from their acceptance of such advertisements, particularly where these contain material advocating either unproven remedies for disease or disability, or the employment of consumers' resources in risky ventures.)

5. When the consumer's response to an advertisement is likely to be directly affected by the appearance of a person whose real-life experiences it describes – as may happen, for example, in connection with a charitable appeal – a model should not be used to represent that person unless the advertiser makes it quite clear that this has been done.

6. On the truthful presentation of comparisons, see B.21 to B.24 below.

Matters of opinion

5.3 The Code's rules on truthful presentation place no constraint upon the free expression of opinion, including subjective assessments of the quality or desirability of products, provided always that
  – it is clear what is being expressed is an opinion;
  – there is no likelihood of the opinion or the way it is expressed misleading consumers about any matter in respect of which objective assessment, upon a generally accepted basis, is practicable (if there is, the provisions of 5.2 above apply);
  – the advertiser is ready to fulfil his obligations under B.1.3 above (substantiation);
  – the advertisement is in conformity with B.3 above (decency); and
  – so far as commercial advertisers are concerned, the Code's rules on fair competition are observed (see B.21 to B.24 below).

Truthful presentation: political claims

6.1 To the extent that any advertisement:
  – expresses an opinion on a matter which is the subject of controversy; and
  – that controversy involves issues within the areas, broadly defined, of public policy or practice,
then neither that opinion, nor any evidence which the advertisement may include in support or explanation of it, is subject to the provisions of this Code on truthful presentation, except as provided in the remainder of this paragraph.

6.2 Assertions of fact and expressions of opinion which are 'political' in the sense of the preceding sub-paragraph will be required to conform to the provisions of B.5 above if they are made in the context of an appeal for funds or are directly linked to the offer of any product in return for payment.

6.3 All advertisements which contain 'political' claims should:
  – be readily recognisable as advertisements;
  – cause no confusion as to the identity or status of the advertiser; and
  – whenever such information is not otherwise readily accessible, state the advertiser's address or telephone number.

Truthful presentation: quotation of prices

[The following paragraph is retained in this edition of the Code in the form in which it appeared in the Seventh Edition. This is done pending the introduction of a new Code on Price Indications (to be made under the Consumer Protection Act 1987) which was close to completion as this edition of BCAP went to press. To the extent that any of the provisions of the forthcoming Code prove to be incompatible with what follows, they will override the corresponding provisions of this paragraph with immediate effect.]

7.1   The provisions of this paragraph apply to advertisements of all kinds. Where appropriate, therefore, 'price' is to be understood as meaning 'charge', 'fee', etc., and references to the sale of goods are to be understood as being applicable also to the provision of services, facilities etc. in return for payment.

7.2   The Code makes no general requirement that the cost to the consumer of an advertised product should be stated in an advertisement (but see C.X below so far as advertisements addressed to children are concerned).

7.3   When any indication of cost is given in an advertisement, regard should be paid to the provisions of the following four sub-paragraphs.

Clarity

1. If reference is made in an advertisement to more than one product, or more than one version of a single product, it should be clear to which product or version any quoted price relates.

2. If a product is illustrated, and a price quoted in conjunction with the illustration, advertisers should ensure that what is illustrated can be purchased for the price shown.

Inclusiveness

3. Except when those addressed by an advertiser are likely to be able to recover VAT, prices should normally be quoted inclusive of VAT. When prices are quoted exclusive of VAT, that fact should be stated with no less prominence than the prices themselves. The same principles apply in the case of other taxes and duties.

4. When an advertised product cannot be purchased unless the consumer is willing to make associated purchases from the advertiser (e.g. where a case has to be purchased with a camera), the price of the advertised product should normally be quoted on a basis which includes such unavoidable costs. Where it is impracticable to include such costs in the quoted price, because, for example, they are variable while the price of the advertised product is not, the consumer's liability to pay them should be stated with no less prominence than the price of the advertised product itself.

On price comparisons, see B.21 and especially B.21.3 below.

Truthful presentation: use of 'free'

8.1 When a product is advertised as being 'free', incidental costs which will necessarily be incurred in acquiring it, and which are known to (or can be accurately assessed by) the advertiser, should be clearly indicated; and when such incidental costs exceed those that would typically arise if a comparable product was *bought* from a comparable source, the product advertised should not be described as free.

8.2 Advertisers should not seek to recover the cost to them of a product which they describe as free
   - by imposing additional charges they would not normally make;
   - by inflating any incidental expenses they may legitimately recover (e.g. cost of postage); or
   - by altering the composition or quality, or by increasing the price, of any other product which they require to be bought as a pre-condition of the consumer obtaining the 'free' product.

8.3 Except in the context of a free trial, the word 'free' should not be used if payment for an advertised product is only deferred.

8.4 Any offer which consists in the giving without cost of one product on condition that another is paid for should normally be temporary, otherwise if such a combination offer is continuous, the use of the word 'free' may become misleading.

Truthful presentation: use of 'up to . . .' and 'from . . .'

9. Expressions such as 'up to x miles per gallon' and 'prices from as low as y' should not be used if, as a result, consumers may be misled about the extent to which the benefits claimed are in practice attainable by them or are available to them.

Truthful presentation: testimonials and other indications of approval

10.1   In this paragraph 'testimonial' embraces any reference made by an advertiser to the favourable opinion of another in circumstances in which the consumer is likely to give added credence to that opinion because of the ostensible independence of the person or institution said to hold it.

10.2   Except when the opinion quoted is available in a published source, in which case a full reference should be made available on request, the advertiser should be able to provide substantiation for a testimonial in the form of a signed and dated statement, containing any words which appear in the advertisement in the form of a direct quotation, and with an address at which the author of the statement may be contacted.

10.3   Testimonials should not be used unless the advertiser has good reason to believe that they represent the genuine and informed opinion of those giving them.

10.4   A testimonial may become misleading if the formulation of the product concerned, or its market environment, changes significantly after the date on which the testimonial was given. As a general rule, therefore, testimonials should relate only to the product as currently offered.

10.5   The fact that a testimonial is given by a person or body independent of the advertiser is not, in itself, sufficient to demonstrate the accuracy or truthfulness of any claim it may contain about a product; and advertisers should be prepared to provide objective substantiation for such claims in the normal way (see B.1 and B.5 above). They should also ensure that, in all other respects, what is quoted by way of testimonial in an advertisement conforms to this Code.

10.6   When fictitious characters in an advertisement express satisfaction with the advertiser's product, care should be taken to avoid consumers confusing them (or their ostensible experiences) with real people or their experiences.

10.7   Advertisers are reminded that testimonials by persons named or depicted in an advertisement may be employed only when the consent of these persons has been obtained in advance (see further B.17 below).

Royal approval

10.8 Attention is drawn to the provisions governing the use of the Royal Arms and Cypher, and references to the Queen's Award to Industry. (Details may be obtained from the offices of the Lord Chamberlain and the Queen's Award to Industry respectively.)

10.9 The Royal Warrant does not imply either personal endorsement or use of the product concerned by H.M. The Queen (or such other royal person on whose behalf the warrant is issued) and no suggestion that it does should appear in any advertisement.

Truthful presentation: recognisability of advertisements

11. An advertisement should always be so designed and presented that anyone who looks at it can see, without having to study it closely, that it is an advertisement.

Truthful presentation: identity of advertisers

12.1 Except in respect of
  – "political" advertisements (see B.6 above);
  – mail order and direct response advertisements (see C.VI below); and
  – the advertisements of itinerant traders (see C.XI.3 below),
  the Code makes no requirement that the name or address of an advertiser be given in an advertisement. (As regards advertisements for sales promotions, see the British Code of Sales Promotion Practice.)

12.2 When an advertiser *is* named in an advertisement, the way in which this is done should not be such as to cause confusion about his identity or mislead as to his status or qualifications.

12.3 In some cases there may be a legal requirement that an advertisement names the advertiser. Advertisers are advised to seek professional advice on this point.

Truthful presentation: guarantees

13.1 In this paragraph 'guarantee' includes 'warranty'.

13.2 Advertisers are urged to take legal advice on any reference they wish to make to a guarantee.

13.3 1. Words such as 'guarantee' should not be used in an advertisement if, in consequence, there is any likelihood of consumers mistakenly believing, when such is not the case, that it is the advertiser's intention to confer on them, or procure for them, a legal right to recompense or reimbursement.

2. Where it *is* intended that such a legal right be created, it should be made clear to the consumer, before he is committed to purchase, whether his right lies against the advertiser or against a third party (as it may do, for example, where insurance schemes are used to prolong product warranties).

3. Subject to the provisions of the two preceding sub-paragraphs, there is no objection to the use of 'guarantee' in a colloquial sense ('Guaranteed to cheer you up' of a film, for example).

13.4   When an advertisement offers a legally enforceable guarantee as to the quality, life, composition, origin, etc. of any product, the full terms of that guarantee should be available for inspection by the consumer before he is committed to purchase, and should be offered for his retention on purchase.

13.5   If the applicability of any guarantee is subject to a substantial limitation (e.g. one-year; parts only), the nature of that limitation should be given adequate prominence in advertisements referring to the guarantee.

13.6   1. When he uses a phrase such as "money-back guarantee", the advertiser should be ready to make a full refund of the purchase price to a dissatisfied customer at any point during the expected life of the product, unless a shorter period of time was stated in his advertisement. The payment of such a refund may reasonably be made dependent upon the return of the unsatisfactory product.

On mail order advertisements see further C.VI below.

2. Money-back guarantees should not be offered in respect of medicines or by betting tipsters.

Truthful presentation: availability of advertised products

14.1   1. Except in circumstances a) in which the advertisement makes clear that any advertised product is subject to a limitation on availability, or b) in which such a limitation is inherent in the nature of the product (e.g. theatre tickets), advertisers should be able to show that they have reasonable grounds for supposing that they can supply any demand likely to be created by their advertisement.

2. Products which cannot be supplied should not be advertised as a way of assessing potential demand.

3. Advertisers will be required, in the event of challenge, to demonstrate that they took adequate steps to monitor the adequacy

of stocks of all products mentioned in an advertisement between its creation and its publication.

4. Advertisers, when advertising on behalf of a number of outlets, should be able to demonstrate that they have used their best endeavours to ensure that the offers contained in their advertisement have been adequately explained to those outlets and that each has sufficient stock to service them properly.

5. When it becomes clear that an advertised product is not available in sufficient quantity to meet demand, immediate action should be taken by the advertiser to ensure that any further advertisements for the product are promptly amended or withdrawn.

Switch selling

14.2   An advertisement may be regarded as misleading if an advertiser's salesmen seriously disparage or belittle the article advertised, recommend the purchase of a more expensive alternative, indicate unreasonable delays in obtaining delivery or otherwise seek to put difficulties in the way of its purchase.

ALL ADVERTISEMENTS SHOULD BE PREPARED WITH A SENSE OF RESPONSIBILITY TO THE CONSUMER AND TO SOCIETY

Fear and distress

15.1   Without good reason, no advertisement should play on fear or excite distress.

15.2.1. When an appeal to fear is properly made in an advertisement – as, for instance, when it is made with the object of encouraging prudent behaviour – the fear evoked should not be disproportionate to the risk addressed.

15.2.2. An advertisement should excite distress only in circumstances in which the seriousness and importance of the subject matter unarguably warrant such an approach. Distress should never be occasioned merely in pursuit of an attempt to attract attention, or to shock.

Violence and anti-social behaviour

16.1   Advertisements should neither condone nor incite to violence or anti-social behaviour.

16.2   Advertisements for weapons and for items, such as knives, which offer the possibility of violent misuse, should avoid anything, in copy or in illustration, that may encourage such misuse.

Protection of privacy and exploitation of the individual

17.1   1. Except in the circumstances noted in paragraphs 17.2 to 17.5 below, advertisements should not portray or refer to any living persons, in whatever form or by whatever means, unless their express prior permission has been obtained.

2. 'Refer' in the preceding sub-paragraph embraces reference to a person's possessions, house etc. in any manner which unambiguously identifies their owner to prospective readers of the advertisement.

17.2   The circumstances in which a reference or portrayal *may* be acceptable in the absence of prior permission, are the following:
– generally, when the advertisement contains nothing which is inconsistent, or likely to be seen as inconsistent, with the position of the person to whom reference is made, and when it does not abrogate his right to enjoy a reasonable degree of privacy;
– in the special case of advertisements the purpose of which is to promote a product such as a book or film, when the person concerned is the subject of that book, film etc.

A complaint from a person represented that an advertisement falling within either of these exclusions is none the less offensive, harmful or humiliating, will be weighed by ASA or CAP when deciding whether the advertisement concerned is within the spirit of the Code.

The applicability of these two exceptions to the general rule is further considered in sub-paragraphs 17.3 to 17.5 below.

17.3   It follows from the above that complaints from those who occupy positions or exercise trades or professions which necessarily entail a high degree of public exposure, such as actors, sportsmen and politicians, can be entertained only
– when it can reasonably be argued that the advertisement concerned suggests some commercial involvement on their part which is of a kind likely to be generally perceived as inconsistent with their status or position; or
– when the effect of the advertisement is to substantially diminish or to abrogate their right to control the circumstances or terms upon which they may exploit their name, likeness or reputation on a commercial basis.

17.4 The use of crowd or background shots, in which individuals or their possessions, houses etc. are recognisable, is not regarded under the Code as inconsistent with the right of such individuals to enjoy a reasonable degree of privacy, provided that there is nothing in the depiction which is defamatory, offensive or humiliating. Advertisers should be ready to withdraw any advertisement in respect of which they receive a reasonable objection on such grounds from a person affected.

17.5 Advertisements in which reference may properly be made to members of the Royal Family include:
- those which incorporate a reference to royal approval which satisfies the provisions of B.10.8 and B.10.9 above;
- those for which express permission has been granted by the Lord Chamberlain's office;
- those for, or depicting, products such as stamps or commemorative items which have received royal approval; and
- advertisements for books, films, articles and the like which deal with a member or members of the Royal Family.

17.6 It is not regarded as contrary to the principle set out in 17.1 above for unsolicited advertising material to be addressed to a consumer personally.

17.7 References to individuals with whom the advertiser is personally acquainted, and which he has no reason to suppose will be resented, are not regarded as infringements of the privacy of such individuals, but should be withdrawn if any reasonable objection is received.

17.8 Advertisers should seek to avoid unnecessary offence to the susceptibilities of those connected in any way with deceased persons depicted or referred to in any advertisements.

Unsolicited home visits

18. When an advertiser intends to call on those who respond to his advertisement, with a view to making a sale, he should either make this clear in the advertisement or should explain his intention in a follow-up letter. In both cases, respondents should be given an adequate opportunity to refuse the salesman's call and the advertiser should help the respondent to communicate his decision by providing either a reply-paid postcard or instructions as to how to make telephone contact. (See also the Financial Services Act 1986 in respect of investment advertising).

Safety

19.1   As a general rule, advertisements should not show or advocate dangerous behaviour or unsafe practices except in the context of the promotion of safety. Exceptions may be permissible, in circumstances in which emulation is unlikely. Special care should be taken with advertisements directed towards or depicting children or young people (see further C.X below).

19.2   There should be no suggestion in any advertisement
   – that there is a 'safe' level for the consumption of alcohol; or
   – that a product can mask the effects of alcohol in tests on drivers,

and all advertisements for breath test products should include a prominent warning on the dangers of driving after drinking.

19.3   The alcohol content of some 'low alcohol' drinks is none the less such as to make it unwise to consume them in quantity before driving or engaging in any other activity for which complete sobriety and command are needed. Advertisers should take care that such drinks are not advertised in any way which may lead to such inappropriate consumption.

(And see, on the advertising of alcoholic drinks in general, Section C.XII below.)

Children

20.   Advertisements should contain nothing which is likely to result in physical, mental or moral harm to children, or to exploit their credulity, lack of experience or sense of loyalty (see further C.X below).

ALL ADVERTISEMENTS SHOULD CONFORM TO THE PRINCIPLES OF FAIR COMPETITION GENERALLY ACCEPTED IN BUSINESS

Comparisons

[The following paragraph is retained in this edition of the Code in the form in which it appeared in the Seventh Edition. This is done pending the introduction of a new Code on Price Indications (to be made under the Consumer Protection Act 1987) which was close to completion as this edition of BCAP went to press. To the extent that any of the provisions of the forthcoming Code prove to be incompatible with what follows, and particularly with the requirements of sub-paragraph 21.3, they will override the provisions of this paragraph with immediate effect.]

21.1 1. So that vigorous competition may not be hindered and that public information may be furthered, comparisons, whether between products themselves or between the prices of products, are regarded as in conformity with this Code provided that such comparisons do not conflict with the requirements of this paragraph and of the following three paragraphs (B.22 to B.24). This is so even in circumstances in which the comparison identifies a competitor of the advertiser or that competitor's product.

2. The requirements of this paragraph and of paragraphs B.22 to B.24 apply also, where relevant, to comparisons made by an advertiser between two or more of his own products, or between the price at which one of his products is sold, and the price at which it was sold, or is to be sold.

21.2 Advertisements containing comparisons should deal fairly with any competitors involved and should be so designed that there is no likelihood of a consumer being misled. In particular:
   – it should be clear with what the advertised product is being compared, and upon what basis;
   – the subject matter of the comparison and the terms in which it is expressed should not be such as to confer any artificial advantage upon one product as against another (this is of especial importance in comparisons between branded and unbranded products and between natural products and substitutes for them);
   – claims to objectively superior or superlative status should be expressed in terms which accurately reflect the extent and the nature of the evidence available to substantiate them; and
   – no claim that a competitive product is generally unsatisfactory should be based on the highlighting of selected advantages only of the advertised product.

21.3 1. When a price for a product is quoted in a way which may suggest that the product concerned is a bargain, and particularly when one price is compared directly with another, there should be no exaggeration of the extent to which a purchaser may benefit by buying at that price.

2. Specifically, comparisons may be regarded as unfair when one (or both) of the elements in the comparison have been artificially selected or manipulated so as to maximise any apparent saving.

On the quotation of prices generally, see B.7 above.

Denigration

22.1   Advertisers should not seek to discredit the products of their competitors by any unfair means.

22.2   In particular, no advertisement should contain inaccurate or irrelevant comments on the person, character or actions of a competitor.

22.3   Nor should an advertisement describe or show the products of a competitor as broken or defaced, inoperative or ineffective. The only exception to this rule is where the description or depiction is based upon the outcome of fair comparative tests to which the advertiser's product also has been subjected and the results of such tests are stated.

Exploitation of goodwill

23.   Advertisements should not exploit the goodwill attached to the trade name or mark of another, or his advertising campaign, in any fashion which may unfairly prejudice his interests.

Imitation

24.   No advertisement should so closely resemble another advertisement as to be likely to mislead or confuse.

Section C. VI
Mail order and direct response advertising

Scope

1.1 This section (C.VI) sets out the rules governing transactions of all kinds, whether for goods or services, in which the trader and his customer, having been brought into communication through an advertisement, conduct their business through the post or other intermediary, and not face to face at the trader's place of business.

1.2 In this section 'advertiser' includes, where appropriate, all who are involved in the preparation of the advertisement and the servicing of the response.

1.3 The supply of self-liquidating and other premium offer goods is subject to separate rules set out in the British Code of Sales Promotion Practice.

1.4 Paragraphs 2 to 8.3 below set out the requirements to be met by the advertiser in respect of all mail order advertisements, while paragraphs 9.1 to 10.4 set out the obligations of the advertiser in transactions in which the consumer is required to send all or part of the charges to the advertiser before receiving the goods or services concerned (cash with order). An exception is made only when payment of a nominal sum is required by an advertiser for the provision of information by way of a catalogue, brochure, price list or the like. In such cases only the provisions of 7.1 below (concerning name and address) shall apply.

Conformity to BCAP and BCSPP

2. Mail order advertisements should conform to all applicable sections of this Code and of the British Code of Sales Promotion Practice.

Conformity of goods to relevant standards

3.1 When an accepted standard (e.g. a British Standard (BS)) has been developed for a given product or class of product, goods falling within the scope of that standard which are advertised for supply by mail order should, in all normal circumstances, comply with it, particularly if it relates to safety. *Special attention is drawn to Regulations made under the Consumer Safety Act 1978 and the Consumer Protection Act 1987.*

3.2   Advertisements for articles made of precious metal may, at the discretion of media, be required to state the amount of the metal involved. *Attention is drawn to the requirements of the Hallmarking Act 1973.*

Conformity of goods to description

4.1   All goods despatched in response to orders received should conform both to the description given in the advertisement and to any sample which may have been supplied to the publishers of the advertisement. Substitutes may be supplied only with the express consent of the person who ordered the goods for which they are replacements.

4.2   When a physical characteristic would be likely to influence the decision of a prospective customer whether to order a product (e.g. size or weight in the case of certain goods), it should specifically be indicated in the advertisement.

Goods sent on approval

5.   When an advertiser offers to supply goods on approval, the prospective customer will be expected, subject to 9.1.4 below, to bear the cost of return of unwanted goods unless the advertiser has indicated in the advertisement his intention to refund such costs.

Goods unacceptable for offer in mail order advertisements

6.   Some goods or services, for safety or other reasons, may not be acceptable at all for offer in mail order advertisements, or may be acceptable only if offered under special conditions, e.g. with supervision or tuition (see also C.I.5.8 above, medicinal products). Media may at their discretion refuse to publish such offers. Attention is drawn to the Post Office Act 1953, Section 11.

The advertiser's address

7.1   Mail order advertisements should clearly state in the body of the advertisement (i.e. in a place other than a coupon) the true name (with or without first name or initials) or business name, as appropriate, of the advertiser and the full address at which his business is managed and at which he can be contacted during normal business hours. For the purposes of this section, this address should normally be that of the advertiser himself.

7.2   This requirement does not prevent an advertiser from also stating in his advertisement another address to which consumers are to send their orders, and this address need not be a full address but may be in the form of a Box Number or Freepost Number. *See also, in this connection, the Mail Order Transactions (Information) Order 1976 and the Companies Act 1985, Section 351.*

Mailing and packaging

8.1 Advertisers should take care to ensure that any enclosing medium for an advertisement, or any special means for effecting its delivery, is not materially misleading as to the nature of the advertisement.

8.2 Advertisers should carefully consider mail order goods and their packaging in relation to the fact that children often have access to packages delivered to the home. *See also C.X below and the British Code of Sales Promotion Practice.*

8.3 Mailing lists should be kept accurate and up-to-date.

Cash with order

9.1 The mail order advertiser is under an obligation, subject only to the conditions in 9.2 below, to return all money paid in advance by the consumer:

1. when unwanted goods are returned, undamaged, within seven working days of their receipt by the consumer;

2. when attention is drawn to the benefit of a money-back guarantee (however expressed) and no limit is placed in the advertisement upon the period during which such a guarantee is to be effective. In such a case, the advertiser should be prepared to make a refund at any reasonable time, having regard to the nature of the product;

3. when the consumer expresses a wish to be reimbursed because of delay in the fulfilment of the order as provided for in 10.1 below; and

4. when, for whatever reason, the product received by the consumer does not conform to the description of it in the advertisement, or the advertiser is otherwise in breach of his contractual obligations. In such cases the consumer should not be expected to bear the cost of return postage or carriage.

9.2 The conditions referred to in 9.1 above are these:

1. the advertiser should make clear to consumers whether or not they may try out goods, subject to their remaining undamaged. If no indication is given, it will be assumed that trial by the consumer is permitted. Particular care should be taken to express clearly the terms upon which goods sold for self-assembly are offered;

2. there is no requirement that an advertiser should accept responsibility for goods returned by a consumer, but which he has not received, unless the consumer can produce proof of posting or of receipt by a carrier, in which case the advertiser should accept that proof as a sufficient basis for a refund to be paid; and

3. bespoke and made-to-measure goods are normally exempt from the provisions of 9.1, provided the advertiser is not in breach of his contractual obligations to the consumer.

9.3   All refunds which the advertiser is required to make should be made promptly upon receipt of the consumer's request.

Fulfilment of the order

10.1   All mail order advertisements should indicate the period within which the advertiser undertakes to fulfil orders, or, when appropriate, provide services. Except in the circumstances noted below, or any others in which CAP is satisfied that it would be unreasonable, the period should not be greater than 28 days from receipt of order.

10.2   An advertiser should never take longer than 28 days to fulfil an order, except:

1. when security for the purchaser's money is provided, whether through stake-holder or other schemes; in such circumstances longer periods than 28 days may, at the discretion of the publishers, be permitted to elapse, provided that the advertiser prominently and clearly explains this in the advertisement, and in the same place gives a realistic estimate of the delivery time;

2. when the advertisement makes clear that a series of items is to be despatched in sequence and states the intervals between consignments. In such cases only the first delivery need be made within the 28-day period;

3. when, at the discretion of the publisher, the advertiser is permitted to state a period in excess of 28 days during which despatch will be effected. This exclusion applies only to goods in the following categories:
–   plants;
–   bespoke and made-to-measure goods;
–   goods the manufacture of which is not to be commenced unless sufficient response is forthcoming, in which case the advertiser's proposal should be clearly expressed in his advertisement and will be subject to the provisions of B.14 above.

4. in circumstances that are covered by, and comply with, the provisions of C.IX below on Limited Editions.

10.3 Where bespoke and made-to-measure goods and goods subject to special manufacture are concerned, media may require to see examples of similar work, or models in lieu of samples of the articles to be supplied.

10.4 If it becomes clear that an order cannot be fulfilled within the period stated in the advertisement, the advertiser should immediately offer the consumer a refund. If the consumer none the less elects to wait, he should either be given a firm date for despatch or the progress of his order should be reported to him at intervals of not more than 14 days.

Media requirements

11.1 Advertisers should be aware that in the area of mail order advertising media bodies will, in respect of cash with order advertisements, require special undertakings under mail order protection schemes currently in operation, over and above the requirements set out in this section.

11.2 Publishers will require undertakings that advertisers have made adequate arrangements to handle all orders efficiently.

Section C. VII
Advertising of financial services and products

1.1 The rules in this section of the Code (C.VII) apply to advertisements for the following:
- financial services and products;
- investment opportunities;
- credit facilities; and
- financial information.

Such advertisements are required to conform also, wherever appropriate, to the other provisions of this Code. It is not to be assumed that such conformity will necessarily be achieved by conformity with the various legal requirements referred to in paragraph 2 below.

1.2 All advertisements within the scope of this section should be prepared with care and with the conscious aim of ensuring that members of the public fully grasp the nature of any commitment into which they may enter as a result of responding to an advertisement. Advertisers should take into account that the complexities of finance may well be beyond many of those to whom the opportunity they offer will appeal and that therefore they bear a direct responsibility to ensure that in no sense do their advertisements take advantage of inexperience or credulity.

1.3 Advertisers inviting an immediate commitment (e.g. by coupon), whether or not this involves the sending of money, should take particular care to ensure thorough comprehensibility, and should clearly state, in the body of the advertisement and not only in the coupon, if one is included, their full postal address.
(See also C.VI above)

2.1 Advertisements for **credit** are subject to stringent requirements under the legislation referred to below. These requirements are described in booklets available from the Office of Fair Trading but advertisers are advised that it may be necessary also to seek professional advice on the interpretation of the Consumer Credit Act and the relevant regulations.

2.2   Attention is drawn to Consumer Credit Act 1974 (Sections 43 to 47 and Section 151 (1) and (2) of the Consumer Credit (Advertisements) Regulations 1980 (SI 1980 No. 54)). Written quotations of terms for credit and hire business are subject to the Consumer Credit (Quotations) Regulations 1980 (SI 1980 No. 55.) As this edition of BCAP goes to press, the Regulations referred to above are under revision with the object, in particular, of providing that where any loan is secured upon property this fact shall be adequately disclosed.

2.3   Many investment advertisements are affected by stringent legislative provisions, notably under the regime established by the Financial Services Act 1986 and administered by the Securities and Investments Board (SIB).

The rules in this section, which apply to a wider range of advertisements than does the Act, enshrine the same principles of fair dealing. Conformity with these rules, however, must not be assumed to guarantee conformity with any other provisions, whether made in or under the Act or imposed by SIB, or by any of the financial self-regulating organisations, whether SROs or professional bodies, which exercise responsibilities under SIB.

3.1   Any advertisement which may lead to the employment of consumers' money for the purchase of any **financial product or service from which profit, interest or benefit is expected** should comply with the conditions below.

3.2   Advertisements which are limited to indicating in general terms the availability of financial opportunities are acceptable as long as full explanatory material concerning the facilities or opportunities available is provided to the consumer, free of charge, before any contract entered into becomes finally binding.

3.3   Advertisements which go beyond a general indication of the availability of an opportunity, and especially those which invite immediate investment or commitment, should clearly indicate, in particular:
- any limitations on eligibility;
- the type of contract forming the basis of the product or service offered; and
- any charges, expenses or penalties attached: and in particular the terms upon which withdrawal, if permitted, may be arranged.

Whenever the nature of the investments underlying the contract, or to which it is linked, may be material to the consumer's choice, a fair description of investment objectives and of such investments should be given.

3.4   When an advertisement contains any **forecast or projection,** whether of a specific growth rate, or of a specific return or rate of return, it should make clear the basis upon which that forecast or projection is made, explaining, for instance:
  −   whether reinvestment of income is assumed;
  −   whether account has been taken of the incidence of any taxes or duties (and if so, how); and
  −   whether the forecast or projected rate of return will be subject to any deductions, either upon premature realisation or otherwise.
Likewise, if reference is made to any rate of interest other than the rate actually payable on the sum invested (the contractual rate), the basis upon which that other rate has been calculated should be explained and that rate should be given no greater prominence than the contractual rate.

3.5   Advertisements which may lead to the **employment of money in anything the value of which is not guaranteed** should clearly indicate that the value of the investment can go down as well as up and that the return upon the investment will therefore necessarily be variable. Where values are guaranteed, sufficient detail should be included to give the reader a fair view of the nature of the guarantee.

3.6   All advertisements which make reference to past performance or experience should do so in a manner which gives a fair and representative picture and should include a warning, given due prominence, that neither is necessarily a guide to the future. Nothing in the rest of the copy should have the effect of undermining or removing the impact of such warning.

3.7   When an advertiser reserves the right, in certain circumstances, to **defer requests for repayment** of any sum invested (and for which, in normal circumstances, immediate repayments might be expected by the investor), the maximum period during which repayment may thus be withheld should be stated in the advertisement.

3.8   When investors are offered the facility of **planned withdrawal from capital** as an income equivalent (e.g. by cashing in units of unit trusts) the advertiser should ensure that the effect of such withdrawals upon the investment is clearly explained.

3.9   When **claims to investment skill** are based upon an asserted increase in the value of particular items purchased (or recommended for purchase) by the advertiser in the past, he should be able adequately to substantiate that the purchase or recommendation upon which his assertion is based was made at the time claimed, and that the present value asserted for the investment corresponds to the price actually obtained for identical items when sold in the open market in the period immediately preceding the appearance of the advertisement. No claim to increase in the value of investments or collectibles should be based upon the performance within a given market of selected items only, unless substantiation for the claim can be provided in the form set out above. (See also C.IX 'Limited editions' below.)

3.10 Phrases such as **tax-free, tax-paid** should not be used
   –   unless it is made clear which particular tax(es) and/or duties are involved, and
   –   the advertiser states, as clearly as possible, what liabilities may arise and by whom they will be paid.

3.11 When the achievement or maintenance of the **return** claimed or offered for a given investment is in any way **dependent upon the assumed effects of tax or duty,** this should be clearly explained; and the advertisement should make it clear that no undertaking can be given that the fiscal system may not be revised, with consequent effect upon the return offered.

   (Attention is drawn to the requirements of the Code in relation to comparative advertisements and in particular the need to make clear the basis on which any comparison is made. (See B 21–24 above.)

   Attention is also drawn to the Code of Practice for the Advertising of Savings and Deposit Accounts and Money Market Accounts as adopted and implemented by the Building Societies Association, the British Bankers' Association and the Finance Houses Association, under the aegis of the Bank of England and the Registry of Friendly Societies.)

Section C.IX
Limited editions

Advertising of 'collectibles'

1. A 'collectible' is a product advertised in terms of its interest as a collector's item, with the emphasis being placed primarily upon factors such as scarcity or aesthetic quality and not, or not solely, upon practical considerations (e.g. utility).

2. Great care requires to be taken in the advertising of 'collectibles' so as to avoid prospective purchasers being misled about the scarcity or about the current, or likely future, value of the item(s) on offer. Claims about the investment potential of a 'collectible' should conform to the rules set out in C.VII above.

3. In particular, advertisers are under an obligation not to trade upon any lack of knowledge among the general public as to the nature and extent of the market for items of the kind advertised or about the criteria for assessment employed within that market.

Limitations on availability

4.1 When an advertiser claims that an edition of any item is subject to a limitation on production, the nature of the limitation imposed must be immediately evident from the description used in the advertising material. The two most common methods of limitation of articles are by pre-announced number, or by application or subscription within a stated period, but other means of limitation may be imposed upon special editions.

4.2 When an edition is limited by number, the advertiser must clearly state the maximum number of articles to be produced in all advertising material containing any claim that the edition is limited. If the offer is to be made both within the United Kingdom and outside, the worldwide total should be given; any UK allocation may also be indicated.

4.3 When an edition is limited by the number of persons applying within a given period of time, the description 'limited', or its derivations, should not be used without qualification.

4.4 When an edition is claimed to be limited by any means of production, the effect of which will not be clear from the method employed, both the nature of the limitation and its effect must be clearly explained in all advertising material containing any claim that the edition is thus limited.

4.5 In either of the cases contemplated in the sub-paragraphs 4.3 and 4.4 above, the advertiser should offer to inform all interested purchasers of the numbers of articles eventually produced worldwide and should publicise his willingness to provide this information in the advertising material.

4.6 Information about the period during which the offer is available should be unambiguous. Where an offer is to be made in more than one stage, the final closing date should be clearly stated at an early point in the advertisement, and prior to any information regarding other dates by which the initial orders are being limited.

4.7 When the same item is to be (or has been) offered elsewhere, this should be made clear.

4.8 Claims as to the 'scarcity' or 'rarity' of items not produced directly by or for the advertiser should be capable of substantiation by reference to the testimony of those expert in the particular market concerned and should, in appropriate cases, take into account the situation worldwide.

Articles containing precious metal

5.1 Advertisements for articles made of precious metal are required to conform to the provisions of the Hallmarking Act 1973.

5.2 Any advertisement which claims, directly or indirectly, that goods are of value by virtue of the amount of precious metal they contain should give an indication of the weight of precious metal contained in the goods concerned.

And see generally the provisions of C.VI above on Mail Order and Direct Response Advertising.

Section C.X
Children

General

1.1 Direct appeals or exhortations to buy should not be made to children unless the product advertised is one likely to be of interest to them and one which they could reasonably be expected to afford for themselves.

1.2 Advertisements should not encourage children to make themselves a nuisance to their parents, or anyone else, with the aim of persuading them to buy an advertised product.

1.3 No advertisement should cause children to believe that they will be inferior to other children, or unpopular with them, if they do not buy a particular product, or have it bought for them.

1.4 No advertisement for a commercial product should suggest to children that, if they do not buy it and encourage others to do so, they will be failing in their duty or lacking in loyalty.

1.5 Advertisements addressed to children should make it easy for a child to judge the true size of a product (preferably by showing it in relation to some common object) and should take care to avoid any confusion between the characteristics of real-life articles and toy copies of them.

1.6 Where the results obtainable by the use of a product are shown, these should not exaggerate what is attainable by an ordinary child.

1.7 Advertisements addressed to children should, wherever possible, give the price of the advertised product.

1.8 No advertisement, especially one offering a product for supply by mail order, should appear in a medium directed at children if, for whatever reason, that product is unsuitable for purchase or use by the children who are likely to see the advertisement.

Safety

2.1 Special care should be taken to avoid the likelihood of children copying any practices which are either inherently unsafe, or likely to become unsafe when engaged in by children. The following paragraphs highlight some particular danger areas in advertisements likely to appeal to children.

2.2 No advertisement, particularly for a collecting scheme, should encourage children to enter strange places or to converse with strangers in an effort to collect coupons, wrappers, labels and the like.

2.3 Children should not appear to be unattended in street scenes unless they are obviously old enough to be responsible for their own safety; they should not be shown playing in the road, unless it is clearly shown to be a play-street or other safe area; they should not be shown stepping carelessly off the pavement or crossing the road without due care; in busy street scenes they should be seen to use the zebra crossings when crossing the road; and otherwise they should be seen in general to behave, as pedestrians or cyclists, in accordance with the Highway Code.

2.4 1. Children should not be seen behaving dangerously, e.g. leaning far out of windows, standing on the parapets of bridges or climbing without adequate supervision or protection.

2. Small children should not be shown climbing up to high shelves or reaching up to take things from above their heads.

2.5 Medicines, disinfectants, antiseptics and caustic substances should not be shown within reach of children without close parental supervision, nor should unsupervised children be shown using these products in any way.

2.6 Children should not be shown using matches or gas, paraffin, petrol or any mechanical or electrical appliance which could lead to their suffering burns, electrical shock or other injury.

2.7 Children should not be shown driving or riding on agricultural machines (including tractor-drawn carts or implements), so as to encourage contravention of the Agriculture (Avoidance of Accidents to Children Regulations) 1958 SI 361.

2.8 An open fire should have a fireguard clearly visible when a child is included in the scene.

Section C.XI
Media requirements

1.1   Publishers require all **betting tipster** advertisers to disclose to them their real name and permanent address. Where the business is conducted in any other name, that name is also required.

1.2   Publishers require copies of all forecasts or selections to be in their hands and time-stamped by the Post Office before the event or events to which they refer have taken place. Systems are also required to be in the hands of publishers before any advertisement referring to them can be published. Such literature will be checked, and if found to be incorrect, the advertisement will not be accepted.

1.3   Publishers will permit only verified results of selections or forecasts to be quoted in advertisements. They will not permit any reference to successes or profits based upon a staking plan to be included in an advertisement unless the details of the plan have been deposited with the publishers before the date on which the advertisement is to be published. (See also B.13.6.2 above, which requires that betting tipsters do not offer money-back guarantees.)

2.1   Advertisements of **business opportunities,** including franchises, which require a financial investment by an applicant are not acceptable unless, in advance of publication, the advertiser has provided publishers and/or their media organisations with satisfactory supporting information. (See further C.VIII above.)

2.2   Advertisements for **home-work schemes** are not acceptable unless, when offered to media, they are accompanied by full details of the work involved and the conditions imposed upon the home-worker. (See further C.VIII above.)

3.   Advertisements by **itinerant advertisers** will not be accepted by media unless the following information is made available:
   –   in the case of a limited company, the registered address;
   –   where the advertiser is trading in a name other than his own, that name;
   –   where the advertiser is not a limited company or registered business, his own name and a verifiable permanent address.

4.   See further, generally:
   –   on mail order, C.VI above;
   –   on physically invasive treatments, C.I.6.2 above;
   –   on slimming, C.IV above and particularly 1.3, 2.4.3, 2.6.1 and 5.3.2.

Section C.XII
Advertisements for Alcoholic Drinks

Preamble

1. This section is concerned with accepted restraints upon the advertising of alcholic drinks; and in what follows, except when the context does not permit, words such as 'advertisement' and 'drink' are to be understood as relating to alcoholic drink, and the way in which it is advertised.

2. The rules in paragraph 5 below are based upon those which were drawn up by the drinks industry in 1975 and which appeared most recently as Appendix 2 to the seventh edition of the Code. As they appear here, they have been substantially reorganised and redrafted and contain new material.

Scope

3.1 This section is concerned with the promotion of drinks the alcohol content of which exceeds 1.2% by volume. It applies to:

 –   advertisements for such drinks;
 –   sales promotions for such drinks, and sales promotions in connection with which such drinks are distributed, whether as gifts or prizes, or otherwise; and
 –   other advertisements, to the extent that they show people drinking or give particular emphasis to the name or visual identity of any brand of drink.

3.2 As appropriate, advertisements and sales promotions within the scope of this section are required to conform also to all relevant provisions of the rest of this Code.

Interpretation

4   Both the drinks industry and the advertising business are concerned to ensure that, in appealing to the many who buy and enjoy alcohol in moderation, advertisements avoid anything that can reasonably be seen as likely to lead to the adoption of styles of drinking that are unwise for the drinkers or a source of social and medical problems for the community. No set of rules can cater for every circumstance, but those responsible for the rules which follow understand the power of alcohol to do harm as well as good. They accept a commensurate responsibility for ensuring that these rules are always

applied in the spirit as well as in the letter. They do not believe advertisements need to be devoid of humour, but they will not tolerate the use of humour as a way of circumventing the clear intention of the rules.

Rules

5.1   Advertisements should be <u>socially responsible</u> and should not encourage excessive drinking. In particular, they should not exploit the young, the immaturė, or those with mental or social incapacities.

5.2.1   Advertisements should not be directed at <u>people under eighteen</u> whether by selection of the medium or context in which they appear, or by reason of their content or style of presentation.

5.2.2.   No advertisement should feature any <u>characters,</u> real or fictitious, who are likely, whether because of their apparent youth or otherwise, to attract the particular attention or admiration of people under eighteen and thereby, in any way, to encourage them to drink.

5.2.3.   People who are under eighteen should not appear in advertisements except when their presence would be neither illegal nor unusual; for example, as participants in such events as <u>family celebrations</u>. When they are so shown, it should always be obvious that they are not drinking.

5.2.4   <u>People shown drinking</u> in advertisements should always clearly be adults; and to ensure that this is the impression created, advertisers should not engage as models people under twenty-five, or people who look as though they may be under twenty-five, if these people are to be shown in any advertisement either drinking or about to drink.

5.3.1.   Advertisements should not suggest that drinking, or the choice of a particular drink, leads to <u>social acceptance</u> or popularity; or that alcohol is the main reason for the success of any event or occasion.

5.3.2.   It is legitimate to promote the consumption of particular drinks on particular occasions, or under particular circumstances (for example, champagne at <u>celebrations</u>), but if this is done, the advertiser must take care not to allow the implication to be drawn that the choice of a given drink is anything more than an evidence of the good taste of the drinker – that, for example, it can make him better liked or more successful than those who do not drink, or who drink something else.

5.3.3.   No advertisement should be capable of being understood as a challenge to people to drink. In particular, suggestions that drinking is an essential attribute of masculinity should be avoided, as should anything which suggests that the brave, the tough and the daring owe these characteristics to their drinking. No advertisement for a drink should depict or refer to it in the context of aggressive or anti-social behaviour.

5.3.4.   No advertisement should suggest that the femininity or attractiveness of women is enhanced by drinking or by the choice of a particular drink.

5.4.1.   While it is legitimate for them to give factual information about alcoholic strength, advertisements should not suggest that it is sensible or desirable to prefer a drink merely for its high alcohol content or intoxicating effect. To that end, high alcohol content should not be the principal basis of the appeal of any advertisement.

5.4.2.   Advertisements should not suggest that immoderate drinking, however portrayed, is sensible, admirable or amusing. Particular care requires to be taken with advertisements for sales promotions which require multiple purchases.

5.5.   Advertisements should avoid any implication, particularly when showing men and women together, that alcohol generally, or a particular drink, offers the key to success in personal relationships of any kind, or that it can make drinkers more attractive or successful in such relationships than non-drinkers, or those who drink something else.

5.6.1.   Advertisements for drink should not suggest the enhancement of mental ability or physical capacity. In any advertisement which features sportsmen, particular care is required to avoid the implication being drawn that their performance, or success, is related to their alcohol consumption.

5.6.2.   Advertisements should not suggest that drink has therapeutic properties or that it can resolve personal problems; in particular that it is acceptable to use it as a means of removing inhibitions, resolving tension or soothing agitation. Advertisements should not suggest that regular solitary drinking is advisable.

5.6.3.   It is legitimate to base an advertisement upon the ability of an alcoholic drink to slake the drinker's thirst.

5.7. Advertisements should not depict <u>activities or locations</u> in connection with which the consumption of any drink whatever would be unsafe or unwise. Particular care requires to be taken with advertisements which depict powered vehicles of any kind and especially motor cars.

See also B.19.2 and 3 above in relation to breath-tests, 'safe' levels of alcohol consumption and low alcohol drinks.

3

British Direct Marketing Association Code of Practice

The following extracts have been taken from the BDMA Direct Marketing Code of Practice, 1st edition, 1989, pp. 7–31 and 34. The full text is available from the British Direct Marketing Association Ltd, Grosvenor Gardens House, 35 Grosvenor Gardens, London SW1W 0BS.

CODE OF PRACTICE

1.0 INTRODUCTION

1.1 A Code of Practice has been drawn up by The British Direct Marketing Association Ltd and the Association of Mail Order Publishers in consultation with the Director General of Fair Trading. The Code has been adopted separately in 1989 by both Associations with such minor modifications as are necessary to adapt it to their respective constitutions.

1.2 Members of each Association undertake to adhere to the Code and accept that a breach of its terms may result in disciplinary proceedings.

1.3 The purpose of the Code of Practice is to lay down principles to be adhered to by Members in their direct marketing and also to set out the limitations in the conduct of their business which the Members accept as being in the interests of their customers and the public.

1.4 The Code of Practice is also the reference manual to which recourse will be taken in any dispute between a Member, its customers, and the general public.

1.5 The British Direct Marketing Association Ltd has set up the BDMA Conciliation Service to assist in the resolution of complaints against Members.

1.6 The Council of the BDMA is responsible for the supervision and monitoring of the Code and for taking action in relation to breaches of this Code, of the Codes administered by the Advertising Standards Authority, and of other relevant provisions.

1.7 The Council of the BDMA will report annually to the Director General of Fair Trading on the operation and effectiveness of the Code.

1.8 Nothing in this Code of Practice shall remove any right of either party to a dispute to refer the matter to the County or Sheriff Court or, jointly, to arbitration.

1.9 Members and their customers may, of course, at any time seek help and guidance from Trading Standards Departments, Consumer Advice Centres and Citizens Advice Bureaux.

2.0 INTERPRETATION

2.1 Members shall honour the Code of Practice both in the letter and in the spirit.

2.2 For the purpose of the Code, the word 'advertisement' includes all forms of selling communication, written, visual, electronic or oral, between a Member, its customers and the general public.

2.3 The term 'offer' includes an invitation to treat.

2.4 Some of the provisions in the Appendices to the Code have the same force as provisions in the Code proper; others are of a more advisory nature: the difference is evident from the language in which they are expressed. Nevertheless, those of an advisory nature are regarded in the same way as a Court regards the provisions of the Highway Code: the breaching of them may, in the circumstances of a particular case, result in a breach of the section in the Code which the provisions in the Appendices are intended to amplify.

2.5 Members may adopt any or all of the recognised forms of direct marketing, eg.
- display advertising or inserts in newspapers or periodicals
- advertising by post or hand delivery service
- inserts accompanying other companies' material
- telephone marketing (Appendix 1)
- advertising on television, radio or cable services
- electronic advertising

3.0 OBLIGATIONS OF MEMBERS

3.1 Members undertake to support the Code in the spirit as well as in the letter; in other words, not to treat its provisions as obstacles to be circumvented by legal ingenuity. Furthermore Members undertake to accept, in the context of any complaint referred to the BDMA Conciliation Service, the interpretation of any term of the Code given by the Director General of the BDMA; and to respond to the complaint accordingly.

3.2 Members acknowledge, in addition to the obligation to their customers, an obligation to the general public, and to each other.

3.3   This obligation comprises the use of selling-methods that are consistent with the public interest, in promises that are honest and intelligible, in performance that matches promises, in terms that are fair and equitable and in products that match claims.

3.4   The obligation further accepts the view that in certain areas of operation legal limits may insufficiently define what public taste permits; in particular, Members will at all times respect the reasonable privacy and personal notions of taste of consumers.

3.5   Members are expected to comply in all respects with legislation affecting their businesses. Any breach of such legislation resulting in a conviction or the serving of an order or notice may be considered by the Council of the Association as a disciplinary matter. In such a case the procedure in Section 8.0 would apply.

3.6   The attention of Members is drawn to a listing of principal legislation affecting direct marketing in Annex 1. This list is not necessarily exhaustive and is intended only as a guide to Members.

3.7   Members are required to comply with the provisions of the British Code of Advertising Practice and the British Code of Sales Promotion Practice administered by the Advertising Standards Authority.

3.8   Members are required to comply with the Code of Practice on the use of Personal Data for Advertising and Direct Marketing Purposes issued by the Advertising Association in consultation with the Data Protection Registrar.

3.9   Members must, where applicable, subscribe to the Mailing Preference Service and abide by its Rules of Membership.

3.10   Members must, where applicable, subscribe to the Telephone Preference Service (when it becomes available) and abide by its Rules.

3.11   Members shall not copy one another's material so that there might be confusion between them in the public eye. Nor shall they, without permission, use one another's trade marks, trade names, lists, slogans, or devices, whether protected or otherwise.

3.12   Members are recommended to include in a legible size in all advertisements and selling communications the Association's logo and are urged to display it in all correspondence to their customers and the public.

Members' Offers

4.0 GENERAL RULES

4.1 Members shall, where applicable, in addition to the specific provisions of Section 3 above, comply with Codes of the Independent Broadcasting Authority and the Cable Authority and successor bodies.

4.2 As an advertiser, a Member shall express itself clearly and without ambiguity so that members of the public shall know exactly what they are being offered and to what they are committing themselves when replying to an advertisement. The advertisement should, where appropriate, include accurate details of quality, quantity, supply, price and terms of business, that would apply to any respondent.

4.3 A Member shall not issue a misleading advertisement nor give false or misleading indications as to price, worth, value or quantity.

4.4 Every advertisement that could result directly in a respondent entering into a contractual commitment for goods or services should include a short, simple statement of the essential points of the offer, clearly displayed, for the respondent to keep. Such statement should include the Member's name and the full address at which the Member's business is managed.

4.5 Where it is not possible to include these points except on the order form to be returned to the Member, the Member shall supply the respondent with such a statement together with the goods; this statement should display the Association's logo if this was shown on the advertisement.

4.6 A Member shall not make factual claims in an advertisement unless they can readily be substantiated.

4.7 No testimonial shall be used unless the Member is able to substantiate its authenticity. No testimonial or endorsement shall be used unless it is genuine and related to the personal experience of the person giving it.

4.8 Testimonials given by employees of the Member or agency shall not be used unless the interest of such an individual is explicitly declared.

4.9 Testimonials which are obsolete or otherwise no longer applicable shall not be used.

4.10 Nothing in any advertisement, catalogue or other material should lead respondents to believe that their rights at law are in any way diminished or removed.

4.11 Claims as to the fitness of goods for a particular purpose should be made bearing in mind the need for caution in respect of goods of unusual design or manufacture and those with a wide range of uses. Reference should be made to the manufacturer in cases of doubt.

4.12 Samples of goods advertised should be available for public inspection during normal business hours.

4.13 Where bespoke or made-to-measure goods are advertised, or where the Member intends not to commence manufacture unless sufficient public interest is shown in the goods offered, (in which case this must be clearly stated), models or examples of similar work should be available for public inspection in accordance with Paragraph 4.12.

4.14 Instruction material, catalogues and lists of goods and/or services for sale shall state clearly the Member's name and the full postal address at which the Member can be contacted during normal business hours.

4.15 The requirements of this section of the Code do not preclude a Member from also stating in an advertisement another address to which consumers are to send their orders.

4.16 The full name of the Member shall be displayed prominently at the premises identified in advertisements, in instruction material, catalogues and other listings intended to be made available to the public.

5.0 SPECIAL RULES

5.1 **Incentives** are gifts, unconditional or conditional, premiums or opportunities to take part in a prize draw or competition.

5.2   **Gifts** and **Premiums** The terms on which a gift or a premium form part of any offer must be clearly stated, particularly whether it is conditional upon order (as in approval offers) or purchase.

5.3   **"Free"** An advertisement shall not describe goods or samples as "free" unless they are supplied at no cost or at no extra cost (other than actual postage/carriage) to the recipient.

5.4   A conditional gift or premium may be described as "free" only when the conditions are defined in close proximity to the word "free".

5.5   A premium shall not be described as "free" if the article to be purchased is increased in price or decreased in quantity or quality as a result of the premium offer.

5.6   **Prize Draws** and **Competitions** Any offer involving the opportunity to participate in a Prize Draw or a Competition is not permitted unless the Rules governing entry are clearly stated and any special conditions that apply are clearly explained. Detailed provisions on Prize Draws and Competitions are set out in Appendices 2 and 3 respectively.

5.7   Children under the age of 18 should not be eligible to participate in a prize draw or competition in which prizes such as, for example, holidays, pet animals, goods or cash which may be likely to cause problems between parent (or guardian) and child are offered, unless the Rules require the written consent of parent (or guardian).

5.8   **On Approval** An offer of goods "on approval" or "on trial" or similar terms must be honoured in the ready acceptance of goods returned within the period specified in the advertisement, and this period shall be calculated from the date on which the customer may reasonably be assumed to have received the goods.

5.9   **"Free" Approval, Trial, etc** In the context of an offer of the kind described in Paragraph 5.8 above, the inclusion of the word "free" indicates that the goods can be examined and returned without cost to the customer and shall not be used unless the Member either:

(a) automatically refunds the cost of postage or carriage, or

(b) supplies the respondent with a prepaid device to cover the cost of returning the goods, or

(c) gives the respondent instructions how to secure a refund of the cost of returning the goods.

5.10 **Guarantees** No advertisement shall contain the word ''guarantee'', ''guaranteed'', ''warranty'' or ''warranted'' or words having a similar meaning, unless the full terms of the guarantee are clearly set out in the advertisement or are supplied to the purchaser in writing with the goods. In all cases the terms should include details of the remedial action available to the purchaser.

5.11 No guarantee (which includes any document or form of words) shall be issued by a Member which might convey to the purchaser that any rights in respect of fitness for purpose, merchantable quality, etc were limited to those described in the guarantee and, to this end, all guarantees shall advise the purchaser that any statutory rights are in no way affected by its terms.

5.12 **Prepayments** Advertisements which request a prepayment should clearly state in the body of the advertisement (i.e. in a place other than on a coupon) the true name (with or without first name or initials) or business name, as appropriate, of the Member and the full address at which the business is managed and at which the Member can be contacted during normal business hours. For the purpose of this section, this address should normally be of the Member.

5.13 This requirement does not prevent a Member from also stating in an advertisement another address to which respondents are to send their orders, and this address need not be a full address but may be in the form of a Box Number or Freepost Number. (See also, in this connection, the Mail Order Transactions (Information) Order 1976 and the European Communities Act 1972)

5.14 Where a prepayment for goods is involved, Members should take steps to ensure that they do not create a demand for goods which cannot be met. A careful assessment of likely demand should be made before goods are advertised and when stocks are exhausted further advertising should be discontinued.

5.15 All advertisements or other offers which require any prepayment for goods or services must indicate the period within which the Member undertakes to despatch orders. Except in circumstances noted in the following Paragraph, the period must not be greater than 28 days from the receipt of the order.

5.16   Where a prepayment is required a Member should never take more than 28 days to despatch the order except:

(a)   when the advertisement makes it clear that a series of items is to be despatched in sequence and states the intervals between consignments; in such circumstances, only the first despatch need be made within the 28 day period; or

(b)   when there are special circumstances and the advertisement states prominently and clearly the latest date on which (or period within which) despatch will be effected; or

(c)   when it becomes clear that an order cannot be despatched within the period stated in the advertisement.

The Member should then immediately offer the respondent a refund. If the respondent nonetheless elects to wait, the respondent should either be given a firm date for despatch or the progress of the order should be reported to the respondent at reasonable intervals.

5.17   **Non-optional Extra Charges** No advertisement shall quote a price for goods or services which omits a postage and packing charge (or any other extra charge) which the customer is required to pay.

Where the amount of postage and packing is not included in the advertisement headline, a phrase such as '(plus p&p)' should be included in the headline sufficiently prominently to ensure that no respondent could be in doubt as to the application of such charges to the transaction advertised.

Such a postage and packing charge should be detailed clearly on the order form or coupon and in every other place where the terms of the sale are set out.

Where a postage and package charge cannot be determined in advance the order form should show clearly how it will be calculated or refer to the place in the catalogue etc where the information is given.

A Member may quote a price which is inclusive of postage and packing.

5.18   **Club Schemes** The supply of the Editor's or other choice to subscribers to a Book or Record or other Club shall be subject to the following conditions:

(a)   the terms of business relating to such supply must be stated clearly to the respondent before any contractual commitment to membership is entered into, and

(b) the Club Member must, on each occasion, be given reasonable advance notice of such main choice and, at the same time, be supplied with the opportunity to exercise an alternative choice, or, where applicable, to decline the main choice.

5.19 **Continuing Series** An open-ended commitment offered by a Member to a respondent to receive a continuing series of goods or supply of services shall be subject to the following conditions:

(a) the nature of the contractual commitment shall be set out prominently in the advertisement or in a statement provided with the initial supply of goods when they are supplied on approval.

(b) the option to cancel shall be available at all times after the discharge of any initial contractual commitment.

(c) the Member shall accept cancellation, even during the period of contractual commitment, if the price of the goods has to be increased to an extent that the buyer could not reasonably have expected when the commitment was undertaken.

(d) the Member shall, on reasonable notice, accept such cancellation even if he is unable to prevent the despatch of further goods; and in such case the Member shall agree to refund the cost of returning the goods.

(e) the Member shall refund at the time of cancellation any monies received for goods or services not provided.

5.20 Changes in the rate or quantity of goods from those advertised are not acceptable except where:

(a) the Member intends to supply more than one item at one time and this is clearly stated as a term of the offer; or

(b) the Member does not know whether it will be possible to supply more than one item of a series at one time and prominently states as a term of the offer that more than one item will be supplied if possible. The Member may, nevertheless, not effect such supply without giving the buyer adequate advance notice of such quantity supply together with a facility for the buyer to reject it; or

(c) the Member, not having intended to supply more than one item at one time and having therefore made no reference to it in the initial offer, finds it possible to do so and clearly invites the buyer to accept or reject this facility.

This procedure is subject to the condition that such quantity supply may not be proceeded with unless it is expressly accepted by the buyer.

5.21   The three forms of changing the despatch programme permissible under the Code are subject to two general conditions:

(a)   no such quantity supply in a series may be commenced less than three months after the initial offer, except where, under Paragraph 5.20 (a), an earlier date is explicitly stated in the initial offer and

(b)   the original terms for frequency of payment and amount may not be varied in the absence of the express agreement of both parties.

5.22   Paragraphs 5.20 (b) and (c) are subject to the further requirement that any notice or invitation relating to such quantity supply in a series of goods shall be accompanied by a reply paid envelope or other reply paid device.

5.23   A Member offering a series of products should not in the advertising describe items in the series which may not, in fact, be produced, unless it is clear in the advertisement that they might not become available.

5.24   **Offers of Services** shall include details of the nature, duration, extent and cost of the service concerned.

5.25   Offers requiring prior payment relating to holidays, travel facilities, or entertainment shall include full information as to the date, time, true nature, cost and any supplementary charges. Such offers must where relevant comply with the provisions of the Codes of Conduct of the Association of British Travel Agents and the Air Transport Operators' Association.

5.26   **Fixing or Installation of Goods** Where goods are offered which may require fixing, installation or assembly other than by the purchaser, information shall be given in the advertisement, catalogue or other promotional material as to the nature and extent of the work involved. If the Member is able to do the work either directly or through an agent at an additional cost to the purchaser the approximate cost of fixing, installation or assembly shall be stated.

5.27   **Collectibles** A collectible is a product advertised in terms of its interest as a collector's item, with the emphasis being placed primarily upon factors such as scarcity or aesthetic quality (and not, or not solely, upon practical consideration; eg. utility). Special rules attaching to the advertising of collectibles are set out in Appendix 4.

5.28 **Special physical characteristics** Where such a characteristic may be likely to influence a respondent whether to place an order, the size or weight etc. shall be specifically indicated.

Members' Customer Service

6.0 CUSTOMER SERVICE

6.1 **Service** Members shall at all times aim to give prompt and courteous service to a respondent.

6.2 Members shall keep an adequate record of orders received for goods or services.

6.3 **Queries and Complaints** Members will recognise that many complaints, when taken in isolation, are intrinsically minor; but these can quickly assume major proportions when coupled with a train of events involving failure to reply, broken promises, vague assurances and a defensive or evasive attitude. In a minority of cases, complaints do arise which cause a high degree of frustration, leading to criticism of the industry. This damages the public image of direct marketing, reflects upon the quality of its goods and services and is liable to bring the Member and the Association into disrepute.

6.4 Members should therefore investigate complaints received from customers promptly to assess their validity and, if substantiated, settle them quickly, effectively and courteously. When a complaint is not justified, the Member should explain politely why that is the case.

6.5 If the customer is still not satisfied, the Member should advise the customer of the service provided by the Association (Section 7.0 below) and that the local Trading Standards Office, Citizens Advice Bureau, Consumer Advice Centre or other similar body may also be prepared to help.

6.6 Members shall maintain an adequate system of monitoring consumer queries and complaints about their goods and standards of service so that appropriate remedial action can be taken promptly.

6.7 **Unsolicited Goods** Members shall under no circumstances send goods for which payment is required to any addressee without first having received an instruction for the supply of the goods.

6.8 Members shall operate reasonable verification procedures to minimise irritation resulting from a hoax order. Where such an order results from a handwritten application, Members should ensure they can supply a complainant with a copy of the order, if the complaint is made in reasonable time, and provided that the complainant provides adequate information to enable the Member to identify the order.

6.9 **Billing and Collection Procedures** Members shall keep these under constant review to ensure that at all times they are conducted as efficiently as possible.

6.10 Before threatening or instituting legal action for the collection of debts, Members shall take action to ensure that the identity of the debtor has been established correctly and that the debt has not been settled. Where a debt collection agency is employed, Members shall ensure that it holds the appropriate licence and exercises the same degree of care before any proceedings are taken on their behalf.

6.11 **Refunds** A Member shall, subject to Paragraph 6.12 below, return all money paid in advance by the consumer upon the return of the advertised goods:

(a) where goods are returned to the Member undamaged, within seven days of their receipt by the consumer (except in the case of bespoke and made-to-order goods);

(b) where the consumer has fulfilled the terms of an advertised money-back guarantee;

(c) where, for whatever reason, the product or service received by the consumer does not conform to the description of it contained in the offer;

(d) where the consumer has expressed a wish to be reimbursed because of unreasonable delay in the despatch of his order;

(e) where the Member is otherwise in breach of his statutory or contractual obligations.

6.12 The conditions referred to in Paragraph 6.11 above are:

(a) The Member should make it clear to consumers whether or not they may try out goods, subject to their remaining undamaged. If no indication is given it will be assumed that trial by the consumer is permitted;

(b) Where a Member does not intend to return money paid in respect of goods claimed returned but not received back by the Member, unless the consumer can produce proof of despatch, the Member shall so advise the consumer, at a time no later than that at which the goods are despatched, to obtain such proof of despatch.

6.13 **Mailing Lists and Data Protection Requirements** Members shall adhere to the Data Protection Principles set out in Schedule 1 to the Data Protection Act 1984. The attention of Members is also drawn to the obligations set out in Paragraphs 3.8 and 3.9 above.

6.14 On request, Members should suppress on their mailing list those who ask for their names to be deleted, so long as those making such requests supply the Member with adequate details to identify them.

6.15 Members should also, where possible, exclude such names from other lists which they may use.

6.16 Particular care should be taken not to send to minors offers suitable for adults only.

The British Direct Marketing Association Ltd and Complaints Against Members

7.0	BDMA CONCILIATION SERVICE

7.1 The British Direct Marketing Association Ltd has, in consultation with the Director General of Fair Trading, drawn up this Code of Practice. The Council of the Association is responsible for the supervision and monitoring of the Code.

7.2 The Council of the Association has also set up a Conciliation Service to which either members or consumers may apply in the event of their failure to reach a satisfactory conclusion to problems arising between them covered by this Code.

7.3 **Action by Members**

7.4 Members should, where appropriate, advise consumers that if they feel they have a problem they should write, in the first instance, to their address in the Member's advertisement or other communication quoting all relevant details and any reference number which relates to the transaction.

7.5 **Action by the BDMA**

7.6 If the Member is unable to resolve the problem, the Member shall advise the consumer of the Conciliation Service provided by the Association and send the consumer a copy of ''Information Notes for Members of the Public on the Code of Practice and Complaints Against Members''. (Copies are available to Members; the text of the Notes is contained in Annex 2).

7.7 Either party may then refer the problem to the BDMA Conciliation Service, by writing to the Director General of the BDMA.

7.8 On receipt of a written complaint the Director General of the BDMA will:
—assure himself that the complaint has already been referred to the Member by the complainant.

—then, if he feels that there may be a prima facie case of breach of the Code, put the complaint to the Member inviting a written explanation and/or prompt remedial action. The Member will co-operate fully with the Director General of the BDMA in his efforts to effect a satisfactory conclusion and will, for purposes of conciliation, accept his interpretation of any relevant term of the Code of Practice and respond to the complaint accordingly.

—if he is not satisfied that a breach of the Code has occurred (either on the basis of the written complaint without referring the matter to the Member or after investigation of the complaint with the Member), inform both parties accordingly.

For purposes of conciliation:

(i) the expression "Director General of the BDMA" shall also include any other person nominated by the Director General and approved by the BDMA Council for such purposes.

(ii) nothing in the conciliation procedure shall constitute the Director General an arbitrator.

7.9 If the BDMA Conciliation Service is unable to effect a conciliation between a complainant and a Member, or otherwise fails to satisfy the complainant, the complainant will be reminded that nothing in the Code of Practice affects the right of either party to refer the matter to the County or Sheriff Court or, jointly, to arbitration.

8.0 BREACHES OF THE CODE OF PRACTICE—CONSEQUENCES FOR MEMBERS

8.1 If the BDMA Council, after considering a report from the Director General of the BDMA, is satisfied that any breach was unintentional and an undertaking is given by the Member that it will not be repeated, it may decide to take no further action.

8.2 If the BDMA Council concludes that a breach of the Code has taken place, in circumstances not covered by Paragraph 8.1, it may admonish the Member formally and, if it considers it appropriate, publish a statement to that effect.

8.3 The BDMA Council may, however, conclude that the circumstances of the case—because of the seriousness of the breach or the previous record of the Member in regard to breaches of the Code and/or undertakings—may give rise to consideration of the expulsion of the Member from the Association in accordance with the Articles of Association of the BDMA.

8.4 The procedures outlined in Paragraphs 8.1 to 8.3 above may also be applied in circumstances described in Paragraph 3.5 of this

Code, without prejudice to the generality of Articles 11 (c) and 12 of the BDMA's Articles of Association.

8.5 Upon the expulsion of a Member from the Association under Paragraphs 8.3 and 8.4 the Council may issue a public statement giving reasons for its action.

9.0 OTHER SELF-REGULATORY BODIES

9.1 The BDMA Council will take note of adjudications by or proceedings of other self-regulatory bodies, in particular those by the Advertising Standards Authority, insofar as they relate to a Member's activities.

10.0 ANNUAL REPORT TO THE DIRECTOR GENERAL OF FAIR TRADING

10.1 The BDMA Council will make an annual report to the Director General of Fair Trading on the operation and effectiveness of the Code.

Appendix 1
Telephone Marketing Guidelines

1.0 Introduction

1.1 These Guidelines for Telephone Marketing Practices are intended to provide Members making use of Telephone Marketing to both Consumers and Businesses with principles of ethical and professional conduct and have been drawn up by the British Direct Marketing Association Ltd. in consultation with the Director General of Fair Trading.

1.2 Members shall comply with any relevant legislation which may supersede these Guidelines.

1.3 In addition, all Members shall comply with the following Guidelines in respect of activities not covered by specific law, or when legal requirements are less restrictive than the Guidelines.

2.0 Disclosure

2.1 The name of the Member on whose behalf a sales and marketing call is made or received should be voluntarily and promptly disclosed, and this information repeated on request at any time during the conversation.

2.2 The purpose of the call should be made clear at the start, and the content of the call should be restricted to matters directly relevant to its purpose.

2.3 The name, address and telephone number of the Member responsible for the call should appear in the telephone directory, or be available through directory enquiries, or be readily available through another source. This information shall also be given on request.

2.4 If a telephone marketer is acting as an agent of a Member the name, address and telephone number of the agent should be disclosed upon request at any time during the conversation.

2.5 If a person telephoned was recommended by a third party, the identity of the third party should be voluntarily and promptly disclosed.

3.0   Honesty

3.1   Telephone marketers should not evade the truth or deliberately mislead. Any questions should be answered honestly and fully to the best of the knowledge available.

3.2   Sales and marketing calls should not be executed in the guise of research or a survey. In cases where the words ''research'' or ''survey'' are used the information obtained must not be used to form the basis of a direct sales approach either during or after the call.

3.3   Members should accept responsibility for statements made by their sales staff or agents.

4.0   Reasonable Hours

4.1   Telephone marketers should avoid making sales and marketing calls during hours which are unreasonable to the recipients of the calls, bearing in mind that the OFT recommends that calls to consumers should not be made later than 9.00 pm unless expressly invited and that what is regarded as unreasonable can vary in different parts of the country and in different types of households or businesses.

4.2   When sales and marketing calls are initiated by a Member or its representatives, telephone marketers should ask whether the timing of a call is convenient. If it is not, they should offer to ring back at a more convenient time.

5.0   Courtesy and Procedures

5.1   Normal rules of telephone courtesy should be observed. Telephone marketers should avoid the use of high pressure tactics which could be construed as harassment.

5.2   Telephone marketers should always recognise the right of the other party to terminate the telephone conversation at any stage, and should accept such termination promptly and courteously.

5.3   If, as a result of a telephone contact, an appointment is made whereby a representative of a Member is to visit a consumer at home, the consumer should be provided with a clearly identified contact point in order to facilitate possible cancellation or alteration of the appointment.

5.4   Confirmation of any order placed should be sent to the customer and any documents forwarded in accordance with the prevailing legislation (e.g. The Consumer Credit Act 1974 and the Consumer Protection (Cancellation of Contracts concluded away from Business Premises) Regulations 1987).

5.5   Telephone marketers should take particular care not to seek information or to accept orders or appointments or invite any other action from a minor.

5.6   When consumer sales and marketing calls are made by a Member or its representatives, there should be a cooling off period of at least 7 days for oral contracts resulting from such calls, and the recipients of the calls should be so informed.

6.0   **Restrictions of Contacts**

6.1   Sales and Marketing calls should not be generated by random or sequential dialling manually or by computer.

6.2   Sales and marketing calls should not knowingly be made to unlisted or ex-directory numbers.

6.3   Unless expressly invited consumer calls should not be made to individuals at their place of work.

6.4   Members making use of telephone marketing should subscribe to the Telephone Preference Service (when it becomes available).

6.5   Members should delete from their telephone contact lists those persons who have specifically requested not to be contacted by telephone for sales or marketing purposes.

6.6   When sales and marketing calls are initiated by a Member or its representatives and automatic message and recording equipment is used, it is necessary, subject to the requirements of the Branch Systems General Licence, either to:

(a)   Immediately effect an introduction on the lines of ''This is a computer call on behalf of . . . ''
or
(b)   Have a ''Live'' operator introduce the call under those circumstances where the nature of the call is of a personal or a sensitive nature.

7.0 Definitions

7.1 **Business Calling:** Sales and marketing calls, for an individual as a representative of his or her company.

7.2 **Consumer Calling:** Sales and marketing calls for an individual not as a representative of his or her employer or company.

7.3 **Sales and Marketing Call:** A call designed to generate a sale of a product or service, or to lead toward a sale of a product or service to the specific company or consumer as a result of the information given during a telephone conversation.

Appendix 2

Prize Draws

Application of Paragraph 5.6 of the Code of Practice to any scheme involving the distribution by chance of prizes to members of the public at no charge to them (i.e. 'prize draws') and involving no breach of the Lotteries and Amusements Act 1976.

1.0 Structure and Operation

1.1 A copy of the Principles and Procedures to be adopted in any Prize Draw should be lodged with the Association in advance of the publication of any advertisement of the Prize Draw to the public.

1.2 The important stages of any Prize Draw, such as the drawing of winning numbers and the checking of returned claims, should be conducted strictly in accordance with the Procedures.

1.3 These stages should be observed by an independent official (e.g. an accountant or solicitor) so that a certificate of compliance with the Procedures may be issued.

1.4 The same official should certify the results when the Prize Draw has been completed.

1.5 A full list of winners (excluding winners of consolation prizes) must be produced, and a certified copy lodged with the Association as soon as possible after the completion of the Prize Draw.

1.6 Where the Prize Draw involves the issuing of numbers to the public, each number must be unique, and the drawing procedures should be appropriate to this requirement.

1.7 The chances of success for any recipient of the advertisement should be absolutely independent of acceptance or rejection of any merchandise offered.

1.8 Apart from the supply of goods to an acceptor and any procedure necessary to expedite delivery thereof, there should, unless otherwise expressly indicated, be no distinction made in the handling of responses.

1.9 No person in any way connected with the operation or administration of a Prize Draw shall be eligible to receive a prize in it.

1.10 All prizes must be awarded as advertised.

2.0 **Advertising the Prize Draw**

2.1 'Advertising' includes any means by which a member of the public may be invited to take part in the Prize Draw.

2.2 No advertisement for a Prize Draw shall be such as to raise unjustified expectations in any recipient that he or she has won a particular prize if it is not known that it is so.

2.3 In any advertisement for a Prize Draw in which every participant is entitled to claim goods without consideration to the Member, care must be taken to avoid any recipient reasonably concluding that he is entitled to anything other than one of the 'gifts'.

2.4 Goods of minor value which are to be supplied to all participants must be described as 'gifts', not as prizes, and the term 'win' (or any grammatical variation thereof) may not be used in relation to such goods.

2.5 In any advertisement in which one or more of the prizes is dramatised by any 'document' which is likely to be taken to be of intrinsic value (e.g. 'cheques', 'airline tickets', 'Savings books') such documents shall indicate conspicuously that they are by way of example only.

2.6 All advertisements must make it clear that the chances of winning any prizes are absolutely independent of whether the recipient orders any goods.

2.7 All advertisements which invite orders shall include clear devices for accepting or rejecting the offer and no one such device shall enjoy undue prominence over the other.

2.8 Conditional gifts may be included and advertised in such schemes, but only goods can be described as gifts; discounts and any other special terms of business must be presented as such and not as gifts.

2.9 Where any prize category is subject to special conditions (e.g. a cash alternative) these must be made clear in the advertisement.

2.10 Where the Member intends to offer cash in lieu, this fact, and the amount, must be stated in any advertisement.

2.11   The quantities of prizes to be given away must be stated in any advertisement.

2.12   Where in any scheme it is possible that not all prizes advertised will be awarded to participants, this must be clearly stated.

2.13   The Prize Draw part of any advertisement should be regarded as one of the essential parts of an offer and should therefore comply with Paragraph 4.4 of the Code of Practice, that is to say, the essential points of the Prize Draw should be included in a short, simple statement, clearly displayed, for the participant to keep.

2.14   All Prize Draw advertisements must include information that a list of prize winners (see Paragraph 1.5 above) will be available on request and indicate approximately when, from where and how the list may be obtained.

Appendix 3

Prize Competitions

Application of Paragraph 5.6 of the Code of Practice to Prize Competitions (i.e. promotional schemes complying with S.14 of the Lotteries and Amusements Act 1976) and open to members of the public. Such competitions must not involve betting nor amount to a lottery.

1.0 Structure and Operation

1.1 Adequate resources should be made available for the running of Prize Competitions so that consumers have no reasonable ground for complaint as regards the administration of such schemes.

1.2 A copy of the Rules of the Prize Competitions must be lodged with the Association in advance of the publication of any advertisement of the Competition to the public.

1.3 A panel of judges should be set up by the Member and it should include a person with special knowledge of the field covered by the task demanded on the entry form.

1.4 The judging of entries must take place promptly and winners should be informed as soon thereafter as practical.

1.5 Entrants must be supplied with a copy of the rules no later than the time at which they are expected to complete their entries.

1.6 The prizes available must clearly be identified.

1.7 The results of any Competition must readily be available to entrants.

1.8 A copy of the results must be certified by the judges and lodged with the Association.

1.9 Any Competition involving gifts as well as prizes shall clearly distinguish between the two so that the consumer is left in no doubt as to the difference between them.

1.10 In any advertisement for a Prize Competition in which participation is dependent upon a purchase being made, the exact nature of what it is an entrant is required to do shall be clearly explained.

1.11 Goods of minor value which are to be supplied to all participants must not be described as prizes, nor may the Member state that all entrants have 'won' or will 'win' them.

1.12 No person in any way connected with the operation or administration of a Competition shall be eligible to receive a prize in it.

1.13 The Member must take care to ensure that entrants are given adequate time in which to complete and submit their entries.

2.0   The Rules

2.1 The Rules for the Competition should be set out clearly and should, where applicable, deal with the matters covered in the following paragraphs.

2.2 If the Member requires the judges to award prizes only to entries of a sufficient standard (and therefore possibly not to award all prizes advertised), a statement to this effect must be included in the Rules.

2.3 If it is intended to limit the number of entries that may be submitted by any one competitor, this must be stated.

2.4 If it is intended to limit the number of prizes any single participant may win, this must be made clear.

2.5 When cash alternatives are available, the value of such alternatives must be indicated.

2.6 In any Competition in which those who do not order products are permitted to compete, any special conditions that may apply to such competitors must be stated.

2.7 Where the judges will be required to have regard to any special factors relating to entries, these should be indicated.

2.8 A statement that copies of the results will be available must be made and such statement should indicate when these copies will be available and how they may be acquired.

2.9 A clear indication must be given of the conditions under which the entries may be disqualified.

2.10   The closing date for the receipt of entries must be stated, as well as the date by which it is intended to announce the results.

2.11   Where the Member intends to limit, or disclaim, responsibility for entries that may be lost, this must be clearly stated.

2.12   If the organiser intends to acquire copyright in all or in certain entries, this must be indicated.

2.13   A statement must be made that no one in any way connected with the running of the competition is eligible for a prize in it.

Annex 1

Principal Legislation Affecting Direct Marketing

Trade Descriptions Act 1968
Unsolicited Goods and Services Acts 1971 and 1975
Consumer Credit Act 1974
Unfair Contract Terms Act 1977
Sale of Goods Act 1979
Supply of Goods and Services Act 1982
Data Protection Act 1984
Consumer Protection Act 1987 and Code of Practice thereunder for Traders
on Price Indications 1989

Consumer Transactions (Restrictions on Statements) Order 1976
Mail Order Transactions (Information) Order 1976
Consumer Protection (Cancellation of Contracts concluded away from
Business Premises) Regulations 1987
Control of Misleading Advertisements Regulations 1988
Trade Descriptions (Place of Production) (Marking) Order 1988

4

Direct marketing: industry statistics

Table A4.1 Direct mail: inland volume (millions of items)

	1980	1981	1982	1983	1984	1985	1986	1987	1988	1989	1990
Mail order origins	251	294	333	264	276	330	348	393	441	520	612
Other origins	734	740	769	820	986	973	1053	1233	1325	1597	1760
Total volume	985	1034	1102	1084	1262	1303	1401	1626	1766	2117	2372

Source: Royal Mail.

Table A4.2 Direct mail: senders, 1988–89

	Total 1988 (%)	Total 1989 (%)
Film processing	0.04	0.04
Publisher	2.5	2.8
Pools	0.04	0.04
Charity	0.1	0.1
Entertainment	0.04	0.04
Legal	0.1	0.1
Post Office	0.04	0.04
Utility	2.3	2.0
Book clubs	3.6	3.7
Estate agent	3.1	2.0
Retailer	6.3	6.3
Travel	5.6	6.2
Other	14.4	16.7
Mail order	37.8	34.8
Bank	5.6	6.0
Building Society	3.1	3.1
Insurance	8.6	9.6
Credit card companies	3.8	3.6

Source: Royal Mail.

Table A4.3 Direct mail: business and consumer percentages

	Consumer (millions of items)	%	Business (millions of items)	%	Total (millions of items)	%
1983	713	66	371	34	1084	100
1984	889	70	373	30	1262	100
1985	933	72	370	28	1303	100
1986	976	70	425	30	1401	100
1987	1161	71	465	29	1626	100
1988	1221	69	545	31	1766	100
1989	1445	68	672	32	2117	100
1990	1612	68	760	32	2372	100

Source: Royal Mail.

Table A4.4 Direct mail: total expenditure (postage and production)

	Postage £m.	Yr on yr % change	Prod. £m.	Yr on yr % change	Total £m.	Yr on yr % change
1981	100.3		198.3		298.6	
1982	119.7	+19.3	221.4	+11.6	341.1	+14.2
1983	112.0	− 6.4	187.8	−15.2	299.8*	−12.1
1984	121.5	+ 8.5	202.4	+ 7.8	323.9	+ 8.0
1985	144.2	+18.7	300.5	+48.5	444.7	+37.3
1986	149.4	+ 3.6	324.6	+ 8.0	474.0	+ 6.6
1987	183.1	+22.6	300.4	− 7.5	483.5	+ 2.0
1988	203.7	+11.3	326.0	+ 8.5	529.1	+ 9.4
1989	273.0	+34.0	485.0	+48.7	758.0	+43.2
1990	311.0	+13.9	668.0	+37.7	979.0	+29.1

* The reason for the apparent decline in 1983 was the reduction during that year in the use of direct mail by the larger mail order companies. (See Table A4.1 for direct mail volume split between mail order companies and other users.)
Source: Royal Mail.

Table A4.5 Direct mail: expenditure per item

	Postage (pence per item)	Index	Production (pence per item)	Index	Total (pence per item)	Index
1981	9.7	100	19.18	100	28.88	100
1982	10.86	112	20.09	105	30.95	107
1983	10.33	106	17.33	90	27.66	96
1984	9.63	99	16.03	84	25.66	89
1985	11.10	114	23.03	120	34.13	118
1986	10.66	110	23.17	121	33.83	117
1987	11.00	113	18.00	94	29.00	100
1988	12.00	124	18.00	94	30.00	103
1989	12.89	132	22.90	119	35.79	123
1990	13.11	135	28.16	146	41.27	142

Source: Royal Mail.

Table A4.6   Direct mail: share of total UK advertising expenditure (£million)

	Total DM spend (£m.)	Total UK adv. spend (ex direct mail) (£m.)	Direct mail % share of spend
1980	260	2555	9.2
1981	299	2818	9.6
1982	341	3126	9.8
1983	300	3579	7.7
1984	324	4059	7.4
1985	445	4455	9.1
1986	474	5138	8.5
1987	483	5823	7.7
1988	530	6831	7.2
1989	758	7555	9.1

Source: Advertising Association.

Table A4.7   Media expenditure analysis (all media)—retail and mail order by product group (£000)

	1984	1985	1986	1987	1988	1989
Book clubs	8 101	7 912	8 651	8 553	10 922	14 425
Retail and mail order						
Collectors, limited editions	5 000	3 221	5 499	7 016	12 151	18 445
Direct response catalogues	7 859	8 267	11 349	12 686	17 496	16 745
Film process—retail and mail order	6 826	6 069	4 418	6 071	3 459	3 580
Direct response mail order	41 540	40 371	48 114	53 222	61 262	84 974
Mail order agencies	10 236	12 244	11 295	10 409	11 537	10 339
Mail order retail stores	1 725	2 501	1 720	1 395	2 971	2 195

Source: Media Expenditure Analysis Ltd (based on rate card).

Table A4.8 UK advertising expenditure

	Press (£m.)	TV (£m.)	Direct mail (£m.)	Posters/ transport (£m.)	Radio (£m.)	Cinema (£m.)	Total (£m.)
1980	1684	692	260	107	54	18	2815
1981	1816	809	299	115	60	18	3117
1982	1986	928	341	124	70	18	3467
1983	2236	1109	300	137	81	16	3879
1984	2558	1249	324	150	86	16	4383
1985	2801	1376	445	164	82	18	4886
1986	3136	1675	474	196	91	19	5591
1987	3560	1872	483	216	111	22	6264
1988	4292	2127	530	244	139	27	7361
1989	4806	2286	758	270	158	35	8313

Source: Advertising Association.

Table A4.9 UK advertising expenditure—by media (year on year % change)

	Press (%)	TV (%)	Direct mail (%)	Posters/ transport (%)	Radio (%)	Cinema (%)	Total (%)
1981	+ 7.8	+16.9	+15.0	+ 7.4	+11.1		+10.7
1982	+ 9.4	+14.7	+14.0	+ 7.8	+16.6		+11.2
1983	+12.6	+19.5	−12.0	+10.5	+15.7	−11.1	+11.9
1984	+14.4	+12.6	+ 8.0	+ 9.5	+ 6.2		+13.0
1985	+ 9.5	+10.2	+37.3	+ 9.3	− 4.7	+12.5	+11.5
1986	+12.0	+21.7	+ 6.5	+19.5	+11.0	+ 5.6	+14.4
1987	+13.5	+11.8	+ 1.9	+10.2	+22.0	+16.0	+12.0
1988	+19.2	+13.6	+ 9.7	+12.9	+25.2	+22.7	+16.6
1989	+11.9	+ 7.4	+43.0	+10.6	+13.6	+29.6	+12.9

Source: Advertising Association.

Table 4.10 UK advertising expenditure—by category (% share of total)

	Press	TV	Direct mail	Posters/ transport	Radio	Cinema	Total
1980	59.8	24.6	9.2	3.8	1.9	0.6	100
1981	58.3	25.9	9.6	3.7	1.9	0.6	100
1982	57.3	26.8	9.8	3.6	2.0	0.5	100
1983	57.7	28.6	7.7	3.5	2.1	0.4	100
1984	58.4	28.4	7.4	3.4	2.0	0.4	100
1985	57.3	28.2	9.0	3.4	1.7	0.4	100
1986	56.1	30.0	8.5	3.6	1.6	0.3	100
1987	56.8	29.9	7.7	3.4	1.8	0.4	100
1988	58.0	29.1	7.2	3.3	1.9	0.4	100
1989	57.8	27.5	9.1	3.2	1.9	0.4	100

Source: Advertising Association.

Table A4.11 European comparisons: addressed direct mail volume 1981–89 (millions of items)

Country	1981	1982	1983	1984	1985	1986	1987	1988	1989
Belgium	312	344	409	449	474	506	533	566	750*
Yr on yr ±%		+10.3	+18.9	+9.8	+5.6	+6.3	+5.4	+6.1	+34.9
Denmark	130	135	140	150	180	190	200	215	240
Yr on yr ±%		+3.8	+3.7	+7.1	+20.0	+5.6	+5.3	+7.5	+11.6
Finland	154	156	171	199	213	179	197	216	236†
Yr on yr ±%		+1.3	+9.6	+16.4	+7.0		+10.0	+9.6	+9.3
France	1 401	1 553	1 603	1 737	1 973	2 000	2 407	2 684	2 850‡
Yr on yr ±%		+10.8	+3.2	+8.4	+13.6	+1.4	+20.3	+11.5	+6.2
Ireland	N/A	7.0	7.1	9.0	13.0	19.0	20.0	30.0	40.0‡
Yr on yr ±%			+1.4	+28.6	+44.4	+46.1	+5.3	+50.0	+33.3
Netherlands	444	454	451	512	541	558	680	780	850‡
Yr on yr ±%		+2.2	−0.6	+13.5	+5.6	+3.1	+21.9	+14.7	+9.0
Norway	105	108	121	135	177	204	215	216	192
Yr on yr ±%		+2.9	+12.0	+11.6	+31.1	+15.3	+5.4	—	−11.1
Portugal	N/A	83	58	58	61	66	85‡	85‡	105
Yr on yr ±%			−30.1	N/A	+5.2	+8.2	+28.8		
Spain			480					647	650‡
Sweden	373	383	404	434	457	481	511	541	606
Yr on yr ±%		+2.7	+5.5	+7.4	+5.3	+5.3	+6.2	+6.0	+12.0
Switzerland	467	496	534	542	565	582	620	652	671‡
Yr on yr ±%		+6.2	+7.7	+1.5	+4.2	+3.0	+6.3	+5.2	+2.9
United Kingdom	1 034	1 102	1 084	1 261	1 303	1 401	1 626	1 766	2 117
Yr on yr ±%		+6.6	−1.6	+16.3	+3.2	+7.5	+16.1	+8.6	+19.9

	1981	1982	1983	1984	1985	1986	1987	1988	1989
West Germany	3 013	2 996	3 004	3 113	3 078	3 261	3 352	3 609	3 704
Yr on yr ±%		−0.6	+0.3	+3.6	−1.1	+5.9	+2.8	+7.6	+2.6
Total	7 433	7 817	8 466	8 599	9 035	9 447	10 446	11 997	13 011
Yr on yr ±%		+5.1	+8.3	+1.5	+5.1	+4.6	+10.6	+14.8	+8.4

* Belgium changed their method of calculation in 1989.
† Change in volume as bulk publications no longer included 1986 and 1987 volumes adjusted.
‡ Estimate.

Source: Services Postaux Européens.

Table 4.12 European comparisons: addressed direct mail volume per head of population (number of items per year)

	1981	1982	1983	1984	1985	1986	1987	1988	1989
Belgium	32	35	41	45	48	51	54	57	76
Denmark	25	26	27	29	32	37	43	45*	47
Finland	32	33	36	41	44	46	50	45	48
France	26	28	29	32	36	37	41	45*	50*
Ireland	N/A	2	2	2.4	4	5	6	6	11
Netherlands	30	31	31	35	37	38	40	56	58
Norway	25	26	29	32	42	49	52	55	46
Portugal	N/A	8	6	6	6	6	8	8*	11
Sweden	45	46	49	52	55	58	62	66	73
Switzerland	72	76	82	83	87	90	95	96	102
United Kingdom	18	20	19	22	23	25	29	32	38
West Germany	49	49	49	51	50	53	55	59	60
Spain			13						17

* Estimate.
Source: Services Postaux Européens.

NB: These figures include business-to-business mailings as well as business-to-consumer mailings. The figures cannot be used to work out receipt of direct mail items per household.
Only the UK produces figures which can identify consumer receipt of mailings. At present per household receipt of direct mail items in the UK is 5.6 items per four-week period (January 1989–December 1989).
Source: Direct Mail Information Service.

Table A4.13 European comparisons: direct mail expenditure and percentage share of advertising spend figures in local currencies (millions)

	1982		1983		1984		1985		1986		1987		1988		1989	
	DM	% share	DM	% share	DM	% share	DM	% share	DM	% share	DM	% share	DM	% share	DM	% share
Belgium (BF)	3808	17.4	4380	17.2	4730	16.8	5064	17.1	5376	17.3	5724	17.9	6075	18.4	—	—
Denmark (K)	1683	30.0	2166	31.7	2728	33.0	2810	30.0	2945	31.0	3135	33.0	—	—	4820	35.0
Finland (Mk)	505.9	11.5	599.3	11.6	719	11.6	805	11.7	886	15.0	950*	15.0*	1040*	15.0*	1170*	14.0*
France (FF)	2600	9.5	2935	9.5	3410	9.8	3800	9.5	4200	9.5	4990*	9.6*	—	—	—	—
W. Germany (DM)	1485	11.1	1699	11.1	1759	11.7	1847	11.8	1948	12.0	2030	12.0	2235	11.8	2400*	12.0
Ireland (£I)	1.74	1.8	1.79	1.9	1.9	1.8	2.8	2.3	5.2	4.4	5.4	4.7	—	—	—	—
Netherlands (G)	920	18.4	1031	19.9	1224	21.1	1217	18.4	1253	—	1389	20.7	1644	22.0	—	—
Norway (Kr)	1200	27.9	1500	30.0	1800	30.0	2200	28.9	2600	29.4	2900	28.6	2900	28.8	2800	28.3
Portugal (Esc)	873	15.4	666	9.4	814	8.6	786	6.2	976	5.3	1386	4.6	—	—	2000	3.8
Spain (Ps)	—	—	—	—	—	—	—	—	48000	—	52000	—	95000	12.6	—	—
Sweden (Kr)	1953	31.0	1860	30.0	1944	27.0	1894	28.7	3631	21.6	4066	22.0	4021	20.0	—	—
Switzerland (SF)	1000	35.0	—	—	—	—	1250	35.0	—	—	—	—	—	—	—	—
UK (£)	341	9.8	299	7.7	328	7.4	445	9.1	474	8.5	483	7.7	530	7.2	758	9.1

* Estimate—Definitions changed in 1986.
Source: Services Postaux Européens.

Table A4.14 All couponed direct response advertising

	1988	1987	% Change last year
Number of advertisers	7 287	7 118	+ 2.4
Number of brands	19 670	19 464	− 1.1
Number of advertisements	126 430	128 509	− 1.6
Rate card expenditure (£000s)	495 458.3	453 981.2	+ 9.1
Number of publishers	179	191	− 6.3
Number of titles	606	557	+ 8.8
Number of title issues	10 318	10 001	+ 3.2
Number of pages in issues	678 495	631 000	+ 7.5
Number of advertising pages	63 904.9	64 227.6	− 0.5
Circulation reached (000s)	99 158 855.3	104 444 886.3	− 5.1
Cost per thousand circulation reached	£4.99	£4.35	+14.7

Source: Nationwide Market Research.

Table A4.15 Couponed direct response advertising: the top ten spending product/ service types by rate card expenditure

Product/service type	1988 (£000s)	1987 (£000s)	% Change on 1987 (±)	Position 1988	Position 1987
Secured loan and second mortgage	15 710.2	11 680.5	+34.5	1st	6th
General fashion (female)	14 140.3	11 766.4	+20.2	2nd	5th
Contemporary cars	12 956.8	11 953.4	+ 8.4	3rd	7th
Life insurance/ assurance	12 382.0	13 667.0	− 9.4	4th	3rd
Fashion catalogues (agency)	10 653.2	10 290.9	+ 3.5	5th	9th
Kitchens	10 206.7	10 967.6	− 6.9	6th	8th
Unit trusts	9 538.6	29 254.6	−67.4	7th	1st
Pensions	8 505.0	4 135.6	+105.7	8th	20th
Motor insurance	7 832.2	4 290.4	+82.6	9th	18th
Building societies (saving and investment)	7 821.2	11 976.4	−34.7	10th	4th

Source: Nationwide Market Research.

Table A4.16 Couponed direct response advertising: product/service group rate card expenditure as a percentage of all rate card expenditure

Product/service group	1988 (%)	1987 (%)
1. Personal financial	23.0	29.5
2. Household and home interest	14.1	13.2
3. Leisure and entertainment	10.7	10.4
4. Clothing and fashion accessories	7.3	6.2
5. Holidays and travel	6.8	6.9
6. General merchandise	6.0	5.2
7. Motor vehicles and products	4.2	4.1
8. Business equipment and services	4.2	3.6
9. Catalogue houses	3.7	3.4
10. Business services and products	3.6	2.8
The top ten total as a percentage of all rate card expenditure	83.6	85.3

Source: Nationwide Market Research.

Table A4.17 Couponed direct response advertising: changes in rate card expenditure for the top ten product/service groups

Product/service group	1988 Rate card expenditure (£000s)	1987 Rate card expenditure (£000s)	% Change on last year
1. Personal financial	116 021.0	134 056.5	−13.5
2. Household and home interest	71 085.7	59 919.1	+18.6
3. Leisure and entertainment	54 064.7	47 292.2	+14.3
4. Clothing and fashion accessories	36 634.8	28 142.1	+30.2
5. Holidays and travel	34 122.2	31 347.9	+ 8.9
6. General merchandise	30 422.4	23 763.5	+28.0
7. Motor vehicles/products	21 269.1	18 767.6	+13.3
8. Business equipment and services	21 113.1	16 158.1	+30.7
9. Catalogue houses	18 512.0	15 486.8	+19.5
10. Business services and products	17 914.5	12 862.9	+39.3

Source: Nationwide Market Research.

Table A4.18 Couponed direct response advertising: rate card expenditure by product/service types as a percentage of total rate card expenditure

1988	%	1987	%
1. Secured loan and second mortgage	3.1	1. Unit trusts	6.4
2. General fashion (female)	2.8	2. Equity (sales and investment)	4.0
3. Contemporary cars	2.6	3. Life insurance/assurance	3.0
4. Life insurance/assurance	2.4	4. Building societies (saving and invest)	2.6
5. Fashion catalogue (agency)	2.1	5. General fashion (female)	2.6
6. Kitchens	2.0	6. Secured loan and second mortgage	2.6
7. Unit trusts	1.9	7. Contemporary cars	2.5
8. Pensions	1.9	8. Kitchens	2.4
9. Motor insurance	1.6	9. Fashion catalogue (agency)	2.3
10. Building societies (saving and invest)	1.5	10. Furniture	1.5
Top ten total as percentage of all rate card expenditure	21.8		29.9

Source: Nationwide Market Research.

Table A4.19 Couponed direct response advertising: the top ten BRAD interest groups by rate card expenditure

BRAD interest group	1988 (£000s)	1987 (£000s)	% Change yr on yr (±)
National dailies	157 128.9	153 176.9	+ 2.6
Sat. and Sun. supplements	120 835.4	95 960.5	+25.9
Sunday newspapers	74 299.8	75 564.2	− 1.7
Women's interest	49 003.4	44 642.5	+ 9.8
TV and radio	31 507.7	30 907.3	+ 1.9
General interest	15 420.2	12 665.9	+21.7
Home interests	8 579.4	8 084.8	+ 6.1
Motoring	4 523.2	3 693.8	+22.5
Business management	3 893.7	3 669.9	+ 6.1
Teenage and pop	3 170.5	2 721.4	+16.5

Source: Nationwide Market Research.

Useful addresses

UK Addresses

The Advertising Association
Abford House
15 Wilton Road
London SW1V 1NJ
071-828 2771

The Advertising Standards
Authority
Brook House
2–16 Torrington Place
London WC1E 7HN
071-580 5555

Association of Mail Order
Publishers
1 New Burlington Street
London W1X 1FD
071-437 0706

British List Brokers' Association
Springfield House
West Street
Bedminster
Bristol BS3 4EF
0272-666900

Data Protection Registrar
Springfield House
Water Lane
Wilmslow
Cheshire SK9 5AY
0625-535777

Direct Mail Producers' Association
34 Grand Avenue
London N10 3BP
081-883 9854

Direct Mail Services Standards
Board
26 Eccleston Street
London SW1W 9PY
071-824 8651

Institure of Sales Promotion
Arena House
66–68 Pentonville Road
London W1 9HS
071-837 5340

Mail Order Protection Scheme
16 Tooks Court
London EC4A 1LB
071-405 6806

Mail Order Traders' Association
100 Old Hall Street
Liverpool L3 9TD
051-227 4181

Mailing Preference Service
1 Leeward House
Square Rigger Row
Plantation Wharf
London SW11 3TY
071-738 1625

The Newspaper Publishers'
Association Ltd
34 Southwark Bridge Road
London SE1 9EU
071-928 6928

Periodical Publishers' Association
Ltd
Imperial House
15–19 Kingsway
London WC2B 6UN
071-379 6268

Overseas addresses

Australia

Australian Direct Marketing
Association
GPO Box 3982
10F 52–58 Clarence Street
10th Floor
Sydney, NSW 2000
Australia
(02) 29-2914

Belgium
Groupement de la Vente par
Correspondance
Rue de la Science, 3
1040 Brussels
Belgium
(02) 537-3060

Canada
Canadian Direct Mailing
Association
1 Concorde Gate
Don Mills
Ontario M3C 3N6
Canada
(416) 391-2362

Denmark
The Danish Direct Marketing
Club
Dansk Markedsforing Forbund
Vesterbrogade #24
DK–1620 Copenhagen
Denmark
(01) 224688

Finland
Finnish Direct Marketing
Association
Henry Fordin katu 5m
5F-00150 Helsinki
Finland
(0) 663 744

France
Syndicat des Enterprises de Vente
par Correspondance et à
Distance
60 rue la Boetie
75008 Paris
France
(1) 4256–3886

Hong Kong
Hong Kong Direct Mail and
Marketing Association
GPO Box 7416
Hong Kong
(5) 68-11-77

Italy
AIDIM (Associazione Italiana per
il Direct Marketing)
Corso Venezia, 16
20121 Milano
Italy
(2) 78 31 02 and
(2) 760 15 34

Japan
Japan Direct Marketing
  Association
32 Mori Building
3-4-30 Shiba-Koen
Minato-ku
Tokyo, Mail 105
Japan
(3) 434 4700

The Netherlands
Direct Marketing Institute
  Nederland
Weerdestein 96
1083GG Amsterdam
The Netherlands
(20) 429-595

New Zealand
New Zealand Direct Marketing
  Association
PO Box 437
Auckland
New Zealand
(9) 419-0042

Singapore
Direct Marketing Association of
  Singapore
450 Alexandra Road
#10-00 Inchape Hov
Singapore 0511
4750220

Spain
Association Española de
  Marketing Directo
Provenza 238
Barcelona 08008
Spain
(3) 323-4408 and
(3) 323-4061

Sweden
Swedish Direct Marketing
  Association
PO Box 14038
104-40 Stockholm
Sweden
(8) 661-39-10

United States
Direct Marketing Association Inc.
6 East 43rd Street
New York, NY 10017
USA
(212) 689 4977

West Germany
DDV-Deutscher Directmarketing
  Verband e.v
Schiersteiner Strasse 29
D-6200 Wiesbaden
West Germany
6121-843061

Pan European
European Direct Marketing
  Association
34 rue du Gouvernement
  Provisoire
B-1000 Brussels
Belgium
(2) 217 6309

6

Standards of practice in lists and database management

Introduction

The direct marketing industry is well aware of its obligation to use responsibly the rapidly developing techniques for processing names and addresses and recording marketing information about its customers and prospects. Consumer attitudes to, and concerns about, direct marketing are at least as much to do with the use of personal information as with the advertising content.

The industry has now adopted recommended standards that should be met nationally, with the intention that compliance should in due course form part of the self-regulatory machinery of the Advertising Standards Authority and the Committee of Advertising Practice. In the meantime, the five direct marketing trade associations—the Association of Mail Order Publishers, the British Direct Marketing Association, the British List Brokers' Association, the Direct Mail Producers' Association, the Mail Order Traders' Association and the Mailing Preference Service—have incorporated these standards into their own Codes of Practice, which are mandatory on their members. In addition, the Direct Mail Services Standards Board will be adopting these standards as a condition of its Recognition Scheme.

The standards have been defined in two ways: first, in terms of what the consumer should reasonably be able to expect; second, in terms of what operational practices would be required to fulfil these expectations. They cover the three principal areas of consumer concern: the ways in which information is obtained, the opportunities for getting such information corrected, and the opportunities for getting unwanted mail stopped. They are intended to cover lists and databases used to market consumer products, and not business-to-business lists.

The Data Protection Act 1984 has an important bearing on direct marketing practice, but does not address it specifically. The Advertising Association's Code of Practice for the use of Personal Data for Advertising and Direct Marketing Purposes defines the effect of the Act on direct marketing practice, and the standards now being put forward by the direct marketing industry are entirely consistent with this. But because they start from the needs of the consumer rather than the provisions of the statute, they cover data protection considerations only partially, and operators should continue to refer to and be guided by the A A Code, the Registrar's occasionally published interpretations of the Act, and the Act itself.

It has been acknowledged that the operational requirements will in some cases demand important changes to existing practice, and a period of transition has been agreed. Full compliance will be required with effect from 1st July 1991. In some cases the standards defined are at the minimum acceptable level, and it is expected that significantly improved levels will be possible after an appropriate period allowing for the modification of practices. It will be important to provide for regular and reasonably frequent reviews of the practical experience of compliance, including failures to meet consumer expectations as well as unforeseen operational difficulties.

The operational requirements apply to all mailings to UK consumers, irrespective of the country from which the mailer trades or of the country in which the mailing is made. Those practitioners supplying lists (or other services) to offshore mailers should take particular care to ensure that use is covered by an appropriate warranty and is in all respects acceptable for receipt by UK consumers.

In the longer term, when it is hoped that the Advertising Standards Authority and the Committee of Advertising Practice will issue their own Code of Practice and assume responsibility for regulating compliance, enforcement will be supported by the existence of substantial sanctions. First, mailing houses and agencies recognised by the Direct Mail Services Standards Board will be required to comply, or risk losing their recognition and any commission revenue to which they are currently entitled. Second, mailers who contract with Royal Mail for discounted postage rates will be required by that contract to comply, or risk losing the entitlement to discounted rates. Third, publishers may refuse to carry direct response advertisements from advertisers who have been shown not to comply.

The objective of monitoring compliance should not simply be confined to looking for infringements; it should be a means of encouraging standards, assessing the extent to which direct marketing is better/worse than other industries, and uncovering trends, weaknesses, etc. Further, it must be recognised that pre-operational advice is linked to monitoring and encourages observance.

Finally, those considering compliance will, no doubt, take note of events outside the control of the operator which may prevent strict adherence, particularly to required time limits.

Section I

A. CONSUMER STANDARDS: OBTAINING PERSONAL INFORMATION

(i)   The purpose for which personal information (which includes a name and address) is being requested should be transparently clear to the individual giving it in the context in which the request is made.

Information given in response to an offer of a brochure, goods or services, for example, will necessarily be used for despatch purposes and for billing. In the normal course of events it is to be expected that the information may be used to make follow-up offers.

(ii)   If it is intended that the personal information will also be used for a significantly different purpose (for example, making it available for use by unrelated third parties), the individual should be informed of the possibility, and given an opportunity to object.

(iii) Sensitive personal information (racial origin, political opinions, religious or other beliefs, physical or mental health, sexual life, criminal convictions) should only be used (for any purpose) with great care, and the express consent of the individual concerned should be considered.

(iv)   The amount of personal information requested from an individual should normally be adequate for, but limited to, that which is directly related to the primary purpose of collecting it. Where more extensive personal information is requested (for example, in application forms and 'lifestyle' questionnaires) an explanation of all the purposes of collecting it must be made at the time.

(v)   Personal information that is published (for example, in *Who's Who* or a professional register) is in the public domain and can be used without informing the individual in advance. It is, however, mandatory that names on the Mailing Preference Service suppression list should be omitted from any mailing using names from these sources.

B. OPERATIONAL REQUIREMENTS: OBTAINING PERSONAL INFORMATION

(i)   It can be assumed that when the purpose of collecting personal information is simply and exclusively to enable fulfilment, to make a single transaction and/or to initiate a continuing trading relationship, the invitation to the individual to provide information will normally imply a transparent purpose in the context.

(ii) When it is intended to use the information for additional and significantly different purposes which the individual could not reasonably be expected to foresee, the individual must be informed of the possibility, preferably at the time the information is requested, and given adequate opportunity to object. The information must not be used for such purposes before a reasonable time (at least 21 days) has been allowed for such an objection to be received.

(iii) The definition of 'significantly different purpose' must ultimately be a question of judgement. It plainly includes permitting the use of the personal information by unrelated third parties, and where doubt exists as to the definition of an unrelated third party (for example, in circumstances where subsidiary companies in the same group wish to use the information) the test should be the extent to which the individual can reasonably be expected to recognise or to know of such associations. To this end, it is recommended that steps should be taken to inform customers of such associations where they cannot readily be inferred from trading companies' names. Particularly sensitive categories, such as personal financial information, actual or attributed, should be subject to the most stringent interpretations of this requirement.

(iv) In some circumstances it may be considered impractical to describe the additional purposes at the time when the individual is invited to provide personal information. Examples of such circumstances are:

- direct response press advertisements where space and/or response rates are critical
- direct response TV or radio advertisements
- the acceptance of telephone orders
- face-to-face transactions.

In such cases the personal information obtained may only be used for primary purposes (see (i)) until the individual has been informed of the intention to use the information for specified additional purposes and has been given an opportunity to object to such use.

(v) In circumstances where the intention to use the personal information for significantly different purposes is formed at a stage in the marketing process later than the time when the information was collected, it may not be used for such purposes until the individual has been informed of the intention and has been given adequate opportunity to object to such use.

(vi)   When obtaining, using or disclosing sensitive personal information (racial origin, political opinions, religious or other beliefs, physical or mental health, sexual life, criminal convictions) consideration should be given to whether it is appropriate to see the express consent of the individuals concerned.

(vii) List owners must be able to identify all names which have objected to additional uses and all names which have been given no opportunity to object.

(viii) Users of lists obtained from a third party carry the primary responsibility for ensuring that individuals mailed have been appropriately informed and that none of them has objected, or has given express consent where applicable. Users are therefore advised to require their suppliers to warrant that these requirements have been met, and to require their suppliers to indemnify them against the consequences of breach.

(ix)   Personal information requested from an individual should be limited to that which is directly related to the purposes for which it is being collected. Information should not be collected speculatively unless this purpose is clearly explained, and where detailed personal information is requested (for example, in application forms or lifestyle questionnaires) a description of all the types of purposes for which the information will be used must be made at the same time.

(x)   Personal information compiled from published sources (whether or not the publication is required by statute) is to be regarded as in the public domain, and may be used without giving the individual an opportunity to object.

Section II

A. CONSUMER STANDARDS: LIST MAINTENANCE AND MANAGEMENT

(i)   All mailing companies are required to take all reasonable steps to ensure that their lists are accurate and up-to-date.

(ii)   Requests by individuals for the correction of personal information must be acted on with all reasonable promptness, but allowance should be made for the subsequent use of uncorrected information by those to whom it may already have been supplied.

(iii) Requests by individuals addressed to a particular company to receive no further promotional mailings must be acted on promptly, but will be taken to concern that company's mailings only.

(iv)   If an individual wishes to receive no promotional mailings from any company, he or she may request the Mailing Preference Service to add his or her name to its suppression list. It is mandatory that the names on this list are omitted from mailings, other than those from a company to its own customers.

(v)   If an individual enquires about the source from which his or her name has been selected, the identity of the mailing list must be revealed.

(vi)   All mailing companies are required to make all reasonable endeavours to eliminate the duplication of mailings to the same name and address.

(vii) Personal information must be held securely and safeguarded against unauthorised use, alteration or destruction.

(viii) All companies who make their lists available to third parties, and the intermediaries who may act for them, are required to satisfy themselves as to the intentions and credentials of a prospective user before permitting use. Prospective users must specify particular and legitimate uses before they are permitted to use such lists.

(v)   If a customer is reported to have died, the name must be so marked in the file as soon as possible. If they can be identified, the informants should be told that mailing programmes already in train may delay the suppression of mailings for some months. They should be advised to contact the Mailing Preference Service.

(vi)   Customer files must be kept secure and safeguarded against unauthorised use, alteration or destruction, bearing in mind that security measures appropriate to routine personal information may not be adequate for systems containing sensitive data.

B. OPERATIONAL REQUIREMENTS: LIST MAINTENANCE AND MANAGEMENT

1. Customer lists used in-house

(i)   Requests from customers for the correction of personal information must be acted on promptly. The customer should be informed if mailing programmes already in train will cause delay in corrections taking effect.

(ii)   Customers who have asked to receive no further promotional mailings must have their names so marked in the file.

(iii) Customers who have objected to their names being made available to unrelated third parties must have their names so marked in the file.

(iv) Customers who have not been given an opportunity to object to their names being made available to third parties must have their names so marked in the file.

2. Mailing lists rented-in

(i) Users of rented-in lists carry the primary responsibility for ensuring compliance with these requirements, and are therefore advised to require their suppliers to provide an appropriate warranty.

(ii) Users of rented-in lists are required to make every endeavour to avoid the duplication of mailings to the same name and address. To this end they should rent-in only those lists with adequate levels of identification of individuals and correct postal addresses, including whenever possible a full postcode.

(iii) If an individual whose name has been rented-in enquires about the source from which his or her name has been selected for mailing, the list user is required to reveal the specific identity of the mailing list. In cases of multiple list sources, the identity of the list should be that which has been credited with the rental charge. List users must in any case maintain source records which permit such enquiries to be answered.

(iv) If an individual whose name has been rented-in requests the list user to send no further promotional mailings, his or her name must for a minimum of five years be so marked on a file, maintained if necessary for that purpose only, which must be used to suppress further mailings when the same name is included in lists which are rented-in subsequently. List users should assume that they are authorised to apply this suppression to their own mailings only, and should not inform the list owner. If, however, the nature of a request from an individual implies that he or she wishes to receive no promotional mailings from any source, the list user should refer him or her to the Mailing Preference Service.

(v) If a list user is informed that an individual whose name has been rented-in has died, the name must be so marked in the suppression file (see (iv) above) immediately. If they can be identified, the informants should be told that mailing programmes already in train may delay the suppression of mailings for some months. The list user should also advise them to contact the Mailing Preference Service. The list user must also inform the owner of the list or his or her manager, if known, within 30 days.

(vi)   If an individual whose name has been rented-in requests corrections to his or her personal information, the list user must inform the owner of the list, or his or her manager, within 30 days.

(vii) In order to ensure that at the time of mailing the latest available corrections and suppressions are incorporated in rented-in lists, users should acquire lists no earlier than necessary. The interval between the supply of the list and the date of mailing should preferably be no longer than three months, and in any case must not exceed six months.

(viii) Users of rented-in lists who for any reason are forced to defer the mailing for more than six months from the date of supply must not use the list until the latest corrections and suppressions available to the list owner have been incorporated in it.

(ix)   Prospective users of rented-in lists must satisfy the list owners or their agents that the prospective use is for a specified and legitimate purpose only.

(x)   Prospective users of rented-in lists should have a reasonable expectation that the category of individuals on them is likely to be interested in the products or services they propose to promote. A list may, however, be used for test purposes, provided that the aim of the test is to determine whether such an interest exists.

(ix)   In any case where harm of any kind is likely to result from a particular use of a list, the individuals must first have been asked whether they object to this use.

3. Mailing lists rented-out

(i)   List owners and/or their agents or managers are required to use their best endeavours to ensure that lists available for rental are accurate and up-to-date. They must, in particular, amend their lists in accordance with requests for corrections to personal information and for the suppression of deceased names within 30 days of receipt of such requests either passed on by list users as required by Section II.B.2.(v) and (vi) above, or directly.

(ii)   List brokers, although acting as agents, should use their best endeavours to ensure that list owners compile, maintain and (where appropriate) manage their lists in compliance with these requirements, and should only trade lists which so comply and act only for list owners who agree to comply.

(iii) List owners or their agents are advised to require prospective list users to provide appropriate undertakings, to the effect that:

(a) the mailing is intended to be completed by a specified date, and that proof of mailing can be produced;

(b) if the specified mailing date is for any reason deferred for more than six months following supply, either the rental copy of the list will be returned unused and extracts from it deleted from their files, or they will take steps to incorporate any corrections and suppressions available to the list owner;

(c) the use of the list is for a specified and legitimate purpose only;

(d) the rental copy of the list and copies of extracts made from it will be kept secure and safeguarded against unauthorised use;

(e) requests from individuals for corrections and for the suppression of deceased names will be forwarded by the list users to the list owners or their agents within 30 days.

(iv) List owners or their managers must keep a record of actions taken in regard to each list available for rental in a form which allows compliance with these requirements to be demonstrated.

(v) List owners, their agents and managers are required to ensure that the names of individuals who have objected to their names being made available to unrelated third parties have been either deleted from the rental copy or appropriately marked.

(vi) List owners, their agents and managers are required to ensure that the names of individuals who have not been given an opportunity to object to their names being made available to unrelated third parties have been either deleted from the rental copy or appropriately marked, except in cases where the list has been compiled from published sources.

(vii) List owners, their agents and managers are required to ensure that the names of individuals in the Mailing Preference Service suppression list (in the latest version available at the date of supply) have been appropriately marked in the rental copy, whether or not the list has been compiled from published sources.

Section III

OTHER OPERATING REQUIREMENTS

1. Enquiries and requests from individuals must be dealt with courteously, quickly and knowledgeably. All mailing companies must therefore take steps to ensure that staff at all levels who are likely to be in touch with individuals have been trained accordingly. At least one senior executive must be identifiable as having ultimate responsibility.

2. The analysis of information about individuals, actual or inferred, makes increasingly accurate targeting possible but also carries the risk of

causing alarm, distress or legitimate offence through ill-chosen or inadequately presented material. All users of lists must avoid including references to age, economic status, education, purchasing behaviour, bereavement, marital status or children in the family, where such references risk having this effect.

Section IV

MONITORING AND ENFORCING COMPLIANCE

1. Breaches of national standards will, in many instances, be identified from consumer complaints. However, it will be essential in addition to establish a system of invigilation to monitor compliance.
2. A system of spot checks should be introduced to monitor observance. List users, list owners and list brokers should be required to demonstrate on request positive evidence of compliance.
3. Additionally, the Post Office Consumer Panel provides a selection of physical samples of direct mail collected by a nationally representative sample of 1000 GB households. Material from this source, which is already monitored for compliance with BCAP and BCSPP, should also be monitored for apparent compliance with aspects of these standards. Where such compliance is not apparent, the mailer will be requested to provide positive evidence of compliance.
4. All operators should appoint an appropriate officer or employee with specific responsibility for ensuring compliance.
5. All operators should review their own compliance procedures not less frequently than once every twelve months.
6. A course of conduct which demonstrates serious or persistent breaches of national standards should attract the following penalties as appropriate

   (i) loss of Direct Mail Services Standards Board recognition (together with commission entitlement if appropriate):
   (ii) loss of entitlement to discounted postage rates under Royal Mail contracts;
   (iii) refusal to publish further direct response advertisements;
   (iv) publication of the breach in ASA Case Reports.

7. Procedures for appeal against the imposition of penalties will be instituted.

Further information

Further information or guidance on the requirements of these standards may be obtained from any of the trade associations referred to in the Introduction, or from the Direct Mail Services Standards Board at 26 Eccleston Street, London SW1W 9PY, telephone 071-824 8651.

Bibliography

Andrews, Les (ed.), *The Royal Mail Direct Mail Handbook*, 2nd edn, Exley, Watford, 1988.

Baier, Martin, *Elements of Direct Marketing*, McGraw-Hill, New York, 1983.

BDMA, *UK Telephone Marketing Industry Survey*, McGraw-Hill, Maidenhead, 1990.

Bird, Drayton, *Commonsense Direct Marketing*, 2nd edn, Kogan Page, London, 1989.

Brann, Christian, *Cost-Effective Direct Marketing*, Collectors' Books Ltd, Cirencester, 1984.

Breckman, Malcolm, *Running Your Own Mail Order Business*, Kogan Page, London, 1989.

Copy Testing in the UK, Direct Response Media Ltd, HLY Grey Direct, 1988.

Donovan, Judith, *Back to Basics*, Direct Response Magazine Ltd, Hertford, 1989.

Fairlie, Robin, *The Marketing Person's Guide to Database Marketing Direct Mail*, Exley, Watford, 1990.

Fraser-Robinson, John, *The Secrets of Effective Direct Mail*, McGraw-Hill, Maidenhead, 1989.

Hawkes, Paul, *Hawkes on Strategy*, Direct Response Magazine Ltd, Hertford, 1990.

Hughes, John (ed.), *Mail Marketing File*, Mail Marketing, Bristol, 1982.

Kantz, Bernard, *How to Win More Business by Phone, Telex and Fax*, Hutchinson Business, London, 1988.

Kobs, Jim, *Profitable Direct Marketing*, Crain Books, Chicago, 1979.

Lawson, Richard, *Sales Promotion Law*, Blackwell Scientific Publications, Oxford, 1987.

Leiderman, Robert, *The Telephone Book*, McGraw-Hill, Maidenhead, 1990.

Marks, Pauline, *The Telephone Marketing Book*, Business Books Ltd, London, 1989.

Nash, Edward, *Direct Marketing*, McGraw-Hill, Maidenhead, 1987.

Nash, Edward, *The Direct Marketing Handbook*, McGraw-Hill, Maidenhead, 1984.

Raphel, Murrey and Erdman, Ken, *The Do-It-Yourself Direct Mail Handbook*, The Marketers Bookshelf, Philadelphia, 1986.

Rapp, Stan and Collins, Tom, *MaxiMarketing*, McGraw-Hill, New York, 1987.

Roman, Murray, *How to Build Your Business by Telephone*, McGraw-Hill, New York, 1976.

Shaw, Robert and Stone, Merlin, *Database Marketing*, Gower, Aldershot, 1989.

Simon, Julian L., *How to Start and Operate a Mail Order Business*, 4th edn, McGraw-Hill, New York, 1987.

Stone, Bob, *Successful Direct Marketing Methods*, Crain Books, Chicago, 1979.

Glossary

AMOP Association of Mail Order Publishers. Trade association set up for publishers active in selling by mail order.

Acorn A classification of Residential Neighbourhoods. A consumer list selection and targeting system used on residential property information in areas of at least 150 households (an enumeration district).

Acquisition cost The advertisement cost of obtaining a customer or enquiry.

Advertising Standards Authority The association that regulates, monitors and handles public complaints of all advertisements (except those transmitted by broadcast media).

Agency fee Remuneration based on a negotiated fee, as opposed to commission.

Artwork Material in its final layout, such as type and illustrations, assembled in preparation for making the printing plate.

Average contribution The average total gross income per contribution from those responding to a mailing.

Average customer life The average period of time (or number of buying seasons) during which a customer will continue to purchase.

Average order cost The total cost of orders, divided by the total number of orders.

Average order value The total volume of orders divided by the total number of orders.

BDMA British Direct Marketing Association (trade association for direct marketing users, agencies and suppliers).

BRE Business reply envelope. A pre-addressed envelope to be returned to the mailer. The mailer pays postage on those envelopes that are returned.

Back end 1. Fulfilment procedures carried out after the receipt of an order to complete a mail order transaction. 2. The completion of a campaign or a job. The back-end results or performance includes final figures for paid and unpaid orders.

Back test A 'retest' or 'confirming test', carried out when a sample test was of an acceptable level of success but not so convincing as to justify full roll-out.

Bangtail   A type of envelope generally referring to those formed (often as part of one-piece mailer or self-mailer formats) with an attached perforated 'tail' used as an order or response coupon.

Banker envelope   An envelope with the flap on the long edge. Often used for machine enclosing.

Bill stuffer   Any type of promotional piece inserted with an invoice or statement in order to save postage.

Blow-in card   A loose card with reply device inserted into a publication for advertising purposes.

Bounce back   A further offer enclosed in the fulfilment package. This is an effective device to interest the buyer at a psychologically strategic time.

British Direct Marketing Association   *See* BDMA.

Broadsheets   Publications that measure a maximum of 56 cm wide, and a minimum of 36 cm deep. Often used generally to describe large leaflets folded several times to a small finished size.

Buck slip   A 'dollar-bill'-sized enclosure, generally used to announce a premium or discounted offer for early reply.

CAP   Code of Advertising Practice.

CHADD   Change of address.

CPE   Cost per enquiry. Total cost of a mailing divided by the number of resultant enquiries received.

CPO   Cost per order. Total cost of a mailing divided by the number of resultant orders received.

Camera-ready   A term given to artwork, copy or paste-up that is ready for reproduction.

Cheshire   A make of labelling machine. It cuts continuous stationery to label size and fixes it to material.

Cheshire label   A label produced by a Cheshire machine. Cheshire labels are printed in a continuous form in a special format (generally 4 labels across and 11 down).

Closing out   The final (or closing) results of either a mailing or a direct response advertisement, e.g. it closed out at a two per cent response.

Coin rub   A type of involvement device. A special type of coating is applied to areas of the mailing or advertisement that have already been pre-printed with a phrase or design underneath. By rubbing a coin over the area, the underlying image can be made to appear.

Cold list   A list of people with whom the advertiser has had no prior transaction or contact.

Cold mailing   Mailing to a list of people with whom the advertiser has had no prior transaction or contact.

Collectible An object, or more commonly a series of objects, sold as limited editions through mail order.

Collection series A series of 'reminder' letters or cards sent to mail order buyers who have not paid outstanding invoices.

Compiled lists Lists built up through the research of directories and other published data, as opposed to lists generated as a by-product of direct marketing activity.

Computer letter A computer-printed letter that includes personalised fill-in information from a source file, in predesignated positions in the letter.

Computer personalisation The process of tailoring each piece of correspondence to the needs of the recipient, by filling name, address or other information relating to the recipient into predesignated positions within the correspondence.

Computer record All the information collected about an individual, company or transaction stored on a computer disc or tape.

Confidence level The number of times, out of 100 attempts, that the results' predictions must be correct. This degree of confidence is expressed in terms of the number of standard deviations.

Consumer list A list of individuals' names and home addresses.

Consumer location system A market identification system that gives marketers an indication as to the most suitable areas to target.

Consumer profile The combined characteristics of those who buy or use a given product or service, e.g. their sex, age, class, etc.

Continuation The next step after an initial list test. If a test mailing has been responsive within predetermined financial parameters, the list is ordered again in quantities relating to response.

Continuity series A marketing technique whereby a customer is sold a series of similar products over an extended period.

Contributor list A mailing list made up of names who have made donations in the past to a fund-raising mailing. Otherwise known as donor list.

Control A component in a direct mail package that has been tested before, and was at that time the most successful of two or more packages. The control is used in testing as a true measure against which the effectiveness of new components are gauged. The component can be either the whole package, or elements of a package such as the copy, offer and premiums.

Co-op mailing Two or more products or services (usually non-competitive) mailed in the same envelope to prospects.

Copy control Copy restrictions laid down by the IBA.

Crown British imperial paper size measuring 384 × 504 mm.

DMA Direct Marketing Association. The major American trade association for direct marketers.

DMPA Direct Mail Producers' Association. The trade association for those who produce direct mail packages.

DMSB Direct Mail Sales Bureau. A public limited company set up by the Post Office and industry in order to promote the idea of using direct mail to advertisers and leading agencies.

DMSSB Direct Mail Services Standards Board. A board set up to uphold standards within the industry.

Decoy A unique name inserted into a mailing list in order to verify list usage.

De-dupe The process of identifying and eliminating duplicate names from two or more mailing lists, in order to prevent repeat mailing to an individual's address.

Demographic segmentation Selecting targets on the basis of statistical information such as age, income, sex or lifestyle criteria.

Demographics A statistical description of a group based on common patterns, e.g. geography, socio-economic factors or buying patterns.

Dimensional mailing A high-quality mailing that often includes a high-cost attention-getting device, e.g. including a free gift or sample.

Direct mail Unsolicited mail, usually sent either to advertise or to sell goods or services. It is delivered by the Post Office.

Direct mail advertising Advertising through the post.

Direct Mail Producers' Association *See* DMPA.

Direct Mail Sales Bureau *See* DMSB.

Direct Mail Services Standards Board *See* DMSSB.

Direct mail shot Sending out a collection of direct mailing packages to those on a mailing list at one time.

Direct response Advertising or selling through any medium inviting the consumer to respond to the advertiser.

Donor list A list of people who have donated to a charity.

Door-to-door A type of service, where direct marketing offers are delivered to the target recipients by hand, rather than being stamped or franked and sent through the post.

Dry test A test used to ensure that there will be a demand for the product (a frequent practice among publishers). Consumers are asked to order before the product has been manufactured. The manufacture only goes ahead in cases where the response will guarantee a desired profit level. Where this level is not met and the product never manufactured, compensation is given.

Dummy name A unique name inserted into a mailing list to track list usage. (*See also* Decoy, Seed name.)

Duplication Two or more names and address records that are found to be for the same potential recipient when two or more lists are run against each other.

EDMA European Direct Marketing Association.

Electoral roll confirmation (verification) The use of the electoral roll to ensure a list contains correct addresses, or that the individual is listed (for credit scoring).

Enclosure Anything included in a direct mail package besides a letter.

Enquiries Response to direct marketing solicitations offering further information or other literature, which generally contains the selling message.

Enquiry names A list of those people who requested information to be sent to them, as a result of a direct marketing solicitation, but who did not generally make a purchase.

Enumeration district A geographical area of about 150 households, correlating with the Census breakdown of Great Britain, which can be used for market or list segmentation purposes.

Envelope stuffer Promotional material enclosed in an envelope already containing either business letters, invoices or statements.

Ertma The name of European inserting systems (both gravity/suction-fed systems).

Every-other-name A test where alternate names receive a control and test mailing or advertisement; sometimes known as an A/B split.

File layout The structure and arrangement of data lying within a file (including the size and sequence of the data).

First-class discount The reduction given to presorted mailings, but which receive the same treatment as standard first-class mail (Mailsort 1).

First-class mail Post that should be delivered the following day, if posted by the last collection the previous evening.

Flag To give an indicator against chosen addresses, in order to treat them differently at a later stage (e.g. by selection, or segmentation).

Follow-up mailing A subsequent mailing, sometimes a repeat of the first, sent to those who were non-responders to an original mailing.

Free-flier An additional small insert in a mailing, including as a 'last-minute' offer of a free gift.

Free-keeper A modest gift, given as an incentive in return for placing an order by mail, that can be kept even if the buyer returns the goods ordered.

Free-ride A mailing device with an offer that is inserted into another mailing, often administrative or procedural, in order to capitalise on postage costs.

Free-standing stuffer (insert)   A promotional piece inserted loose into a newspaper or magazine. Also known as free-fall.

Freefone   A British Telecom service. A company offering a Freefone number pays for any call received on the Freefone line.

Freepost   A Royal Mail service. A company offering a Freepost address pays postage on all mail received at the Freepost address.

Fulfilment   The process of dealing with an order or enquiry, from its receipt to delivery. This includes opening, processing, administration, packing and transport.

Fulfilment package   The package containing the goods or the details of the arrangement of the service, which fulfil the order; or containing requested details in response to an enquiry.

Gone-aways   A term given to those mailings sent to an individual at an address where he or she no longer resides.

Guardbook   A book that contains essential information of all an advertiser's advertising activities, and a book that contains copies of all advertisements published for a client.

HDS   Household Delivery Service. The Royal Mail delivery service of unaddressed promotional literature.

Handling house   A company that checks, packs and mails premiums.

Hot line   The most recent names on a mail order buyer or enquirer list. Also a rapid telephone order or enquiry service.

Hotline buyers   Those people who have bought a product or service most recently.

House list   A mailer's own list of people who are either former or current customers or prospects.

House mailing   A mailing to your own house list.

House-to-house   The delivery of unaddressed promotional literature to households.

IBM 3800 laser   A high-speed laser printer, with a continuous stationery feed. One of the most popular types of laser printer.

IBM 6670 laser   High-quality, slow-speed laser printer.

ISBA   Incorporated Society of British Advertisers. An association which voices the collective opinion of advertisers.

ISO sizes   International range of paper and envelope sizes, which replaced the term 'Din sizes'.

ISP   Institute of Sales Promotion.

Impact printer   Printing machine using a printing element hammered onto the paper through a ribbon, in a similar manner to a typewriter.

Inactive buyer A person who has bought from a company, but not within a specified period.

Indicia A mark or frank used in place of a postage stamp. It is printed onto material to be posted, and permits the item to be mailed.

In-fill A word or phrase added to predetermined positions within the main body copy after this has been printed (e.g. in order to personalise a mailing).

In-house Carried out within a company, rather than being bought in from outside firms.

Ink jet A type of printing process. Tiny ink droplets are sprayed from a jet. This process is of a lower quality than laser printing, but can be carried out at high speed.

Inner Common usage for inner envelope. This envelope is included in a mailing for the recipient's use to respond to an offer, as opposed to an outer envelope.

Insert An alternative method of advertising using the published media. A paid-for promotional piece which is placed loose or bound-in to each edition of a magazine issue, or other publication.

Inset A paid-for promotional piece that is bound into a magazine or other publication.

Inter-list duplicate Duplication of a name and address record on two or more mailing lists that have been rented for the same mailing (i.e. other than a house list).

Internal (house) list The advertiser's own list of current or past customers or prospects.

Intra-list duplicate A duplication of a name and address record within a given list.

Job title A title assigned on a mailing list or database to describe a person's position at work.

Johnson box A phrase, sentence or short passage, highlighted by being enclosed in a box, generally formed of asterisks, at the head of a piece of copy.

Jumbo envelope An envelope 324 × 229 mm (more commonly known as a C4 envelope)

Junk mail A term, offensive to direct mailers, used by the media which means unsolicited mail.

Key Or keycode. A reference code (either letters, numbers or other symbols) which enables an advertiser to identify the source of an enquiry from any type of direct response advertising.

Key number A code put on a reply device enabling response to be monitored.

Knock and drop   A term, used incorrectly, for the delivery of unaddressed, unsolicited mail. It is the more exact term used in conjunction with sample distributions.

Landing date   The date on which the mailer targets the mailing package to reach the consumer.

Large post   Standard imperial paper size measuring 419 × 533 mm.

Laser   An acronym for Light Amplification by Stimulated Emission of Radiation. Concentrated light beam of narrow width, used for creating images, engravings, etc.

Laser personalisation   A method of computer printing usually incorporating file data in preplanned positions. (A computer attachment to the laser printer supplies personal data about each record.)

Lead generation   Mailings inviting enquiries for sales follow-up.

Lead sentence   The first sentence in a piece of copy (crucial to gain reader attention).

Lead-in   A phrase or sentence that precedes a headline in a direct response advertisement, or mailing.

Leads   Enquiries for sales follow-up and conversion to sale.

Legal-sized envelope   A term used in the US, Canada and Australia, for the most common direct mail envelope used in mailings to businesses.

Letterset   A printing method where the image transfers from a relief plate, first onto a blanket, and then from the blanket onto paper. It is sometimes known as dry offset, offset letterpress and indirect letterpress.

Lettershop   A company that offers to handle production stages of a mailing for an advertiser, e.g. addressing and enclosing.

Lifestyle   A person's way of life, which has a direct influence on the type of products or services he or she buys or requires.

Lifetime value   The full-term value of a customer to a company. Using direct marketing techniques a customer will often provide a company with sales on a long-term basis. In such cases, the calculation of a customer's lifetime value can be essential to evaluate what initial cost can be spent acquiring a new customer.

Lift letter   A marketing technique to increase the response to a direct mail letter. Often a second letter from an authoritative individual who endorses the product or service.

Limited edition   Products of which a restricted number are produced or available. This increases their perceived value. Such products are successfully marketed by mail order.

List   The collection of people's names and addresses.

List broker   Someone who works for a list user (an advertiser who wishes to rent another company's list) to advise, select and arrange the rental of outside lists.

List cleaning The process of correcting or removing incorrect entries from a mailing list.

List code The code to a list, when lists or list segments are being monitored during a test. The list code is printed somewhere on the reply device.

List conversion Changing one magnetic tape format to another.

List exchange An agreement drawn up by two organisations, in which the lists are mutually exchanged.

List maintenance The process of correcting, removing or adding a record on a list.

List manager The agent retained by list owners to maintain and/or market their list(s).

List owner An individual or organisation that has built or gathered its own list, generally through trading or compilation.

List sequence The order in which names and addresses are kept in a file, e.g. alphabetically or in 'town and county order'.

List source The media from which names for a list are obtained.

List test A test carried out by mailing a sample taken from two or more list segments and/or entire lists.

List user A person who uses someone else's list names for his or her own mailing.

Live names Describes those who are current 'active' customers who have responded recently, and might do so again in future.

Loose insert A method of advertising in published media, where a promotional piece is placed between the pages of a magazine or other publication.

Lottery A sales promotion device that requires a contest containing the elements of chance consideration and prizes.

MGM Member-get-member. A marketing technique where current customers are offered an incentive to enlist a new member.

MOPS Mail Order Protection Scheme.

MPS *See* Mailing Preference Service.

MUA Mailers User Association. An organisation whose role is to protect the interests of members using the postal services.

Machinable envelope An envelope that is designed to be run on an enclosing machine, characterised by a wide 'mouth' and long rectangular gum-flap.

Magalog A catalogue that has a sufficient element of editorial so that its recipients perceive it as a magazine.

Mail date protection Interval of agreed time that a list is not used for mailing, e.g. a week before or after a list is used by a mailer, in order not to vie with other promotions.

Mail house A company that offers all aspects of a direct mail service, prior to its despatch (from idea, printing, packing, through to mailing).

Mail order A buying/selling transaction carried out by mail. Strictly speaking, the placing of the order and the fulfilment should both be carried out by mail. However, often the order is placed via other media (e.g. by telephone) and order delivery may be by other means too.

Mailing date The date direct mail pieces are put into the post (and the date any rented list owner has agreed for his or her list to be used).

Mailing Preference Service An organisation that supervises and administers a service, by which members of the public can have their name added to or removed from suitably screened lists on request.

Mailsort (1, 2, 3) Generic name for presorted mailings for which the Royal Mail offer discounts. There are three service standards: first class, second class and slower bulk rate.

Match code A numerical and/or alpha reference code generated by computer to form a unique identifying code.

Matching-in The process of inserting a name, address or other phrase into pre-positioned spaces within a preprinted piece of text so as to be as nearly indistinguishable as possible.

Mechanical data Information supplied about a publication by publishers to prospective advertisers, e.g. page length, column width, etc.

Mechanicals The material supplied in its final form to a publication for the reproduction of an advertisement, e.g. headlines, pictures, text, etc.

Media Any vehicle for the transmission of a communication, e.g. television, radio, direct mail.

Media data form Established format for presenting comparative data in a publication.

Media independent An organisation that specialises in buying media time and space, in the same role as the media department of a large advertising agency

Media owner A company that owns and operates commercially a media organisation, e.g. television, radio station, newspaper, etc.

Media plan A plan, prepared by an agency, that shows a client the media through which it proposes the budget should be spent, and the rationale behind this.

Media schedule A record or space or other bookings planned and made for a campaign.

Megabyte One million computer bytes (loosely termed one million characters).

Member-get-member *See* MGM.

Merchandising A part of marketing that is concerned with maximising product movement most usually in reference to retail level.

Merge The process of combining two or more mailing lists in order to build one larger one.

Merge and purge The process of combining two or more mailing lists in order to build one larger one, but including the removal of duplication.

Modem Short for modulator/demodulator device, which converts communications (e.g. telephone transmissions) into a digital form, and vice versa.

Multi-mailer A mailing that contains a number of loose single-page promotional sheets.

Multiple regression A statistical technique used to measure the relationship between response and lists or list segments.

NPA Newspaper Publishers' Association Ltd.

Name acquisition Technique used to prompt a response in order to generate new names for a mailing list.

Negative option A buying arrangement in which a customer or member agrees to accept a proposition unless they formally notify the seller to cancel, often within the specified time-period.

Neighbourhood mailing Mailing the neighbours who live next door to or nearby a person who has responded to a mailing in the past.

Nesting Placing one insertion inside another, before inserting into an outer envelope.

Net name arrangement The terms of an agreement between list owners and users. Lists are run together to find duplicate records. The list owner receives payment for the number of new names, or the number of names as percentage of the whole, whichever is the greater. There is generally a specified minimum percentage.

Net names The number of names used for a mailing, after duplicate names have been eliminated.

Netting down The process of merging several lists or list segments in order to find and eliminate duplicate records.

Nixie The direct mail package returned to a mailer because of an incorrect address.

Nth name A method of selecting names to make a sample for list testing. The total list quantity is divided by the quantity of names to be tested, i.e. 10 000 names selected from 100 000 would mean that every tenth name would be selected.

OFT Office of Fair Trading. An association that regulates trading matters in the UK, in order to protect the consumer.

Off-the-page The acquisition of a lead or sale directly from a press ad, without follow-up by any other media.

Off-the-page advertising Advertising using page media, e.g. in magazines and newspapers.

One-stage Short for one-stage sell. A promotion that is designed to sell directly, without any follow-up process.

Outer The container for a mailing piece, e.g. envelope, plastic or wrapper made from other material.

Outward postcode The first half of a postcode identifying the general area for delivery (the first two letters, followed by a number). The remainder of a postcode, called the inward code, identifies the exact location for delivery.

PI deals Payment by results. The number of sales or enquiries generated are paid in accordance with a pre-agreed rate of charge.

PIN Short for Pinpoint Identified Neighbourhoods. A Census-based classification index, used to segment the population and to market products in the most relevant way to each segment.

PMT Short for photo-mechanical transfer. A mechanical method that quickly produces a photoprint from flat originals for use as artwork paste-ups.

POP Short for Post Office Preferred. Describes those envelope sizes that conform to a standard, to assist with processing through automated sorting offices.

PPA Periodical Publishers' Association Ltd.

Package insert A promotional piece that is included in the fulfulment package (i.e. with the shipment of the product, or along with the details of the ordered service).

Page one break A break in mid-sentence at the end of the first page of a direct mail letter, which is designed to encourage the reader to continue reading on to the next page. Also known as a run-on-hook.

Pareto's law The 80/20 rule. The general tendency for the majority of revenue to come from the minority sources.

Passive file A file of those customers who have bought from a company, but have not undertaken a recent transaction.

Past buyer A person who has bought from a company before, but not within the previous twelve months.

Penetration A measure of the uptake of a product in consumer research, i.e. the proportion of homes or the number of individuals who have either bought or used a product.

Personalisation The addition of personal information (e.g. name, address or other personal details about a prospect or customer) incorporated into the copy, usually via computer.

Phillipsburg A make of automatic inserting machine that collates and inserts mailing pieces into envelopes and seals them ready for posting.

Piggy-back The enclosure of an additional promotional effort into a company's own or a second company's mailing package.

Pocket envelopes Envelopes that have the flap along the short edge. These envelopes cannot usually be passed through inserting equipment.

Poly-lope A brand name of a polythene mailing bag sealed by a gummed flap.

Positive option A method of distributing products or services, whereby the order continues to be shipped and the recipient billed until he or she formally cancels the order.

Postcard deck A loose deck of postcards, each with a separate offer and reply device. Generally the person who arranges this type of co-op mailing is the owner of the list to which the mailing is going. The participants pay a fee, plus cost of the printing of the card. Also called Card-deck.

Prestel British Telecom's information service, which is available on screen via a telephone link.

Price point The price people will pay for a product or service, or a level at which it becomes sensitive.

Price test A direct mail test to compare two or more prices for the same or similar product or service.

Printed Postage Impression *See* PPI.

Prize draw Numbers are drawn at random to provide a 'chance' winner of a prize. This technique is popular in direct mail to boost response, often announcing that the draw has already been made.

Probability tables A set of statistical estimates that tabulate the confidence levels that can be achieved.

Product information cards Business reply cards in a booklet, or a deck of loose cards.

Product life-cycle The idea that most products pass through a predictable cycle which is an introductory phase followed by rapid growth, maturity and peak, and lastly decline.

Profile The common format description or picture of a customer typical to a company.

Prospect A person who has either expressed an interest in a company or its product, or whose profile suggests they would be likely potential customers.

Prospecting Mailings whose purpose is to generate leads rather than to make direct sales.

Psychographics   The study of consumers in terms of characteristics and qualities that denote their attitudes and lifestyle.

Publisher's letter   A second letter, which is included in a mailing package, to stress the selling points contained in the first.

Pull   1. A proof.   2. A single print for subsequent photolitho production. 3. The percentage response obtained from an offer.

Purge   The process of eliminating duplicate or unwanted records from a mailing list.

Pyramiding   A method used to test lists whereby a small quantity of names is tested to begin with. If positive indications are received from this initial test, further tests are carried out on larger and larger quantities of names.

Rate of return curve   A graph that records the percentage response from a mailing. This chart allows mailers to determine the point in time when percentage response correlates with the accurate forecast of total response.

Rebate post   The Royal Mail service that preceded Mailsort 3. A postal discount given to second-class letters posted in bulk, providing they were sorted, bundled and bagged in accordance with requirements. The amount of rebate was calculated on a sliding scale based on the number sent.

Recency   The time that has elapsed since a customer either bought from, or entered into another transaction with, a mailer.

Regression   A mathematical technique that produces a functional relationship between two or more correlated variables. It is often used to predict values of one variable when the other values are known.

Rental agreement   An agreement made where one party hires either a segment or an entire customer list that belongs to a second for a one-time use, in return for either a set charge or another form of recompense.

Repeat buyer   A person who has bought from a company more than once within a specified time limit.

Reply-involvement   Various techniques used to involve the recipient of a direct mail shot in replying to a direct mail offer (such as using stickers, rub-down patches, etc.).

Residence list   A list of address records with no names. Direct mail shots are addressed to 'The Resident' or 'The Occupant' instead.

Response curve   The graph produced by plotting the daily intake or responses as a result of a direct response advertisement. This curve can be used to predict the future pull of promotions, as most curves make a similar pattern.

Response rate The percentage of orders or enquiries received of the total number of people who received the promotion.

Return envelope An envelope included in mailing which is self-addressed by the mailer, as distinct from Business Reply or Freepost envelopes which obviate a postage payment by the responder.

Reverse flap The flap that closes a side-seam envelope.

Roll out Mailing to an entire list (or the remainder of the list), usually following a test sample of a list that has proved successful.

Run-on hook A break in mid-sentence at the end of the first page of a direct mail letter, which is designed to encourage the reader to continue reading onto the next page.

SA Short for Self-Adhesive.

Salt name Names and addresses inserted into a mailing list as known decoys (or seeds) to ascertain whether proper usage of the list has been maintained, or to measure speed of delivery, etc.

Sample A limited or trial portion of a whole or of a greater quantity. In direct marketing, the quantity and character of the test portion selected from a larger mailing list. Or a free trial of a product included in a promotion.

Sample error The difference between the test results (of a sample) and the population parameter.

Scamp An idea that has been drawn up roughly. Also known as a rough or first visual.

Seed To insert names and addresses into a list as decoys to ensure that it is not misused, or to monitor its use.

Seed names Those names and addresses inserted into a mailing list for monitoring purposes. *See* Salt name.

Selection criteria Characteristics on which segments or selections are based, e.g. sex, age, class, first-time buyer or a multi-buyer, etc.

Superprofiles A Census-based classification index indicating geographical areas that are most likely to respond to a mailing and can be used for consumer profiling and targeting.

Suppression The removal of name and address records during computer processing in order to avoid inaccuracies such as mailing previously mailed prospects, mailing a prospect twice, or mailing those records that are out-of-date or have requested omission.

Syndicated mailings Mailings or catalogues prepared and sold for the use of more than one advertiser. Usually each participant involved in a syndicated mailing has its own name and address particulars printed, so that the campaign appears to come from that source.

TAN British Telecom telephone answering service.

TGI Target group index. An aid to media and sales planning. A service that provides information on the purchasing and other behaviour of individual consumer segments.

TVR Television rating. A unit of measurement that indicates the level of audience viewing a particular spot.

Tab-pull envelope An envelope that is opened by pulling a tab that tears open along perforation lines.

Tag The marking of a record with given criteria, which allows for subsequent suppression or selection.

Take one Leaflets displayed at point-of-sale or dispensers placed in areas where potential customers gather.

Tape conversion The change of data from one format to another.

Tape density The number of bytes that are included in each unit of magnetic tape.

Tape dump A printout of typical record data held on magnetic tape in order to check its suitability, readability, format, correctness and accuracy.

Tape format layout A map of the specific or relative location of data within each record.

Tape merging The combination of a master tape with a correction tape to produce a third, error-free tape or new master.

Target group index *See* TGI.

Targeting The process of identifying audiences or markets or specific sections or clusters of them to match known or assessed profiles or characteristics of the buyers of a product or service.

Teaser A device (either a phrase or an illustration) intended to entice a reader to open an envelope and read its contents.

Telemarketing The use of the telephone as a marketing medium for any activity such as list building, lead generation or selling.

Telephone selling The use of the telephone to sell, rather than to receive, enquiries.

Testimonial A favourable comment made by a customer or a known personality. It is made to reassure the reader or to add emphasis or credibility to the product or proposition.

Testing The process or trying new ideas, lists or copy approaches by testing one against a second or more and comparing results of one against another and/or against previous results.

Third party letter A letter that is signed by someone other than the mailer or company employee, endorsing the subject of the promotion. This procedure is frequently used for mailings to the membership or customer list of the third party.

Tie-breaker A device used in competitions to ensure that only a certain number of people win prizes. This usually involves a quasi-skill activity composing a slogan, completing a sentence, or demonstrating knowledge about the subject, product or service.

Tip in An insert that is placed loose between the pages of a publication.

Title addressing A form of addressing on a direct mail letter in which a person uses a job title (or styling), rather than a name.

Topping and tailing Hand-written salutations and signatures applied to typed letters.

Variance The relative importance or priority of differing market factors, determined by a statistical process.

Wallet A type of envelope whose flap lies on the long edge. This type of envelope is more usually suitable for use with inserting machines.

White mail A phrase used to describe those letters received by mail order firms which result in extra administrative work. These include letters from prospects and customers, which are either complaints, enquiries or testimonials.

X date 1. For subscriptions, the date a member or subscriber 'expires'. 2. In direct mail, the date a particular offer will terminate.

Index